The Radical Aesthetic

Isobel Armstrong

With thanks to the staff and drivers of the Harvard University Disability Shuttle Service without whom this book could not have been completed

The Radical Aesthetic

Isobel Armstrong

BLACKWELL *Publishers*

First published 2000

2 4 6 8 10 9 7 5 3 1

Blackwell Publishers Ltd
108 Cowley Road
Oxford OX4 1JF
UK

Blackwell Publishers Inc.
350 Main Street
Malden, Massachusetts 02148
USA

British Library Cataloguing in Publication Data

A CIP catalogue record for this book is available from the British Library.

Library of Congress Cataloging-in-Publication Data

Armstrong, Isobel.
The radical aesthetic / by Isobel Armstrong.
p.   cm.
Includes bibliographical references and index.
ISBN 0–631–22052–6 (alk. paper)—ISBN 0–631–22053–4 (alk. paper)
1. Aesthetics, Modern—20th century. 2. Poststructuralism. 3. Emotions
(Philosophy) 4. Feminist theory. I. Title.

BH201 .A75 2000
1111'.85—dc21   99–056206

Typeset in 10 on 12 pt Sabon
by Kolam Information Services Pvt Ltd, Pondicherry, India

Printed in Great Britain by MPG Books Ltd, Bodmin, Cornwall

This book is printed on acid-free paper

Contents

Acknowledgements

Conversation as much as the written text has been the impetus of this book. I have learned from the friends, colleagues, students, and respondents to conference papers and seminar discussions on both sides of the Atlantic who either initiated or participated in this conversation by being, as Mill once put it, 'great questioners'. Alan Sinfield and Jonathan Dollimore set my thinking going through their development of cultural materialist thought and the questions they asked of my own work. I owe the same debt to Tony Crowley's work on language. Terence Hawkes invited me to give a number of papers at British Council seminars in the early 1990s and provided the opportunity for this book to take shape by creating the intellectual openness of these occasions. Ken Hirschkop was both a stringent and generous reader of early writing, and I learned greatly from his demanding political awareness. At different times Maud Ellmann, Robert Young, Bill Marshall, Joseph Bristow, Cora Kaplan, Helen Carr, Paul Hamilton, Alison Mark and Kiernan Ryan have materially assisted the progress of the book. A. S. Byatt, a constant critic and friend, read and commented on parts of the manuscript. My colleagues, Steve Connor, Tom Healy, Josephine McDonagh, and graduate students participating in successive critical theory seminars at Birkbeck College over the last decade have been inspirational. Mary Jacobus and Margot Waddell set up a Wilfred Bion Discussion Group over the summer of 1997 that was formative for this book.

From the other side of the Atlantic, Mary Jacobus and Dominick LaCapra invited me to the Society for the Humanities at Cornell University in 1995 to speak on what proved to be the book's central chapters. I owe much to discussions at the Bread Loaf School of English, Middlebury College, with Dare Clubb, Jonathan Freedman and Jacques Lezra, whose learning and intellectual adventurousness are a delight. During two periods at Harvard University I learned from the creative thinking of Elaine Scarry and Jonah Siegel. Ingrid Geerken-Nilssen and Sophia Padnos gave me sustaining help and support, both intellectual and practical.

I thank Patricia Brewerton for her patient and meticulous work on the final stages of the manuscript. Anne Hartman worked on the manuscript with astonishing efficiency and critical imagination, turning a burdensome task into an intellectual exercise that made important contributions to the book's eventual form. Both worked with a grant from the Birkbeck College English Department's Research Fund, whose generous help enabled the book's speedy completion. Diana Godden's equanimity and promptitude when faced with sudden transatlantic enquiries was immensely supportive and forebearing. I thank her for help and support throughout the time of writing.

To two friends in particular I owe a great debt. To Mary Hamer for perceptive and rigorous reading of parts of the manuscript at crucial times, and to Laura Marcus, who not only read and commented on large portions of the manuscript, but provided, throughout the period of writing, advice whose depth of wisdom, searching scholarship and creative thinking always enhanced the work. I thank her for the happiest of collaborative relationships and for a lasting intellectual friendship.

The writing of the major part of this book coincided with two periods of disability in the United States. Elena Levin's care of body and mind on both occasions made it possible to continue. A great teller of stories as well as an acute questioner, she provided unforgettable support for which I shall always be grateful.

Thomas Armstrong, my son, helped me with music and philosophy. I thank Michael Armstrong, my husband, the most obstinate questioner of them all, for constant suggestions and advice, but above all for an unending conversation.

Chapter 1 was originally published in *Textuality and Sexuality*, ed. Judith Still and Michael Worton, Manchester, Manchester University Press, 1993. I am grateful to Routledge for permission to publish chapters 2, 3 and 6 from Routledge journals. Chapters 3 and 6 were first published in *Textual Practice* in 1995 and 1998 respectively; chapter 2 was first published in *Women: A Cultural Review* in 1998. Thanks to Allardyce, Barnett Publishers for permission to reprint Veronica Forrest-Thomson's 'Ducks and Rabbits' in *Collected Poems and Translations*, London, Lewes & Berkeley, Allardyce, Barnett 1990 in Chapter 2. Taylor and Francis has kindly given permission for publication of the text of 'Tintern Abbey' in chapter 3, from *Wordsworth and Coleridge, Lyrical Ballads*, ed. R. C. Brett and A. R. Jones, London, Routledge, 1965.

Isobel Armstrong

Introduction: A Case for Rethinking the Category of the Aesthetic

I

...his imagination plunged again and again into the waves that whirled past it and round it, in the hope of being carried to some brighter, happier vision – the vision of societies in which, in splendid rooms, with smiles and soft voices, distinguished men, with women who were both proud and gentle, talked about art, literature and history.

...he has told me that the people may perish over and over, rather than the conquests of civilisation be sacrificed to them. He declares, at such moments, that they will be sacrificed – sacrificed utterly – if the ignorant masses get the upper hand.

Henry James, *The Princess Casamassima*

This book is about the turn to an anti-aesthetic in theoretical writing over the past twenty years. It forges, in response, the components of an alternative aesthetic discourse. The most influential cultural and literary theorists of the last two decades, even when they come from constituencies and traditions inimical to each other, have agreed – and sometimes it is all that they have agreed on – that the category of the aesthetic, together with its foundational philosophers, Kant and Hegel, is up for deconstruction. Marxists, cultural materialists, post-structuralists, and deconstructive psychoanalysts, have converged in what has sometimes looked like a mission in cultural eugenics. For however different in origin, these forms of thought have shared a hermeneutics of suspicion.

Productive as this hermeneutics has been in so many ways – irrigating intellectual culture with new theory – the concept of the aesthetic has been steadily emptied of content. This movement calls out in its turn the project of rethinking the aesthetic.

Such rethinking has become an intellectual necessity because the politics of the anti-aesthetic rely on deconstructive gestures of exposure that fail to address the democratic and radical potential of aesthetic discourse. These strategies effectively undermine aesthetic discourse but refuse to remake it. The result is culturally impoverishing and politically disabling. Disabling, to begin with, because the aesthetic principle uncovered is more often than not a nineteenth-century idealist aesthetic, as I show in a number of chapters, stemming from Kant and Hegel. This was indeed formative, but, as James's cruel parody in *The Princess Casamassima* suggests, it could be seen as an obsolete elitist fantasy about the high bourgeois subject, even in 1886 when his novel was published. '[D]istinguished men, with women who were both proud and gentle, talked about art, literature and history' in 'splendid rooms'. Thus while the energies of extirpation are directed against an inappropriate object, the intellectual and political problems involved in construing a democratic aesthetic fail to be addressed. Second, aesthetic production continues, and always will, whatever the exhaustion of theoretical accounts of the aesthetic. To have lost confidence in the aesthetic as a category, together with the possibility of generating new ideas about it, leaves one without resources of analysis in contemporary culture. Finally, a *dearth* of ideas can be as powerful as any ideological directive in shaping theory and practice. One might connect the narrow instrumentalism of educational policies in Britain, for instance, with the lack of a developed understanding of 'aesthetic education'. Theorists from the tradition of a hermeneutics of suspicion are mostly silent about the politics and poetics of 'beauty'. These questions are implicitly left to the reactionaries – an assumption that makes it more rather than less important to remake aesthetic discourse.

Evolving another poetics means challenging the politics of the anti-aesthetic by remaking its theoretical base and changing the terms of the argument. It does not mean returning to a pre-theoretical innocence. At the same time, to give a new content to the concept of the aesthetic means broadening the scope of what we think of as art. In the four parts of this book I argue that the components of aesthetic life are those that are already embedded in the processes and practices of consciousness – playing and dreaming, thinking and feeling. Or, put another way, ceaseless mediation endows language-making and symbol-making, thought, and the life of affect, with creative and cognitive life. These processes – experiences that keep us alive – are common to everyone, common to what the early Marx called species being. That is why they can become the basis from which to develop a democratic aesthetic. They fund the category afresh, but a new aesthetic discourse redefines them in turn. I draw upon a number of thinkers from different epistemological traditions to renew aesthetic discourse, deliberately seeking a more eclectic group of theorists than those aligned with contemporary critique. This group includes the Russian psychologist and educationalist L. S Vygotsky; John Dewey, the American pragmatist and aesthetician; Object Relations psychoanalysts D. W. Winnicott, Wilfred Bion and André Green, the phenomenology of Paul Ricoeur, Emmanuel Levinas and Surrealist poetics, the revisionary Hegelian, Gillian Rose, Theodor Adorno's cultural poetics.

Quizzically ambiguous statements about aesthetic experience from Henry James's *The Princess Casamassima*, his novel about a working-class autodidact and revolutionary socialist, form epigraphs to this chapter. I have used them to stand in for a familiar modern debate and to elicit some of its difficulties. James is sometimes credited with the sophistication of having defined cultural capital *avant la lettre* – though it would have been difficult not to, in 1886, when the interdependence of intellectual and aesthetic culture, money and privilege was glaringly obvious. Hyacinth Robinson, James's 'tormented' precursor to Jude, kills himself. Part fantasized, part the hunger of the imagination – James calls it 'the world of his divination and his envy together' (p. xxix) – his pursuit of aesthetic understanding is one of the things that destroys him. But if his fictional character transcendentalized the aesthetic, James's Preface did not, assuming brutally, though with deep irony, that aesthetic understanding depends on money and class, describing the cultural capital from which Hyacinth was excluded – the doors of 'freedom and ease, knowledge and power, money, opportunity and satiety' had not opened for him. 'For one's self, all conveniently', he adds with suave deprecation, 'there had been doors that opened' (p. xxviii) (though with an interesting tact he does not associate his own case with 'satiety'). The savage irony is that Hyacinth is a man of greater intellectual depth, learning and aesthetic sense than any of the aristocrats he meets. His dream of the intellectual aristocracy is a dream, conflating high art and high status. But nothing in James is simple. The 'vision', with its 'soft voices' and 'distinguished' men, is a banally deferential reading of cultural privilege (having nothing to do with the culture of the music halls James visited), and at the same time it is the product of passion and longing, a famished desire.

Thus in a text written over 100 years ago a modern dilemma opens. Hyacinth fatally identifies the achievement of aesthetic understanding with class privilege. For him they cannot be disjoined. Because privilege and the material circumstances that sustain power control access to the aesthetic and its delights – and perhaps one of these delights is that privilege itself is aestheticized. He reneges on his politics and class loyalty. Working-class victory, he is reported by his disappointed mentor to have said, will overturn the great cultural trophies of our civilization. And so as far as he is concerned, the people 'may perish over and over', rather than that 'the conquests of civilisation' should be destroyed by the ignorant masses. Eighteen years later, in the First World War, 'the people' did indeed 'perish over and over' in the name of those very 'conquests', a historical irony that makes the novel the more disturbing. A trick of James's syntax makes it momentarily unclear what is being 'sacrificed' (a thrice repeated term): the people or the great cultural trophies of civilization. But only momentarily. The Benjaminian reading that deconstructs the union of art and power gives way to a cruder proposition on Hyacinth's part. It is better for the people to perish to save culture rather than the other way round. Nevertheless, the possible outrage engendered by mass sacrifice that flickers in the prose, begotten by the suppressed reading, becomes available.

The tragedy allows itself to be complex because the novel follows through this suppressed reading. Hyacinth's 'divination' of beauty is contaminated with contempt for the ignorant masses, and by his misrecognized elision of high art and privilege. This understanding, one supposition entailing the other, is simultaneously correct and fallacious. In a condition where the doors of freedom and knowledge do not open, and where access to the aesthetic is conditional upon material wealth and privilege, Hyacinth cannot but be caught in his destructive reading. Yet at stake in his tragedy is the proposition that the aesthetic is not *intrinsically* bound to wealth, privilege and power, that it does not *depend* for its existence on class and money – as a penniless autodidact he could never have experienced such longing if that had been the case. He was a dreamer, but he was not deluded. The possibility of uncoupling the aesthetic and privilege glimmers in James's prose.

That such an uncoupling of the aesthetic and privilege can and does take place is an axiom of this book. Not a few nineteenth-century educationalists and working men, including the Chartists who claimed Shakespeare as their own, took a democratic reading of the aesthetic for granted.[1] But this tradition has been lost in the dominant analysis of the category that has come from the left in recent years. The uncoupling James envisaged is deemed to untether the aesthetic from history and ideology, and so the distopian association of culture and privilege that ultimately prevails in his novel has also prevailed in contemporary analysis.

I consider some of these analyses in the chapters that follow – those stemming, for instance, from English and French Marxisms (Terry Eagleton, Pierre Bourdieu) and from American cultural critique (John Guillory). But here the point to be emphasized is that the 'Jamesian' paradigm of the aesthetic remains almost intact in these discourses. It is essentially a derivative, over-simplified Kantianism. This remains equally the case of those who have purified the aesthetic from political analysis, and who tend to write as if the political does not exist at all in the context of aesthetic experience. The traditional definition has not shifted much, whether it is inflected as radical or conservative, undermined or confirmed. Neither radical critique nor conservative confidence works with the possibility that social and cultural change over the last century might have changed or might change the category itself. Both in its deconstruction and consecration the model of the aesthetic remains virtually the same. And so the dialectics of left and right converge in an unspoken consensus that is unable to engage with democratic readings.[2]

The book's project, therefore, arises from the impasse of both conservative and left-leaning thinking about the aesthetic. The second section of this introduction examines two contemporary discussions standing as exemplary cases. Section three briefly explains the structure of the book and charts the sequence of the argument. In the following discussion Roger Scruton and Mark Cousins represent accounts of the aesthetic in, respectively, conservative authoritarian and left libertarian theory. Inevitably this is an immanent reading of their writing and one which neither is likely to accept.[3] Although they come from deeply opposed positions, they are fundamentally alike. For different reasons they arrive at an inward-looking exclusiveness that is indifferent to theorizing the radical potential of aesthetic work.[4]

II

To begin with there is Roger Scruton's determined photographobia. 'The medium of photography, one might say, is inherently pornographic.' So Scruton ends his essay on 'Photography and representation' in *The Aesthetic Understanding* (pp. 102–6). Scruton's conservatism is argued with exactitude and asks for a serious reading.[5] His coolly provocative exclusion of photography, and as a corollary, film and television, from the status of art and aesthetic understanding – effectively the exclusion also of those for whom it is the staple pleasure – is arrived at by a series of scrupulous vetos. The argument is as follows:

In photography only the empirical world provokes our recognition of the picture's meaning; in painting the picture itself initiates our recognition. From this backwards mimesis it follows that photography is tied to the logic of the temporal, and, as the product of one moment and one moment only, cannot synthesize moments of experience. Another veto follows from this first act of exclusion: photography is denied the possibility of thought, which constitutes true representation, because it is tied by a causal logic to the particulars of the empirical world. By a reversible action you can substitute the real thing for the image, just as the copy can be a substitute for the real thing. In the sense that it is a copy, a simulacrum, of a literal object, photography is only a practical craft, tied to the literal.

Photography's dependence on the empirical world leads to a further veto, this time in the order of the emotions. Incapable of representing anything 'unreal', photography is also incapable of imbuing a subject with feeling or emotion, or of charging an ugly subject with beauty or transforming violence into a serenely contemplated act. Because it has to represent facts, what is ugly will *be* ugly in the photograph, transparent as it is to the literal. If the photographer does transform, as in surrealist use of photo cut-outs, the nearer to art will his work become, cheating the simulacrum into art.

Painting, on the other hand, even representational painting rather than abstract painting, does not have a reversible relation with its subject. This, paradoxically, is true mimesis. For it 'stands in a certain "intentional" relation to its subject' (Scruton, p. 103). There can be no direct reference to an external subject because the representation is created in and meant to be recognized in and through the painting itself. The representation is for its own sake: we recognize a 'man', not the record of a particular man at a particular time; therefore we do not have to go beyond the picture to make the act of recognition. Even when the subject is recognized as Napoleon or the Duke of Wellington, the spectator is not recognizing a particular man, x = y, but seeing the subject *in* the picture, seeing the image *as*, because there is no equivalent beyond the picture. Despite his disavowal of painting as surrogate and his understanding that painting is indifferent to literal truth, Scruton is, nevertheless, concerned to show that painting's connection with its subject is not accidental. It tells us something truthful about the thing depicted – the barmaid's hands in Manet's *Bar aux Folies-Bergère*, for instance – precisely because of the irreplaceability of the thing depicted. It shows us something we will not see in anyone's hands but only in those in the picture. (And perhaps we could say the same thing of the glass bottles in the painting as well.) If the photograph is enslaved to the empirical world, the painting has a free relationship to it.

Here Scruton has transposed an almost too well-known distinction between literature and history to painting and photography. Tragedy is more 'philosophical' than history, Aristotle said, because history is tied to empirical fact, whereas literary texts can deal with the typical, can generalize and universalize. Photography is less 'philosophical' than painting, so the parallel argument goes, and is the victim of random detail that it cannot control or select, whereas painting is not. If the labels on the bottles stand out as clearly as the lines on the barmaid's hands, the result is an undiscriminating glut of visual detail. Both Aristotelian generalization and Gombrichian conventional representation (the way objects in art are stylized and formalized over time according to patterns that become commonly recognized) are alike. Generalization and convention alike, synthesizing and ordering reality, make thought constitutive of the representational image. They have that 'objectivity and publicity' (p. 105) that characterizes language. Photography, by contrast, is illiterate, a stutter. Art has to use conventions to offer a complete expression of a thought about a fictional content, creating (though Scruton recognizes that painting has no 'grammar') the equivalent of a sentence. Photography, which simply points to an object, is 'fictionally incompetent' (p. 112) and has no language, because language precisely comes into being from the separation of thing and word.

Scruton then extrapolates an ideological reading from Gombrich's purely formal account of 'style' and the formalization of convention, a reading it was never intended to bear. Conventions constitute the 'philosophical' element in painting, he argues. We recognize the conventions rather than the objects they formalize through the 'common knowledge' (p. 105), built up through a cultural tradition that teaches us how to know and recognize objects. This binding tradition requires, of course, initiation and training. We have to be socialized to recognize conventions, and conventions themselves are socializing.[6] Gombrich's notion of style is first Aristotelianized and then Aristotle becomes Burke. Conventions become the rules.

But why is photography pornographic? Because its dependence on the literal makes it the ready gratification of fantasy. Fantasy needs the literal, fetishizing the immediacy of the thing obsessing it, its realization in the actual. Photography is inherently pornographic because it is always at the service of fantasy by providing the fulfilment of desire in the semblance of the thing, which can be mistaken for the thing itself, or substituted for it. Only convention, only the lifting of the artwork into form, can break the circuit of fantasy, refusing it the gratification of immediacy. Form, convention and the cultural traditions that create them are saving agents.

Scruton's photographobia is, of course, derivative of Kant as well as of Aristotle. Or, perhaps a different thing, it represents what we have come to think of as conventionally Kantian ideas.[7] It is not to demean Kant to say that Scruton's reading of photography, though sophisticatedly argued, is conceptually naïve. The photograph does not, for instance, produce the reversibility he describes. The very fact that it emerges from a fleeting moment in time means that that time is irrevocably lost. Even to exchange the photographed rose with the real rose a few hours later is to expose the delicate ravage of time in a disposition of pollen or fallen petal or the transformation of light. Photographs are celebrations of the uniqueness of every moment of being, every configuration of shadow and substance, and an elegy upon them. The permanent structures guaranteed by the physics of light, and the impermanent moment when the light never again falls in exactly the same way, are its dialectic. Photographs are as heavily mediated as paintings, depending on light, camera angle, the grain of paper, the mood of the artist. Photographs of the same object by different people are always different, utterances about the play of light, universes exposed in a single lens, epiphanies of transience. Film, despite its repeatability, works the same way – the 'never again' is filmed in a flight of birds. The dialectical image as Walter Benjamin saw it, fraught with contradiction, is as possible in a photograph or film as in any artistic production.[8] It is mere logic-chopping to say that a photograph becomes art only when we cheat. Scruton seems ignorant of a tradition of writing on the photographic image, from Barthes's *Camera Lucida* onwards. For a writer who celebrates the power of traditions this ignorance, one can note in passing, is odd.

The core of Scruton's argument is that photography offers no training in the saving conventions of a cultural tradition. It is not amenable to incorporation in a historical tradition of form and convention, on analogy with the conventions of an artistic style, conventions which control and organize one's recognition and perception of the world, art and culture. Form and the 'common knowledge' of convention built up in shared cultural experience and training, conventions that transmute the troubled particularities of our lives into abstractions, rituals and rules – what in another essay, 'Emotion and culture' (*The Aesthetic Understanding*, pp. 138–52), he calls a 'common culture' – are all-important in his aesthetic. Conventions transcend the literal and resolve it into thought. Training in a common culture and its praxis not only teaches us how to behave and where to put emotions, it also relieves us of the responsibility of deciding on the appropriate social form of feeling. Not only does ritual save us from fantasy and, thereby, from pornography, it brings communality and self together.

Scruton is moved by the collective experience of ritual and writes eloquently about it. His thinking on the emotions in 'Emotion and culture' has hopeful possibilities. He evokes the delayed burial rite for Elpenor in the Odyssey, a communal act followed as reparation for the unburied man at the behest of supernatural law, as an example of common culture's power. Through this (though some would remember the element of self-interest among the mariners) Scruton considers the way a common culture objectifies by bringing subject and object together in a publicly recognized arena of action. Much of our lives, he argues, belongs to the sphere of what Kant calls 'practical reason', experiences of the world that frequently go against the logic and categories of abstract, 'pure' reason (p. 148). A certain kind of knowledge is at stake here, one that involves an understanding of the world as imbued with emotion. He has no doubt that this kind of experience is important. But for him emotions require education. They cannot subsist without support from communal practices that depend on recognized social rules. If emotions are allowed public forms and recognized conventions of expression, these in turn reciprocally train emotion.

Communality looks attractive. Unfortunately, though, there can be by definition only one common culture and shared tradition, and on Scruton's terms this can never be remade. Indeed, there are entry requirements for it. His communality is a consoling and deeply authoritarian conservative fantasy. Scruton's world is rule-bound in a way that refuses to see that tradition, form and ceremony – to use the Shakespearian terms reinterpreted for modernity in the 'ceremony' of Yeats's *A Prayer for my Daughter* – are rarely negotiable. If it is alive, the form and content of a culture is continuously negotiated. Scruton assumes a static world of form and convention. But who legislates for these forms and conventions? How are they authorized? How can they ever be challenged? Barbara Hernstein Smith's critique, in *Contingencies of Value*, of axiological propositions – those assumptions confirmed by a deeply felt intuition of their rightness – is precisely that these ignore the contingency and variability of accounts of rightness, ignore the fact of their continuous negotiation in a culture. 'Evaluation is always compromised because value is always in motion . . . it is constantly variable and eternally indeterminate' (p. 9). It is impossible to rest the full weight of a culture on fixed forms and conventions, much less to see these as a communal mode of ethical training in which the ethical is elided with an abstract aestheticism. Recent examples of cultural negotiation – the death of Diana, Princess of Wales in 1997, the Drumcree marchers in 1998, the Clinton scandals of 1999, the death of John Kennedy in the same year – suggest that the reality is more complex. There are some hopeful ways of thinking about a common culture, but Scruton's 'common culture' is a mode of exclusion rather than inclusion. It legislates for an aesthetic aristocracy. Disenfranchizing from the beginning the millions for whom the photography of a daily paper and the colours of cinema and TV constitute aesthetic pleasure, it rests on an ungenerous formalism.

I now turn to Mark Cousins's essay on artistic representations of violence: 'The culture of fear', published in 1998 in the Tate Gallery's house journal. As a political radical, Cousins is, seemingly, repudiating the coercive fixity and ethical rigidity of a common culture such as Scruton would understand it by affirming the continued 'struggle between regulation and the arts'. He deprecates a situation of repressive censorship where 'morality and lawyers are among the first to the scene of the crime' committed by art (p. 51). For him it follows that 'the breaking of cultural expectations, or...the utter surprise of seeing something radically new' is one of the cardinal prerogatives of the aesthetic (p. 51). Not the known but the unknown is art's domain, not training but the breaking of habit is art's praxis. Cousins's argument centres on the presence – for him the necessary presence – of violence in contemporary art, particularly visual art and its representation of the body. In what looks like a parody of orthodox Kantian aesthetics he writes: 'The gap between the history of art's relation to violence and the public version of art as a life enhancing and transcendent practice governed by the beautiful could not be more comic' (p. 52). (The gap between himself and Scruton, perhaps?) Christianity itself has licensed the representation of violence in the tortured body of the crucifixion, and, he says, drawing on Harold Bloom's masculine theory of the anxiety of influence, art has been characterized by parricide, by the heroic Oedipal necessity to negate the achievement of the previous generation. Art is founded on a necessary system of upheaval. No common culture here, and no formalism.

Cousins emphasizes that 'a great corpus of damage is painted, photographed, installed and performed' (p. 52). Anxieties about the body are 'minutely audited' in an iconography of violence that is not simply descriptive but uses violence itself as a medium. He believes – an important insight – that contemporary art's preoccupation with violence has increased in correspondence with western culture's defensive protection against threats to the integrity of the self and with 'the emergence of a very low threshold of the fear of violence and, indeed, the fear of anything that threatens the integrity of the body' (p. 51). Our culture's obsession with fitness and the use of technology to prolong youth is fed by this fear. The result is twofold, and both consequences have important implications for art. First, violence has been redefined, so that anything that threatens the security of the body is included within the category of violence.

Second, 'related to that tendency, is the erosion of the distinction between violence and the representation of violence' (p. 51). A supreme example is the work of Catharine A. MacKinnon, whose campaign against pornography refuses any distinction between representation of an event – gang rape in a movie, for instance – and the event itself. (Scruton's account of the pornography of the photograph has affinities with MacKinnon's presuppositions.) This fallacious conflation of art and life, he argues, is fatal. Rather than directing energy towards the construction of a more secure society, it unleashes a 'hatred of the art object' (p. 53) itself. He predicts the intensification of a fierce moral campaign against violence in works of art, a campaign that will not even need censorship to be effective because it will invoke criminal and civil law to deal with the 'abuses' of art. These will be treated like violence in real life. In other words, just as in Scruton's account of the photograph, image and object are and will be regarded as reversible.

I share Cousins's anxiety about 'paranoid regulation', but his reasons for exempting the aesthetic from regulation are problematical. Quite simply, art is for him a special category where certain judgements must be suspended. Since the domain of the aesthetic emerged as a philosophical category in the eighteenth century 'we have called art' those productions whose status as representation invites us to think of them as objects ' "to be treated in another way than its mere existence as an object might suggest" '. He hastens to make it clear that he is not thinking of 'representation' as vulgar mimesis, but as that which distinguishes the 'art object from the non-art object as part of a public discourse' (p. 53). (Actually, he could usefully have used Scruton's account of 'free' mimesis and representation here.) He is also very much aware, uneasily aware, that the conceptualization of art as a special category has 'internal weaknesses', though he does not say what these are. (An essentialism laying art open to the charges of transcendence and irrelevance, perhaps? The aestheticism of 'pure' art?) Nevertheless, as his cautious inverted commas suggest, he insists that the aesthetic is in some way between brackets. It is 'legally and socially conceived as a specific domain of objects': it is a 'classificatory device for designating certain objects as art and as such having the right to be treated (legally, politically, etc.) differently from other objects' (p. 53).

'...the right to be treated (legally, politically, etc.) differently'...? By arguing that representation is the element that changes the status of art objects in legal and political terms, Cousins is evidently attempting to avoid the charge of an essentialized aestheticism that claims special privileges for a transcendent experience, the very experience he describes as 'comic'. But in doing this he has fallen into another kind of aesthetic libertarianism, a deregulatory paranoia of his own. Do works of art *have* rights? Can legal rights be assigned to created objects? And isn't the discourse of 'rights' problematical anyway? We have long known that in the liberal version of 'rights' one person's right is another's exclusion. And if the arts are to be treated 'differently' in terms of politics and the law, what kinds of special legal and political treatment can they expect? Is it the case that the practice of the arts in civil society gains a kind of exemption from, can be granted a kind of immunity from, any form of what Cousins calls, with a certain hostility, ' "public concern" '? Something as amorphous as 'public concern' includes so many constituencies and gradations of view that it might well include quite justifiable critique. How is legitimate critique to be distinguished from illegitimate 'public concern', and who has the 'right' to offer it? The cognoscenti? The logical conclusion of the argument is the exclusion of art from all critique except of those who 'know'. This argument ends up with another form of censorship: that created by the protectionism of privileged knowledge, which is merely the complement of public regulation. Indeed, the resignifying of art as a practice outside the public sphere, the domain of a private elite, is one of the dangerous possibilities of Cousin's argument. Strangely enough, he is offering us something like 'pure' art, outside the rubrics of the public sphere. The analogy is with those scientists who claim the same suspension of public rubrics in the name of the freedom of experiment assumed to be the prerogative of 'pure' science.

What kind of radical practice does this amount to? In freeing art from the coercion of philistine critique Cousins has forgotten to consider the meaning of a radical aesthetic. No doubt he would argue that to achieve a condition when artists can paint what they like *is* to have achieved a truly democratic aesthetic state. But to found painting what you like on the censorship of discussion is surely a problematic position to have arrived at.

How has an important argument about 'paranoid regulation' reached this dead end? Despite his political convictions and real belief in the 'radically new', Cousins is working with a left-radical form of Kantianism that posits a sphere of disinterestedness for art as free play just as insistently as the conservative inflection of Kantianism we have seen at work in the writings of Roger Scruton. (Similarly, both the deconstruction and the celebration of common culture arise from the same source.) Cousins's argument comes down to a misrecognition of Kant that allows for the individual's free play, or the autotelic artwork's free play, exempt from societal frameworks. And here Kant, or the Kantian tradition, justifies not the restraints of a common culture but the breaking of cultural expectations. Scruton and Cousins occupy two sides of the same argument, rather than representing different political fields, so that conservative authoritarianism and libertarian militancy belong to opposite forms of the same thinking. Both reserve a special space for art. It is marked with a 'no entry' sign.

III

The first part of this book, 'The Hermeneutics of Suspicion and the "Problem" of the Aesthetic', consists of chapters that address critique of the aesthetic by, respectively, Marxism, and post-structuralism, through the work of Terry Eagleton, Jacques Derrida and Paul de Man. A major concern of these chapters is with the cognitive aspects of artwork, widening the category by drawing on theories of play in Lev Vygotsky and D. W. Winnicott and on the revisionary Hegelianism of Gillian Rose. Part II, 'The Poetics of Emotion', addresses the importance of a reading of the emotions to aesthetic discourse, arguing that the constitutive nature of affect has been ignored or bracketed in contemporary theory because of its seeming resistance to analysis. Two chapters, drawing on Emmanuel Levinas, André Green and Wilfred Bion, consider what an analytical poetics of emotion would look like. Above all, the emotions should be included within a definition of the rational rather than fall outside it. Part III, 'Cultural Capital, Value and a Democratic Aesthetic' moves to the cultural theory that subsumes 'value' under cultural capital. An economic discourse and a discourse of beauty each sees the other as the 'problem' to be solved. In successive chapters I read the work of John Dewey and Theodor Adorno to escape this impasse and reclaim a democratic project. Finally, in the fourth part, 'Feminism and Aesthetic Practice', the last two chapters of the book look at the way second-wave feminism found new modes of affective and analytical language. Its strength was that it looked at gender through the prism of the aesthetic rather than the other way round, discovering a poetics of gender that formed one of the most potent discourses of the aesthetic developed in the last quarter of the twentieth century. These chapters discuss ways of repairing the weakening and narrowing of feminism's project in the last decades.

The first part begins with British Marxism's deconstruction of the aesthetic, represented here by Terry Eagleton. It ends with a reading of Hegel's *Encyclopaedia Logic* as a poetics of thinking. The original impulse of these chapters was a defining moment that altered the terms with which cultural and political life was envisaged: Margaret Thatcher's bracing practical and political version of the hermeneutics of suspicion, the new ethos, that is, created by economic policy both for the arts and for higher education evolved by Thatcher in the 1980s under the influence of Reagan. The move from politics to epistemology in the first part of the book came about because these policy decisions took on a wider cultural meaning than the immediately economic. The questions they initiated resonated in European and American theory. They provoked questions about democratic access to the arts, but also opened this up in turn to questions of definition, questions about what people have access *to*, and *which* people are included under the rubric 'democracy'. Above all, what would a radical aesthetic look like? In 1989 I published two essays that arose from Thatcherite policy, 'Thatcher's Shakespeare?', occasioned by the slashing of public funding for the arts and the reclassification of public funding as illicit subsidy for the 'dependency culture' that this entailed, and 'English in higher education: "justifying" the subject', a discussion of the implications for English studies of the metaphor of the market and the attack on the 'vested interests' of the universities occasioned by the turn to consumerism in education. These essays are very much tied to a particular historical moment and are not included here. But since they motivated further work and form a context for this book, a brief discussion of them is in order.

In these essays I was interested in the convergence of a conservative and left anti-aesthetic, and the way both eroded the possibility of even hypothesizing Raymond Williams's understanding of a common culture, 'a society's confirmation of its common meanings, and the human skills for their amendment', a statement of 1958 ('English in higher education', p. 12). This definition, of course, is in direct opposition to Scruton's later formulation and offers the chance of changing practice. Accordingly, 'Thatcher's Shakespeare?' asked what kind of 'amendment' the new surge of politicized Shakespeare criticism represented. It advertised itself as radical – and, concurrent with it, theatrical productions of Shakespeare claimed the same thing – but was this really a political response to the new conservatism? Or was it in collusion with that conservatism's version of the anti-aesthetic? Did theory and practice diverge? The 'left' aesthetics of cultural materialism was oddly twinned with Thatcherism. Alan Sinfield's analysis in *Political Shakespeare* (1985) of what he astutely termed post-war 'culturalism', in both arts and educational policy – and in particular the public funding of artistic production that privileges a comfortable middle class and endorses its values – ends in a thoroughgoing rejection of cultural patronage and public policy for the arts: 'Culturism is an aspect of the theory of welfare capitalism, within which the market is accepted as the necessary agency for the production of wealth, and its tendency to produce unacceptable inequality is to be tempered by State intervention' (p. 164). 'Culturalism' and its spurious radicalism, he argued, had failed. It was a pertinent and convincing argument, impressively documented. But it weakened those socially emancipatory elements in the tradition of thought derived from Raymond Williams, from which cultural materialism draws so much of its strength, by refusing to redefine the politics and function of public finance or to consider what an 'amended' reading of cultural cohesion would look like.

Moreover, in its deconstruction of the way Shakespeare has been used as a powerful ideological weapon of conservatism, cultural materialism seems incapable of evolving a non-authoritarian account of language that can work not only against but also for the powerless. That the resources of language might be available to the disempowered (as indeed feminist critics had argued as a necessity of women's entry into language), and that Shakespeare's plays could often show how this enfranchisement comes about, is not an admissable argument either to the readings of cultural materialism or to Stephen Greenblatt's new historicist readings, with which cultural materialism has strong affinities.[9] Even the creative energy of the English Shakespeare Company's productions of the Henriad over the late 1980s under Michael Bogdanov, which claimed to be and often were radically innovative, could not always shake itself free of a deconstructive irony that was capable of confirming rather than undermining a linguistically conservative Shakespeare. This was the era of the Scarman Report (1981) and, though a degree of scepticism in response to Scarman's belief that the study of literature could be a socially and racially unifying agency in the wake of the Brixton riots was understandable, to see language purely as the site of power and cultural imperialism was as naïve as Scarman's optimism was itself deemed to be. The argument of 'English in higher education' extends this position on language. Its axiom is that there are democratic alternatives to hegemonic Arnoldian views of literature as the best that has been said and thought in the world, with its corollary in educational practice that a dominant standard language is paramount. Carrying out its analyses with the same materials that are its objects of study, language, literary study necessarily 'will not simply be concerned with revaluation from time to time (like houses or antiques) but the nature of value itself...is being continuously defined and redefined' (p. 15). Because language is both a tool of analysis and the material of analysis it is renewed with every speech act and act of writing. Thus the pursuit of a standard is as much a phantom, philosophically mistaken, as the pursuit of absolute value.

These two essays were predicated on the way a refusal to think through alternative accounts of the state and the aesthetic resulted in strange convergences between new conservatism and new political critique.

They were the preliminary to a more sustained exploration of the status of aesthetic understanding. The project that arises from questions about democratic access to art is actually that of changing the category itself, or re-describing it, so that what we know looks different, and what we exclude from traditional categories of art also looks different. This task is not accomplished simply by bringing the aesthetic under the rubric of cultural production or thinking of it as cultural capital or ideology.

This re-describing project was precipitated by Terry Eagleton's brilliant and infuriating Marxist study, *The Ideology of the Aesthetic* (1990), which questioned the high place given to the aesthetic since the Enlightenment. A major work of suspicious hermeneutics, this book aligns itself with cultural materialism but widens the scope of critique. Nothing less than the impossibility of the category of the aesthetic is its theme. It and Kant's work, in particular, serve a succession of different oppressive systems, bourgeois hegemony, commodity culture and, ultimately, Fascism. Eagleton's study offered a salutary, virtuosic analysis of the intrinsic political and ideological problems of the aesthetic in the history of our culture. But the book was not seriously interested in envisaging alternatives, or in imagining what a changed understanding of the aesthetic would look like. Chapter 1 of my book, 'The Aesthetic and the Polis: Marxist Deconstruction', is a response to Eagleton's argument. It seeks, with deliberate eclecticism, to develop other ways of describing the aesthetic, both cognitively and affectively. Play and its potential, not Kantian free play but the play from which it is derived, the drive to experiment and know that motivates ludic play, provides a way of redirecting the argument. Working with a Blake lyric to clarify the discussion, I build on cognitive accounts of play in the work of the Russian psychologist Vygotsky and the object relations theory of Winnicott.

Confronted with deconstruction of 'aesthetic ideology' (Paul de Man's term) coming this time from post-structuralism, from Derrida's reading of Kant and de Man's reading of Hegel, 'Writing from the Broken Middle: Post-Structuralist Deconstruction' carries forward from chapter 1 an inquiry about the way the cognitive is bound up with aesthetic experience. Both writers (Derrida with greater success) demolish the aesthetic in a flagrantly 'aesthetic' way, as if to demonstrate that it can do little work except to accomplish the gesture of exposure. Their extreme rejection of romantic philosophy and its epistemology suggests that it may indeed harbour alternative possibilities. This chapter reads Hegel's *Encyclopaedia Logic* as a poetics of thinking and thought. Seeking, as in the case of play, to ground the aesthetic in experience everyone must have, it explores what it would be like to think of the artwork as a representation of mediation, that transitive relationship with the world which is built into consciousness and which must involve both thought and affect. Gillian Rose's agonistic, revisionary account of Hegelian mediation in *The Broken Middle* (1992), is my model. Post-modern critiques of Hegel, such as those of Derrida and de Man, accuse him of a banal and authoritarian absolutism. But, for her, post-structuralist discourse itself epitomises the coercive idealism of which it accuses Hegelian thought. Post-structuralism's elision of the difficulties of the middle arrives at the reductionism that abolishes a genuinely mediated world. Her revisionary Hegelianism reworks the labour of the negative. This movement is either to or from something, and thus avoids what Rose sees as the violence of post-structuralism's collapsing of opposition to two unmediated terms, pre-empting the real alternatives opened up in the triune struggle that does not eliminate the middle. Conventionally, mediation is described as a negotiation between self and world, the friction of inimical categories, but for Rose the great inimical experiences of ethical and civil life, such as the opposition between law and freedom, are as important as this primary mediation. Customary accounts of mediation propose that knowledge comes about when the mind moves between opposites, which reciprocally change relationship to one another. Rose, on the contrary, replaces what she sees as a triumphalist dialectic of resolution moving to a new synthesis, with a logic of breakdown. It is at the point of contradiction, where opposites fail to transform one another, that intellectual struggle is at its most perilous and stressful, and where a painful restructuring of relationships comes about at the site of the middle, the third term. The broken middle is, for Rose, always the most significant point of the triune relationship in dialectical thought.

Rose's new understanding of mediation releases discussion from the experiencing consciousness of the subject and moves to what consciousness does, not a self-struggling but the nature of struggle itself; not a representation of the subject but the subject of representation, which is not a self, or an object, or a thematics, but the structuring movement of thought and feeling. Working with Antony Gormley's sculpture and Veronica Forrest-Thomson's poetry, I argue that the broken middle is the constitutive moment of the aesthetic.

Hatred of emotion, Bion said, is a hatred of life. Part II, 'The Poetics of Emotion', is mindful of Amélie Rorty's warning (in *Explaining Emotions*) that emotion is not a 'natural' but a constructed category, and is more a term that attempts to explain a number of disparate phenomena than an account of homogeneous experience. This is a reason, nevertheless, for paying more rather than less attention to it, particularly as the poverty of modernity's accounts of emotion is so striking. Chapter 3, 'Textual Harassment: the Ideology of Close Reading, or How Close is Close?' reads the – mostly male – history of new criticism since the 1930s as a partly politically inspired but deeply gendered resistance to affect. This modernist literary critical tradition, exemplified by I. A. Richards, William Empson and de Man, had cause to invoke a 'hard' rationality whenever a 'soft' reading of experience, such as the somatic and affective states affiliated with the aesthetic, threatened to come too near. Fascism's manipulation of mass feeling may have been reason enough for this. But the result was a failure to develop an adequate *analytical* language for affect. Wordsworth's *Tintern Abbey* is a test case of the stubbornly anti-rational for many new critics, but their readings demonstrate that close reading is frequently not close enough. Emmanuel Levinas explores a different politics of closeness through surrealist poetics. Surrealist aesthetics are as interested in the nature of thought as in the power of affect, refusing to divorce knowledge from affect or to see them as mutually exclusive.

It is because a cognitive account of the emotions as mutually inclusive is the core of a remade aesthetic that chapter 4, 'Thinking Affect', is lengthy. There are currently debates on emotion in a number of disciplines, from the biological sciences to philosophy. Freud and Julia Kristeva and the puzzlement and aporias of their work on affect are the starting point of this chapter because psychoanalysis is our primary discourse of emotion this century. I proceed to André Green and Wilfred Bion to consider ways of discussing emotion. Though other theories are considered (Sylvan Tomkins, Paul Ricoeur, for instance), I remain with object relations as a productive way of thinking of the emotions. The work of André Green is attractive because he works ambitiously with a cognitive theory of affect, arguing that affect precipitates intellectual work. In some ways his dialectical thought, unfashionably Hegelian in character and unusual in psychoanalysis, matches the structure of mediation explored in chapter 2, 'Writing from the Broken Middle' – though I want to indicate a general parallel rather than forcing an affinity. Since Green's writing is one of the few texts to argue at length that affect mobilizes thought, it is possible to bring thinking and affect together through his theory in a convincing way. I work with Clint Eastwood's movie, *Unforgiven*, and a Willian Blake lyric to exemplify Green's theory and explore a visual language of emotion through the representation of shock and trauma. Thus an account of the representation of emotion can be developed. The chapter ends with a social reading of the emotions through Vygotsky's account of 'inner speech' and its relation to community and through Bion's account of myth and dream as 'publication'.

Part III, 'Cultural Capital, Value and a Democratic Aesthetic' begins where the previous section leaves off, with an exploration of the aesthetic grounded in social and cultural practices, the 'publicity' of the artwork and its relation to accounts of 'value'. It would seem, according to some readings, that the discourse of value always doubles as transcendent and economic discourse simultaneously, and always preserves itself from the importunate sensoria by taking refuge in what Bourdieu terms 'restricted' production, what we might term 'high' or avant-garde or elite art. Accordingly, chapter 5, 'Beyond the Pricing Principle', looks at Bourdieu and at John Guillory's work on Bourdieu and Barbara Hernstein Smith (though Guillory oversimplifies her work) in *Cultural Capital: The Problem of Literary Canon Formation* (1993). The tendency of modern theory is either to equate aesthetic value and cultural capital or to counter one with the other as irreconcilable. John Guillory's discussion of cultural capital and his reading of Bourdieu is in danger of bringing teleology in through the back door of Bourdieuian thought by accepting the exclusions of his thought as a given. However, a descriptive-structural analysis and an evaluative-affective analysis of the aesthetic will always be in tension. The one is always the problem to be explained by the other. We will always be at this broken middle, unless the terms can be changed by working from the broken middle itself. There is a democratic thinker who did attempt to change the terms, and for whom the question of value is not a central issue – for whom, indeed, judgement is a massive deflection from the meaning of aesthetic experience: John Dewey. His Harvard lectures of 1932, published in 1934 as *Art as Experience*, and the rigorous, much misinterpreted, radical educational theory from which they stem, is an enormously important remapping of the aesthetic. Often travestied, Dewey's account of experience and of artwork is always hyphenated in the sense that for him both always work on and with the world. His is not an individualist but an intersubjective theory, which he saw as severely exacting because it demanded the arousal of the faculties. The aesthetic, quite simply, keeps us alive. Without it we would lack the form-making propensity, and the heightened energies that precipitate it, which is at the basis of all biomental life. I have been drawn to such transitive theories throughout this book. Dewy's commitment to ideas of community is the impetus for a return to the politics of cultural dreaming.

Cultural dreaming is the bridge to chapter 6, 'And Beauty? A Dialogue'. Adorno's newly translated work, *Aesthetic Theory* (1997), alters perceptions of his work. His costive suspicion of the culture industry looks like a 'classic', even elite, traditional humanist theory with a Marxist gloss. But important differences open up if one looks at his work beside a serious philosophical humanist such as Iris Murdoch (by coincidence her essays, *Existentialists and Mystics*, were published in the same year as the new Adorno translation). There is an impassioned materialist theory of beauty embedded in Adorno's bad-tempered prose, and one of community too. He is one of the few Marxists to speak unapologetically and seriously of beauty.

Part IV, 'Feminism and Aesthetic Practice', argues that second-wave feminist thinkers have developed a reservoir of experimental and expressive language that constitutes a contemporary poetics. It has aroused imagination and thought and mobilized innovative writing as little else has. By celebrating feminist poetics I do not mean, however, that an inherent, unique feminist aesthetic is possible. A long tradition associates women with the emotions and with a devalued affective experience, and a feminist aesthetic is often connected with the manifestation of emotion-centred experience. But I do not mean this when I associate feminism and the aesthetic. It is this association that has driven some feminists to break loose from the bonding of femininity and the passions, and it is those non-rational experiences that signal women's limited participation in the culture. (Like Seyla Benhabib, writing in *Feminist Contentions* (1995), they have repudiated the connection and aligned themselves with the rational. To some, Habermasian reason, for all Habermas's lack of interest in gender, is a lifeline). Second-wave feminist writing has developed a 'strong' aesthetic for its most creative intellectual enterprises, deliberately experimenting with the boundaries of the aesthetic to forge feminist thought. Julia Kristeva, Luce Irigaray and Hélène Cixous are the best known of these experimenters, who have seen gender through the prism of the aesthetic rather than the other way round. In such writing affect and thought are fused. Passions become epistemic.

But this creative energy is on the wane. A 'weak' aesthetic discourse has dominated contemporary discussion.[10] Therefore, Chapter 7, 'Debating Feminisms', sets up a taxonomy of second-wave feminisms in order to see what kinds of philosophical project might renew feminist discourse. Endlessly caught up in tracing and retracing the construction of gender and in resignifying the body, feminist thought has become inward-looking. Judith Butler's work has dominated gender politics, which have often become fixated on issues from which she herself has moved away. Chapter 7 tests out and transposes her theory of resignification from gender to racial identity by making readings of three post-colonial novels by Indian women in which gender and ethnicity meet. Post-colonial culture is hypersensitive to the politics of space. Therefore this chapter tries out alternative ways of theorizing difference through essentially aesthetic accounts of relationship based on concepts of space and the politics of space, from Gaston Bachelard to Henri Lefebvre and their common 'ancestor', Heidegger. These interspatial relations constitute a 'transverse' politics rather than a hierarchical one. Though this politics is worked out in the context of post-colonial texts, it can be returned to the location of gender. Space is the aesthetic principle that organizes a gender politics.

I continue this exploration in Chapter 8, 'Women's Space: Echo, Caesura, Echo', the last chapter of this book. This, of course, deliberately recalls Julia Kristeva's famous essay of 1979, 'Women's time', and sets up alternative categories, working on a poetics of space in order to question her temporal model. Kristeva sets up a temporal narrative for her account of gender, putting what she terms the 'Oedipal sacrifice', the intransigent harshness of violent separation, at the heart of feminine experience, so that it repeats a masculine sequence of power relations, castration and the break from narcissism. I experiment with a different notation from the same mythic structure. This is the caesura of the echo, spatial rather than temporal, which unfolds a very different epistemology. With the help of Wilfred Bion's understanding of the caesura I look at alternatives to the determined power relations to which Kristeva consents.

Finally, there are signs that a dormant discourse of the aesthetic is reviving. A recent (1996) collection of essays, *Negotiating Rapture*, is for instance, subtitled, *The Power of Art to Transform Lives* (ed. Richard Francis), a formulation hard to imagine in the last decade or so. The constant preoccupation of theory with the sublime over the decades suffering the occlusion of the aesthetic, instanced as much in Jean-François Lyotard's fascination with the sublime as with Paul de Man's secret predilection for it, was perhaps a way, albeit one that follows the traditional alliance of sublimity and power, in which limited accounts of the aesthetic leaked back into discussion.[11] But the sublime is a discourse of the past. The radical aesthetic cannot return to the point of no return. It must live in the present and the future.

NOTES

1 The most powerful Chartist Newspaper, *The Northern Star*, ran a series in the spring of 1840 called 'Chartism from Shakespeare', quoting passages from Shakespeare's plays which were deemed to exemplify Chartist principles and issues. See Anne Janowitz, *Lyric and Labour in the Romantic Tradition*, p. 146.

2 In an essay on the politics of the aesthetic written at the time of cuts in university funding in the 1980s, I argued that the same problem – the problem of rethinking the status of works of imagination and aesthetic understanding in our society in democratic terms – is confronted by the academic study of English in the universities. (See 'English in higher education: "justifying" the subject').

Also in 1989 I published 'Thatcher's Shakespeare?', an essay addressing the status of a democratic reading of the aesthetic in relation to seemingly radical critique and performance of Shakespeare in a conservative era. Neither of these essays are included here but are discussed briefly in section III of this Introduction as a context for this book.

3   It is likely that each would challenge my interpretation of their work, but though I am making a symptomatic reading of it I do not think I have misrepresented what they say.

4   It is not the intention of this book to arrive at an abstract and comprehensive definition of the aesthetic. I am not working with 'pure' aesthetics so much as engaging with its dialectical meanings in contemporary debates. Reclaiming the aesthetic for a democratic reading is part of that dialectic. That is why I have begun with a 'practical' definition from Henry James. Not surprisingly, the category of the aesthetic gives rise to what Wolfgang Welsch calls 'contrary definitions' that can be 'continued almost without end' (Welsch, *Undoing Aesthetics*, p. 8): 'Sometimes it is to concern the sensuous, sometimes the beautiful, sometimes nature, sometimes art, sometimes perception, sometimes judgement, sometimes knowledge; and "aesthetic" should mean in alternation sensuous, pleasurable, artistic, illusory, fictional, poetic, virtual, playful, unobligating, and so on.' Of course 'aesthetic' is semantically a protean term, covering the obvious: artworks as material artefacts, extending to the creative experience that gives rise to them, the experience that responds to them, and, in a more devolved sense, metatheories about all three. These metatheories in turn may not only analyse the three elements of the aesthetic in either individual or collective and cultural terms, but can become themselves the object of study. A fair amount of ambiguity inevitably arises. Welsch gets round the problem by proposing a series of Wittgensteinian 'family resemblances' among different modes of the aesthetic (ibid., pp. 10–17) but I mean something relatively straightforward – the Enlightenment category of the aesthetic, which includes the idea of beauty that emerged when 'art' began to be perceived as a separate realm of representation and images, was invested with special value and assigned a special place in culture, so that these assignations became, reflexively, the object of enquiry. These enquiries in contemporary intellectual culture are particularly my concern.

5   In concentrating on this particular area of debate I do not want to suggest that important studies have not gone on elsewhere. Recent studies I have found useful are: Christine Battersby, *The Phenomenal Woman: Feminist Metaphysics and the Patterns of Identity*: Andrew Bowie, *Aesthetics and Subjectivity: From Kant to Nietzsche*; Paul Crowther, *Art and Embodiment: From Aesthetics to Self-Consciousness*: Warren Shibles *Emotion in Aesthetics*.

6   Scruton has been an influential rather than a typical figure in the history of contemporary aesthetic discussion since the 1960s, a period that has actually been dominated by left thinkers adopting very different forms of radical critique, from the relative optimism of Marcuse, for instance (in *The Aesthetic Dimension: Towards a Critique of Marxist Aesthetics*), to a deconstructive

politics that assumes the unusableness of aesthetic discourse. It may be that Scruton speaks for a silent majority in his respect for common cultural traditions, but there is no way of knowing.

7 The disinterest of Kantian free play, its liberation from the contingency of the empirical, its hostility to mimesis, its emancipation from substitution and from an economy of the practical (of craft, that is to say), its refusal of the concept unless this emerges from the configuring of particulars in the art object itself – all this is familiar to us from classical Kantian aesthetics.

8 Susan Buck-Morss, (*The Dialectics of Seeing: Walter Benjamin and the Arcades Project*, p. 259) reminds us that Benjamin used the camera shot and the 'lightening flash' of the flashbulb to explain the 'dialectics at a standstill' that comprise the dialectical image, an image which holds unresolved contradictory meanings in dynamic suspension. Contra Roger Scruton, rather than being enslaved by it, temporality is available to the photograph. Such dynamic dialectical images often resignify the past by allowing new meanings to be released. An example is the double focus in the image of the airplane, which holds contradictory histories together, at once indicative of the destructive modern technology that can bomb cities and the antithesis of Da Vinci's Utopian vision of the liberation of flying (ibid., pp. 244–5).

9 Alan Sinfield and Jonathan Dollimore included Stephen Greenblatt's essay, 'Invisible bullets: Renaissance authority and its subversion, *Henry IV* and *Henry V*', in *Political Shakespeare*. Greenblatt's more Foucauldian argument for containment, however – that subversion ultimately endorses power and the need for containing it rather than contradicting it – always sat slightly uncomfortably with the brisker confrontational politics of cultural materialism, which argued for the conservatism of the Shakespearian text. Though there were occasions when Greenblatt's theory and theatrical practice converged, as in the treatment of Francis by the English Shakespeare Company (*Henry IV*, Part I, II. iv. 34–79) in which the servant is deprived of language by the manipulative Hal at the same time as he is accused of having none.

10 Though, despite the exhaustion of theory, women have continued to undertake innovative work. A new radical form and content for the artwork could be explored through the 1997 Documenta art exhibition in Kassel, curated by Catherine David, where the city itself was transformed into a series of installations. Documenta 1997 is interestingly reviewed by Masao Migoshi in 'Radical Art at Documenta X' in *New Left Review*, 1998. A sign that this mould is being broken is the publication, in 1999, of two brilliant lectures by Elaine Scarry under the title *On Beauty and Being Just*.

11 Lyotard invoked the sublime in *The Postmodern Condition* (1982). Paul de Man makes several circumspect approaches to the sublime in the posthumous *Aesthetic Ideology*. In 'Aura and Agora: on negotiating rapture and speaking between' (1996) Homi Bhabha seeks to reinflect the discourse of the sublime for post-modernity.

Part I

The Hermeneutics of Suspicion and the 'Problem' of the Aesthetic

1

The Aesthetic and the Polis: Marxist Deconstruction

Prologue – Blake: the aesthetic belongs to Hell

Blake calls the Proverbs of Hell 'sayings' which mark the 'character' of Infernal culture and which provide the anthropologist of the infernal regions with an understanding of Hell's national identity. Two sayings in particular offer a laconic comment on a product of the late Enlightenment, a new European/infernal category, the aesthetic:

> The head Sublime, the heart Pathos, the genitals Beauty, the hands and feet Proportion.
> —Exuberance is beauty. (Blake, *The Marriage of Heaven and Hell*, p. 110)

Hell is creative and destructive – in Blake's terms, Prolific and Devouring. On the one hand, a new, 'Prolific' language of the beautiful is being created. On the other hand, the body is mapped and charted, repressively ordered into zones and hierarchies. The zone of the sublime is the head, reason, from which both Kant and Burke explicitly excluded women. The head is separated from the heart, the region of pathos, that new affective area of imaginative empathy which, from Shaftesbury on, was to act as the unifying social bond – I understand your suffering through imagining myself in your place. Intuition, not thought, directs social feeling, both assuaging absolutist law and creating a bourgeois subject capable of checking the unbridled desires of the individual self. Beauty belongs to the zone of the genitals because, from the eighteenth century on, the Beautiful was emphatically gendered. For Burke, the Beautiful is associated with the social, and the social is founded on sexual feeling and the desire for procreation. Women, weak, passive, melting, belong to the genital zone because they arouse sexual feeling, not because they experience it. As well as delimiting the erotic, the genital is the source of sensation and somatic life, the world of sensory experience which was beginning, through philosophers such as Hume, to be appropriated for a new sceptical epistemology. Classical proportion is displaced to the hands and feet, reduced to the status of the artefact, the material object at the base of a hierarchical, idealist world. And proportion is also mechanized, product of the 'hands' which are utilized in the division of labour, a division founded on the fragmentation of functions which are inscribed on Blake's partitioned body. Finally, 'Exuberance' is invoked to redress the alienation created by these newly configured parts – energy, creativity, self-delight. Beauty becomes an emancipatory concept, as Blake's proverbs challenge or redress one another. But this is emphatically a Proverb of Hell because the aesthetic escapes from the ethical: it need not belong to the moral order, it can be neutral, it can belong to evil. In its pure self-justifying freedom it is severed from the ethical and may even do violence to it.

But while Blake's beautiful *can* be emancipatory (another reason, of course, why it belongs to Hell), current thinking on the left generally views the category of the aesthetic as, if not fraudulent, deeply suspect. Terry Eagleton's *The Ideology of the Aesthetic*, a study of the category of the aesthetic in post-Enlightenment Europe, for which Blake's two proverbs might have stood as epigraph, is an example of such thinking, despite some gestures to the contrary. It offers a powerful reading of the aesthetic – the book enabled me, for instance, to read Blake's proverbs afresh – but it is pessimistic on the whole. Can the aesthetic be reclaimed for radical thought? Need it be handed over to the right? Can it be reclaimed for feminist thought and praxis? I begin by taking issue with Eagleton's argument (worth challenging because this is a brilliant book), particularly his chapter on Kant, as a preliminary to setting out an alternative account of the aesthetic and the polis.

The ideology of the aesthetic and the seductions of the imaginary

Eagleton's Kant chapter leads up to a moment he seems to have been waiting for, pliant, to be toyed with in the moment of primary narcissism:

> What else, psychoanalytically speaking, is this beautiful object which is unique yet universal...? The beautiful representation, like the body of the mother, is an idealised material form...with which, in a free play of its faculties, the subject can happily sport. The bliss of the aesthetic subject is

the felicity of the small child playing in the bosom of its mother, enthralled by an utterly indivisible object which is at once intimate and indeterminate, brimming with purposive life yet plastic enough to put up no resistance to the subject's own ends. (Eagleton, *Idelogy*, pp. 90–1)

So that was it after all: the work of Kant's aesthetic comes to this – the omnipotent infant using for its own purposes the mother's body and its illusory plenitude and false unity. Kant's imaginary, it is assumed, will stand as a paradigm for the aesthetic in general. What is interesting is not that Kant is shackled to the mother's body (the founding moment of relationship with the mother's body can perfectly well belong to an account of the aesthetic, as I show later), but that Eagleton seems to think this is the worst thing he can say about the aesthetic. Not only does he retain without questioning (if the irony of the passage is intended to question, it does not work) the insistently denigrating Enlightenment connection of the aesthetic and the feminine, but in invoking Lacanian and Althusserian parallels he manages to ontologize these psychoanalytical structures as universals.

What got into him? Such a clever book, using all the resources of the aesthetic so exuberantly, has rarely been written on a topic so uncongenial, so repugnant to its author. While saying that he is liberating the category of the aesthetic from those on the left, for whom it is simply 'bourgeois ideology', he puts it pretty firmly back there and admits that his project is 'hardly' one of the most urgent facing the left (pp. 8, 11). The first part of the book is actually a skit on the aesthetic as the product of liberal humanist ideology. But Marx, who believed passionately in the aesthetic, is a problem and will not be assimilated into this Marx Brothers' intellectual slap-stick or its compulsively carking ironies. So the scene of masquerade gives way, in the last part of the book, to some of Eagleton's best critique ever, from Heidegger to Adorno, Freud to Foucault.

Sharing with Jacques Derrida and Paul de Man (a strange meeting of the ideologically incompatible) a thoroughgoing dislike of the category of the aesthetic, Eagleton is far more insistent than they are, or in de Man's case ever could be, that a black line runs from the earliest explorations of the aesthetic in Baumgarten to Fascism. He sometimes argues as if the aesthetic *produced* Fascism. Implicit in his discussion is Walter Benjamin's admonition that the documents of civilization are the documents of barbarism, and Adorno's belief that poetry after Auschwitz is impossible. True, this is something we need to be constantly reminded of: the Gulf War, closely following upon Eagleton's book, produced a coolly technologized aesthetic destruction on television screens, as smart bombs, autotelic, self-maintaining, like the Kantian aesthetic subject in free play, found their targets.

Eagleton's is a worst-case reading, and has to be attended to. But the best answer to this case might well be to retheorize a flagrantly emancip-atory, unapologetically radical aesthetic. This would refuse the conserva-tive reading of the aesthetic as that which stands over and against the political as disinterested Beauty, called in nevertheless to assuage the violence of a system it leaves untouched, and retrieve the radical tradi-tions and possibilities with which the idea of the aesthetic has always been associated. I would regard with dismay a politics which subtracts the aesthetic and refuses it cultural meaning and possibility.

Moreover, it is the aesthetics of Enlightenment Europe, as Eagleton discloses, which first made gender apparent, first made the feminine visible, as a topos in philosophical discussion, albeit as a means of severely restricting the definitions of sexual difference, a limitation of which Blake's proverbs are aware. So a consideration of the aesthetic and the polis must include the category of gender. Without it, we have no means of grasping our history, no means of grasping, analysing and understanding those massive energies of cultural production which are apparently non-instrumental (to put it in the most neutral way). Not to have conceptual tools is disabling. Feminists themselves have enumerated the dangers of an analysis of a gendered aesthetic: the pursuit of an illusory essentialism that naturalizes and dehistoricizes the constructed category of art, and the privileging of a merely formal avant-garde textual subversion as the site of the semiotic, consent to the false hierarchy of fine art and mass culture. But this should not prevent us from considering the part gender has played in the evolution of the aesthetic, or speculating on what part it will play in the future.

What is wrong with the aesthetic?

According to Eagleton, two things are wrong with the aesthetic. First, like a kind of deadly virus, the aesthetic will show up in bourgeois culture only when it is combined with something else, confounding what hosts it. It is viscous enough as a concept already: the *process* of creation, the art object, the experience of its reception, the theorizing of it as concept and praxis – all these are comprehended in the term *aesthetic*. But for Eagle-ton the aesthetic is positively *runny*. It is both everywhere and nowhere. It secretly confounds the distinction between fact and value (because it manipulates affect). It collapses sign and thing (because it proposes to fuse representation with what is represented in organic unity). It dissolves cognition and percept (because it slides particulars under the concept and substitutes them for it). It plays havoc with the separate realms of the cognitive, ethical and political, making them permeable by aestheticizing them, so that they are commonly grounded in the aesthetic rather than in propositionality. It pretends to be itself while infiltrating the fiercely contested categories of bourgeois thought – freedom, legality, self-determination, necessity. It adopts the appearance of standing over and against power, while being the very essence of the mystified power by which hegemony maintains itself. The virtuosic feats of hegemony, that look-no-hands trick by which hegemony makes people do what it wants by persuading them that they are doing it voluntarily, are performed through the aesthetic.

If hegemony wants a new, free, independent bourgeois subject to facilitate economic competition, the aesthetic offers a pure model of free, self-referential, autotelic, autoaffective being in the work of art in order to lull the conscience of the new subject. If hegemony wants a paradigm of exchange which enables a formal equivalent between human beings and commodities to be developed for the needs of the market place, then the aesthetic will do the reverse of endorsing a full individual subject and make the individual into an abstract entity to provide a model for the capitalist economy of exchange. The aesthetic is always on hand to become a kind of phantom proxy for whatever manoeuvre hegemony conducts. Indeed, it *is* ideology. And because ideology requires a scene of seduction in which the fierceness of power and the brutality of capital can be disguised, hegemony brings on the dancing girls. The aesthetic is a woman. That is the second thing wrong with it.

Here aesthetic epistemology becomes not a paradigm of political structures but an *allegory* of them, not the cause or consequence of the bourgeois/capitalist order, not an element belonging to a material or intellectual structure but an active *agent* in complicity with hegemony, also heavily personified. As naturalizing allegorizer, Eagleton not only abolishes the saving conceptual distance which makes critique possible but also accepts the feminine as a marked term (bound up in European accounts of the aesthetic almost from the start) without the grounding of historical explanation. Indeed, he appears to believe that an account of the aesthetic in terms of the feminine *is* a historical explanation. True, inverted commas sometimes surround 'feminine' as a deconstructive gesture, but investigation goes no further and he stays with the essentialist feminine. Happiest and at his most lovingly sardonic with those grumpy fellow-allegorizers of, respectively, the Will and the Ironist, Schopenhauer and Kierkegaard, he passes lightly over Kierkegaard's phallophile vengeance on the woman's body, his figuring of woman as sickness. One impetus of the aesthetic in the Enlightenment, the redistribution of gender characteristics across the sexes, and the material explanation for this, gets scant enquiry.

What is wrong with Kant?

Kant instigates the true aesthetic subject of bourgeois ascendancy, the first genuinely hegemonic aesthetics, as opposed to the tyranny which directly controls its subordinates, figured as the unruly somatic life of the body, implicitly the male body. So Kant's aesthetic has to account for, or display, bourgeois ideology, bourgeois morality and bourgeois commodity in homologous relationship. The ruling order, Eagleton says, *needs* Kant's epistemology: it needs a persuasive account of freedom which masks the manoeuvres of the ideology of private capital. The self-identical law of the one, producing the autotelic and abstract free play of the aesthetic as an end in itself, is in dialectical relationship with a regressive, atavistically narcissistic individualist subject which must 'coopt reality' to its own purposes (*Ideology*, p. 86). This individualism is surreptitiously slipped under the protection of the disinterested activity of the aesthetic subject.

Kant, read as cultural symptom, is one of the main actants in the bourgeois farce described in the first part of this book. Thus to remind oneself that Kant's was one of the earliest attempts to see the political and cultural problems around the changed relations between the new civic individual and the modern state, for instance, or the problems around rationality and representation, would be to confuse the genre of the discussion. Systematic, almost coercive, misprision (a little heavy for farce) is part of the game. Nevertheless, it is possible to say that Eagleton constantly situates Kant in comic dilemmas which Kant has already systematically allowed for: furthermore, in his anxiety to align and critique the seductions of commodity and ideology with Kant's aesthetic, he forces Kant's unwilling texts towards the pleasure principle, ignoring a much more fundamental critique, the connection between the aesthetic and *violence*.

The culminating critique of Kant's aesthetic is that it provides a structure for, and consents to, ideology by privileging concrete particulars which are universalized. The Kantian subject (seen over-dramatically) is a split and agonistic being, opening up a series of self-perpetuating fissures which the sensuous and affective life of the aesthetic is invoked to assuage. Thus 'sensus communis', which Eagleton interprets as community of *feeling*, is invoked to assuage both the divided subject, unable to comprehend either itself or the object except in terms of property, and the class division which is a corollary of this state. Acting as a point of exchange between subjects as the only 'non-alienated object' available in society, the aesthetic acts as a 'spiritualised' commodity by the very fact of exchange, thus mystifying the relation between fact and value (*Ideology*, p. 78). A series of consequential and homologous splits opens up, parallel to this 'real' and transcendental commodity: between the phenomenal and the noumenal, between the instrumental and the pure, between the activity of purposeful subordination and the non-purposive end in itself, between the practical and the transcendental, between the free play of formal, abstract morality as pure *Law* on the one hand and nature and praxis on the other. Just like the spiritualized commodity of the aesthetic, this pure law of the transcendental signifier, depending on the self-identical one, forces individuals under the same formal category to facilitate contractual exchange. The aesthetic replaces this unbearable totality with immediacy and the manifold concrete. It heals these fractures by persuading us that, like a commodity, the world is *made* for us.

Eagleton does not pause to consider that the Enlightenment move towards parity and exchangeability also instigates the idea of the vote, democracy and representation, but hurries on to the marriage of ideology and the aesthetic. The concrete manifold of the aesthetic, having no access to the concept possessed by transcendental law, can only mimic the form of reason, not the content. Like ideology, it slips the concrete under the general. It ignores the *propositionality* of reason, raising the individual to the universal, generalizing concrete particulars and short-circuiting the conceptual.

That Kant painfully unpicks the relation between the cognitive and the concrete manifold of the aesthetic and its representations, that he attributes to the orator precisely the short-circuiting of the concept at work in ideology, need not concern Eagleton. Kant thinks rhetoric hood-winks. It has its eye on the concept in an instrumental, non-disinterested way, and manipulates the art of persuasion through an imitation of the free play of particulars. Poetry engages with the free play of the concrete manifold, reaching the concept non-intentionally (Kant, *The Critique of Judgement*, pp. 184–5). But Eagleton is attending to symptomatic structures rather than to particular arguments. He is enthralled by the structure of seduction, by Kant's pleasure principle, whereas it is precisely the connection of the aesthetic with the death wish, or with mourning, at least, which is striking in Kant. Containment, stasis, the refusal of difference, is the essence of his aesthetic. The republican potential and critique available to the aesthetic must be muted to individual self-fulfilment in a civic society with 'a lower degree of civil freedom'; and if that individualism shows its inbuilt tendency for violence in those not 'capable of *managing* freedom' (my emphasis), then state violence is on hand to manage it with a standing army (Kant, 'An answer to the question; What is Enlightenment?', p. 34). This is the modern aesthetic state, and it is worth investigating further.

But bourgeois aesthetics, morality, commodity, ideology, are not connected with transcendental *phallic* law in Eagleton's discussion. No, it is the mother's body and a founding narcissism which is responsible for all this. Only a Kleinian anger, the infant's resentment of the mother's withholding, could find this explanation plausible.

The fear of metaphor

Can this chapter be right about Kant? But this is not the question to ask: it would be better to ask, why does Kant have to mean this in Eagleton's text? The detour of a parenthesis suggests an answer to the first question: the second demands the first of a series of speculative propositions and zig zags.

> To begin with the 'sensus communis': surely this is not the assuaging reciprocity of community (a sentimental account), where class is muted, but an appeal to universal standards of taste, which are the decisions of a social elite? The aesthetic inheres in *taste*, not in the object. Therefore, agreement about the rules (and who makes them) is essential, reinforcing rather than assuaging division. This is one of the many occasions on which, in order for the chapter's argument to be sustained, it has to soften the rigidity – the often cold and rather coercive rigidity – of Kant's distinctions. Kant keeps apart the aesthetic idea and the rational idea, just as he keeps apart representation and nature and art and nature. When he argues that the imagination puts ideas into motion by quickening the cognitive faculty, or that the imagination borrows a second nature out of nature, re-modelling it in a constructed representation, or that the work of art may *look* like nature but is ordered with a self constituting power which nature does not possess (*Critique*, para. 49, pp. 175–80), he is writing with an understanding of the separateness of these categories in order to sustain the connection between representation and the aesthetic. An account of representation does not collapse into ideology but becomes a tool for analysing it. The problem seems to be the reverse of this chapter's complaint and lies in the stiffness of Kant's exclusions rather than in a permeable narcissistic relationship of consciousness and the mother's body: the aesthetic object is oneness and unity in self-maintaining free play all right, but because it brings together categories in a static way, without changing them, it belongs to the phallic one of the self-identical subject rather than to the imaginary. It *does* matter, and is a crucial difference

between the two thinkers, that Jacques Lacan's *subject* experiences lack in the mirror stage but that in Kant's epistemology the *object* is so often drained of coherence. Lacan's subject has no sense of the other, but the Kantian subject has only too much sense of the alien and *abstract* other lying outside it, which maintains the subject's oneness only because it is so thoroughly separate. All this is the reverse of Eagleton.

To cut to Derrida, whose 'Economimesis' in some ways pre-empts the discussion in Eagleton's *The Ideology of the Aesthetic*: both texts, in inverse but parallel ways, are intrigued to the point of fascination with an aesthetic of the one. For Derrida, the self-identical one of the symbolic order defends itself with nausea against that which might force it to entertain difference, whereas in *Ideology* the narcissistic one is arrested indivisibly in unity with the mother's body at the level of the imaginary. In transcendental work over and against the economic (Derrida's Kantian subject hierarchizes play over work and the salaried subject who is marked by class), the aesthetic labours on the exclusion of heterogeneity. In an expressive model of taste predicated on distaste, the aesthetic subject spews forth in untranscendental vomit that which might entertain difference, the other. The work of mourning, Derrida says, in one of those brilliant insights he forgets to follow up, is too easily foreclosed, too easily elided with the self. But for *Ideology* the work of mourning has never begun because the narcissistic aesthetic subject, in a reverse but structurally parallel movement, has fused the other with itself.

Connect this with de Man and his resistance to the Romantic metaphor and symbol which, he thinks, has an essentially narcissistic structure ('The rhetoric of tempolality'). Metaphor fuses mind and world, sign and thing, cognition and percept, in an illusion of unity. Connect this also with a recent extrapolation of both Derrida and de Man to the colonial subject, product of the Kantian exclusion of difference as a positive marker. A formidable unanimity emerges. David Lloyd has recently brought Derrida and de Man together to argue that the Kantian aesthetic produces the colonial subject through the self-identical phallic one because racial difference is excluded as an aspect of the exclusion of heterogeneity. He connects this with a valorizing of metaphor in terms of its capacity to produce 'likeness' between categories. The project of metaphor is to elide rather than separate the unlike: 'Whiteness is the metaphor for the metaphorical production of the Subject as one devoid of properties rather than the natural sign of difference' ('Race under representation', p. 77).

So metaphor both produces and is produced by the self-identical subject. Narcissism, class, racism: are they all to be founded on the totalizing

unity of metaphorical activity? Is the aesthetic to produce and be produced by metaphor? Can such opprobrium be heaped upon a trope?

There is an overdetermined and deeply contradictory anxiety about the
law of the one and its connection with the aesthetic. At the same time as
the law of the one is accepted as a kind of tragic necessity, phallic fate,
reintroducing itself at all levels – in the imaginary, even, whose narcissism
strangely mimics it, in the cultural order, in language – it appears to be
produced and sustained by its opposite. The aesthetic is feared as the
collapse and elision of categories, as a permeable, dissolving meltdown of
difference in the law of the same: the threat of metaphor. Phallic self-
identity is at one and the same time shored up and undermined by the
aesthetic figuring as metaphor.

Does metaphor trope woman for these writers? Is it the threat of the
feminine for them? Hence their opprobrium and anxiety. This is why it is
not necessary to ask, is this really what metaphor is about? For the fear of
metaphor is performing the work of repression.

> (A parenthetical question: Is this powerful convergence of so many mascu-
> line texts in the anti-aesthetic related to the present historical moment of
> feminist thought? This massive attack coincides with the last twenty years,
> when women's creativity has burgeoned, and aesthetic artefacts, writing
> and cultural production have been a huge part of the feminist agenda and
> the energies which have created a feminist counter-public sphere. This
> attack has occurred just when aesthetic productions have been politicized
> for feminist emancipatory writing, just when discursive networks of fem-
> inist production have challenged the managed society, establishing a form
> of communality despite the fragmentation of feminisms. This is a proper
> question, not a recrimination, for the project of reclaiming the aesthetic for
> the left is as important as reclaiming it for feminism: the two are bound
> together.)

But what does metaphor do? And why is it so closely connected with
the aesthetic? Abandon the view of metaphor as deliquescence, the fatal
weakening of distinction into likeness. The play of *unlikeness* is essential
to metaphor. Some people, including Paul Ricoeur, think that metaphor is
about the transformation of categories, not their reconciliation (*The
Rule of Metaphor*, p. 7). It is interesting that Lloyd rather wilfully mis-
reads Ricoeur here, forcing an account of metaphor as the one. And yet
Ricoeur explores metaphor as a transformation, a discovery of new
meaning, new *categories* so important that metaphor is a prerequisite
for cognitive thought. 'A tear is an intellectual thing' – Blake makes a
stark categorical contradiction here (*Jerusalem*, p. 741). The precipitation of mental anguish runs down the face as a fluid, pain's material form

secreted from the body. Blake's statement arrests with the shock of difference. A tear is expelled (we think of Derrida again) as an *expression* of the body, but it is not mere salt water because it *is* grief, and without the tear grief could not find expression, nor could grief begin to understand itself (compare vomit). The puzzling junction of bodily and mental experience is being explored here.

Metaphor is a test case of the aesthetic because it has to do with the questioning of categories. But it is not the aesthetic itself. What would another account of the aesthetic for the left and for feminism look like?

Towards a new aesthetic

First, L. S. Vygotsky (1896–1934), whose work circulated in the 1950s and 1960s in western Europe. Some core texts are translated in *Mind in Society* (1978). Second, D. W. Winnicott (1896–1971), whose *Playing and Reality* (1971) collected essays from the 1950s on. One a Marxist, one a psychoanalyst, both see *play* as a central activity for investigation. The writings of both, significantly, emerge at the beginnings of the postwar managed society, at the moment when capitalism begins to colonize the life world of individuals ever more systematically.

Play, that fundamental activity, is cognate with aesthetic production. It is part of a vital continuum. I understand play not as a simple binary set against work, not as a hierarchy of activity (as in Schiller) subordinating work, not as an epistemological hierarchy subordinated to knowledge (as often in Kant), but as a form of knowledge itself. Interactive, sensuous, epistemologically charged, play has to do with both the cognitive and the cultural.

How does Vygotsky help?

For him, play is not a symbolic system (as in the translations of abstract geometry). Nor is it an alternative world (an escape), for play and reality often coincide. Sisters play at being sisters, mother is made to play at being mother, playing 'what is actually true' (*Mind in Society*, p. 94). Play is rule-bound. Imaginary situations contain rules of behaviour, and 'every game with rules contains an imaginary situation' (p. 95). Play sets up a constant dialectic between rules and freedom. It is thus a constantly questioning activity. But, more than this, it is only in play that it is possible to make an essential cognitive leap which radically changes one's relation to reality.

Children live in a world of immediacy, unable to separate the visual field from the field of meaning. But in play 'things lose their determining force'. It is the experiment of play alone which 'enables the child to act independently of what she sees' (p. 96). Play achieves an extraordinary reversal, a transformation of the very structure of perception. When one thing begins to stand for another (a stick for a horse), that thing becomes a 'pivot' for severing the idea of a horse from the concrete existence of the horse, and the rule-bound game is determined by ideas, not by objects. Play liberates the child into ideas, into an understanding of categories and their *relation* to objects:

> A divergence between fields of meaning and vision first occurs at preschool age. In play thought is separated from objects and action arises from ideas rather than things: a piece of wood begins to be a doll and a stick becomes a horse. Action according to rules begins to be determined by ideas and not by objects themselves. This is such a reversal of the child's relation to the real, immediate, concrete situation that it is hard to underestimate its full significance. The child does not do this all at once because it is terribly difficult for a child to sever thought (the meaning of a word) from object. (Vygotsky, *Mind in Society*, p. 98).

The pivotal object is fundamental in providing a transitional stage in cognitive discovery. It is not a substitute, not an abstraction (the emphasis is not on Lacanian absence): there is still a horse in the stick. It is not metaphor either, because it is bound up with immediate material objects, though it is functionally akin to metaphor:

> Play provides a transitional stage in this direction whenever an object (for example, a stick) becomes a pivot for severing the meaning of a horse from a real horse. The child cannot as yet detach thought from object. The child's weakness is that in order to imagine a horse, he needs to define his action by means of using 'the-horse-in-the-stick' as pivot. But all the same, *the basic structure determining the child's relation to reality is radically changed at this crucial point, because the structure of his perceptions changes* [my emphasis]. (Vygotsky, *Mind in Society*, p. 98)

The child is separating itself out from the world but not escaping from it. It is a materialist and a cognitive account of play. The horse–stick is a pivot for remaking categories and for discovering new perceptions. The stick–horse makes a space which redefines one's relationship to the world and the world itself.

'A child's greatest self control occurs in play', Vygotsky says (p. 99). At the same time, play is liberating through its capacity to be interactive: because the child can create an alienated meaning within the constraints of a specific, concrete situation, play occupies 'the realm of spontaneity and freedom'. This is not simply a semiotic space for subversion/freedom any more than it can be the experience of omnipotence. Nor is it that Kantian form without content, particulars divorced from concepts. It is a cognitive negotiation. Spinoza provides Vygotsky with the notion of 'an idea which has become a desire, a concept which has turned into a passion'. A new perception actually ignites desire and desire creates the possibility of new perceptions, constantly discovering new thresholds of experience. (Elsewhere Vygotsky describes intellectual growth in terms of a zone of proximal development in very much the same way.)

Of course, I am reading Vygotsky partly against the grain. There are repressive implications to his thought. Play is ultimately 'a rule that has become desire', and the experiment that has brought about a 'new relation' can be made to perform the function of cultural conditioning (p. 99). A child grows out of play – it transfers to the world of work all that it has discovered. Play is a transitional stage between the situational constraints of childhood and the freedom of the adult and leads straight to work, to compulsory activity based on rules – and to competitive games. But Vygotsky does make play intrinsic to cognitive experience: the function of the essentially double-sided pivotal object (the aesthetic object?), acting within the constraints of material experience yet able to envisage new categories, emancipates us from the tyranny of the one and the primal ooze of the imaginary. And it is in itself emancipatory.

The piece of blanket and the stick–horse

How does Winnicott help?

He redresses some of Vygotsky's limitations. For example, it is crucial that play continues into adulthood. *Playing and Reality* seeks to find in play a non-orgiastic, non-omnipotent experience (Winnicott insists that he is not writing about narcissism), an intra-subjective space in which meanings are renegotiated. The piece of blanket, the transitional object the child clings to when it is releasing itself from the mother, leads him to speculate on this and on the way we relate to and revise cultural tradition. For play is and creates a shared cultural reality (chapter 7: 'The location of cultural experience'). The transitional object, a thing of paradox, neither subject nor object, opens up a third space, the site of play.

The transitional object has an aspect of interiority and indeterminacy lacking in the pivotal stick–horse, but it has an isomorphic relation to it and is functionally similar. It opens up and contains, however, the contradictions only implicit in the pivotal object. 'But the term "transitional object", according to my suggestion, gives room for the process of being able to accept difference and similarity' (p. 7). It is not me *and* part of me;

it is neither subject nor object; it is neither inner psychic reality nor external reality; it is the union of the baby and mother and the point at which their separation occurs. The transitional object enables the baby to do without the mother yet recalls her. It is adopted, not created *ab initio*. It is not a symbol because it is a real, literal object, but it can stand in as the symbol; it can stand in for the mother's breast.

The transitional object is the primal experience of culture, the beginnings of representation and its phantasmic mobility and resourcefulness. 'The place where cultural experience is located is in the *potential space* between the individual and the environment (originally the object). The same can be said of playing' (p. 118).

A mode of release from, not a fetishistic encounter with, the mother's body, not at the mercy of the body's functions but attentive to its experiences, moving from continuity to contiguity to non-omnipotent relations and to the renegotiation of *boundaries*, the transitional object mediates a life-creating, culture-modifying space which is at once transgressive and communal. 'In order to study the play and then the cultural life of the individual, one must study the fate of the potential space between any one baby and the human (and therefore fallible) mother figure who is essentially adaptive because of love' (p. 118). The transitional object cannot be a fetish except where it fails to be a transitional object, for, as Julia Kristeva has reminded us, the fetish stops with the literal. It is where meaning ends, not where *meanings* are infinitely remade.

Where now?

So between them, the pivotal and transitional objects (do these relate respectively to the symbolic order and the imaginary, and does the aesthetic conflate these two orders?) establish the category of the aesthetic as *play*, with all its cognitive and representational potential, its specific cultural space, its interactive possibilities. Yet, as Winnicott emphasizes, the transitional object can be part of a continuum which includes madness. The prolonged absence of the loved object causes the infant's derangement. When the transitional state goes badly the toleration of anxiety and ambiguity passes over into fetishizing and persecution. Such an admonition reminds us that if we accept the aesthetic state on these terms it is not a privileged condition producing privileged objects, but is amorphous, part of a continuum in which madness subsists at one end and ideology at the other – and only becomes art, perhaps, when we *choose* to call it so, just as the infant's possession of the transitional object occurs by a priori agreement. Nevertheless, our play is *play*, not simply subversive linguistic play, but the transformation of categories, which constitutes a change in the structure of thought itself: it is not only an aspect of knowledge but the prerequisite of political change.

A number of theses concerning the aesthetic and the polis can be generated from what has been said, going in a number of directions. They are all capable of further development. But since this discussion is a prolegomenon, they will be expressed laconically.

1. The aesthetic is emancipatory because access to the change of categories is possible in many ways and in many different areas of our culture and its productions. Categorical experiment – new kinds of knowledge – breaks down the binary of high and low culture because it is produced incessantly.

   (In parenthesis, two examples: (i) rave: dancing, that almost universal activity because all it needs is the body, and other bodies, re-invents the body and subverts its function as the pure instrumentality of labour. The body plays at being the body, and in rave's preoccupation with styles of *posing*, the categories of commodified display find themselves not only mocked by exaggeration and hyperbole but also transposed from the beckoning allure of *objects*. They are manipulated by subjects, by people who are in control of their bodies, recognizing and changing the rules of commodity, (ii) Veronica Forrest-Thomson's post-structuralist poem 'Ducks & Rabbits', a 'dialogue' with Wittgenstein, whose impossible hybrids, Duck/Rabbits, one representation only for two mutually exclusive figures, take on a bizarre literal being as it/they swim in the river at Cambridge (*Collected Poems*, p. 22). The poem is a meditation on the transformation of categories in metaphor, on the impossible/possible co-existence of difference, and the kind of knowledge it creates. Just like the Duck/Rabbit, it flickers between two figures for metaphor. Note: neither dance nor avant-garde poem has a special dispensation from mania or ideology.)

2. If the aesthetic enables and empowers, then this implies profound educational change. That is, men and women need to be able to create and tolerate paradox in order to create change.

3. If revisionary ambiguity is at the heart of cognitive experience, then it looks as if a truly populist manifestation of the aesthetic (yet to come) will discover a cultural production which will be as *different* as possible from what Rita Felski calls the pragmatic constraints of everyday discourse (*Beyond Feminist Aesthetics*), pp. 156–64). Like Felski, I do not see the Adorno-endorsed high modernist avant-garde as intrinsically revolutionary simply because it exists. But, in my view, the further away some of our discourses are from everyday discourse through the transformation of categories, the nearer they

]   are to critique. It is harder to make a critique from within a discourse
    than through the drama of difference in linguistic experiment.
4. This then presupposes that everyone needs to be freed into language.
5. But at this point in our culture men and women enter into lang-
    uage, into the symbolic, in different ways and on different terms: as
    Cora Kaplan has argued convincingly, girls enter into language cir-
    cuitously, with more complex negotiations with repression and
    absence than do boys ('Language and gender', *Sea Changes*, pp.
    69–93). I wonder if as a consequence girls are asked to take the
    strain of language, to tolerate linguistic ambiguity, uncertainty, para-
    dox. Language's affinity with the pivotal and transitional object
    would be foregrounded for them as the site of paradox and dissolve.
    I wonder if those who do learn to speak are made more aware both of
    the uncertainty and the *possibilities*, through metaphor and meto-
    nymy, of language's connection with those vital cognitive shifts and
    the transformation of categories which I have called a central com-
    ponent of the aesthetic and the prerequisite of all revisionary
    thought, all cultural transmission which is capable of redefinition
    as well as assimilation. I wonder if women of different class and
    colour are subject to the same conditions – whether there is a greater
    understanding of difference and contradiction as a result of our
    culturally learned roles. Women may well have a greater responsi-
    bility to *play* with contradiction as critique.
6. If women at this specific cultural moment are hypersensitive to con-
    tradiction, then a feminist aesthetic will not be one that is confined
    within pre-given feminine experience (always the problem with a
    feminist counter-public sphere) but one which changes the polis
    because sexual difference itself is what is being redefined. (This also
    means finding new modes of aesthetic production and dissemination
    – networks, informal groups – circumventing commodified pro-
    cesses.)
7. It is surely our present task to *play* with contradictions. If, at this
    moment of upsurge in neo-conservatism, when hypertext and virtual
    reality in particular encourage the union of art and ideology, then
    that is not an argument for an anti-aesthetic but for more of it. A
    counter-aesthetic, using the aesthetic against itself rather than ban-
    ishing it from the polis (though not as a Lyotardian guerrilla but as a
    political subject) is the answer. And women, with, if I am right, that
    heightened sense of contradiction, may have a great part of the work
    to do in redefining communality and formulating critique. Women's
    first object must be to disband the gender-neutral language round the
    classless society built on privilege, with its free choice predicated on

an underclass, and to ask where women function in this structure –
poor women, Black and Asian women. We will not do this if we lose
one of our strengths, a politicized aesthetic. The aesthetic is not the
political, but it may make the political possible.

Coda: to return to Blake...

Infant Joy

'I have no name—
I am but two days old.'
What shall I call thee?
'I happy am,
Joy is my name.'
Sweet joy befall thee!

Pretty joy!
Sweet joy but two days old—
Sweet joy I call thee.
Thou dost smile,
I sing the while—
Sweet joy befall thee!
(Blake, *Songs of Innocence*)[1]

Infant Joy: a *reciprocal* dyadic relation. If the aesthetic belongs to Hell,
then *Songs of Innocence* at least afford a glimpse of an emancipatory
aesthetic, a revisionary creativity so radical but so immediate that – an
essential for that rare thing, a populist reading – the challenge to categories is widely available. 'Joy is my name': throughout this dialogue, as
adult and child make and remake each other's experience, sharing each
other's projections, the parent knows too well that Joy is a *name*, the child
that it is an immediate condition. Joy as pivotal object (as joy the
child itself comes to play the pivotal object) causes a lesion, an easing
away of concept from state, and state from person, the first intimations of
metaphor. Separation happens without phallic violence: it is *space* which
orders separation: and creates transitional ambiguities. The carefully
arranged typographical column of 'Joy' (four repetitions of the word
are placed at the same point in each successive line) divides the poem
vertically. The poem aligns a series of 'o's which are ambiguously circles
and noughts, indivisible continuities and blanks. The identity of both
mother and child – for this does seem to be a female world – trembles
round those indeterminate figures. The child names herself with a non-

patriarchal name, the mother likewise. Yet the nought in the 'o' hovers. We remember that the mother has no identity in law at this time, and with that sinister understanding the repetition of internal rhyme insists upon the missing rhyme word – 'joy', 'boy'. The 'boy' hidden in the internal rhyme threatens to dominate. But such a collocation, a girl's name and a boy's sex, shocks the order of gender. And if 'joy' is a generic term for emotion and not fixed to gender, could it be that this challenging of categories enables the boy to achieve identity without the threat of phallic violence, just as the girl and the mother have momentarily created an emancipatory world by refusing conventional categories? Could the father have access to this world by becoming a nurse, a carer? The emancipatory moment opens – and closes – the final sentence is subjunctive. Though not before the enormity of the change that would be necessary for this alteration to occur is apparent. For if the repressive law of the father were to change and *were* to enact the mother's part without violence, this would imply, in Blake's world, different legal, social and economic structures, different power relations, both for boy child and for father, girl child and mother. God would be different. The angel standing beside the baby (in the pictorial engraving of the poem) would be different.[2]

NOTES

1 William Blake, *The Complete Poems*, ed. W. H. Stevenson, pp. 55–6.
2 William Blake, *Songs of Innocence and of Experience*, ed. Geoffrey Keynes, Plate 25.

2

Writing from the Broken Middle: Post-Structuralist Deconstruction

A coincidence? The beginning of the 1980s, it is now history, saw late capitalism in a new phase of confident aggrandizement. The beginning of the 1980s saw the circulation of two brilliant post-structuralist critiques of the category of the aesthetic. Jacques Derrida took on Kant in the robustly ludic 'Economimesis', a deconstructive project published in 1975 but introduced to Anglo-American criticism when it was translated in *Diacritics* in 1981. Paul de Man, cultivating a rigorous anti-aesthetic asceticism, took on Hegel in a lecture published in *Critical Inquiry* in 1982. The satisfaction granted by the 'relief' experienced when theory and aesthetic 'appreciation' seem to match is deceptively easy, he argued, as if reader and text succumb to the gratifications of the mirror stage: 'one should not be too easily satisfied with one's own satisfaction'.[1] Marxists apparently agreed. Michèle Barrett conceded, rather grudgingly, in *New Left Review* in 1981, that the 'category of the aesthetic is here handed back to us as a legitimate object of materialist analysis' (p. 93). But she meant that the cultural production and reception of aesthetic objects was amenable for materialist analysis rather than that the concept of the aesthetic itself might be reworked: the category of the aesthetic would merely be subsumed under cultural production as ideological work. So it might seem, once we add to this body of critique Terry Eagleton's *The Ideology of the Aesthetic* (1990), which insisted that the concept of the aesthetic is an unusable bourgeois notion, that we are thoroughly into a post-aesthetic condition. 'Art is dead', Baudrillard announced, 'because its critical transcendence is gone' (*Simulations*, p. 151). I have argued elsewhere that Eagleton's position effectively concedes the concept of the aesthetic to the right (see chapter 1). But what of the anti-aesthetic of Derrida and de Man? What do these essays look like over a decade later?

Both are devastating and consummately skilful readers. There is not much to be gained by returning to the foundational texts they deconstruct, Kant's third *Critique* and Hegel's *Introductory Lectures on Aesthetics*, by demonstrating that these were misinterpreted. Whether they were or not, what Kant and Hegel *really* meant is not the point. It is not simply that the post-aesthetic realm is 'beyond the reach of value judgement', as one analyst has argued, for that would bring discussion to a stop: these critiques demonstrated that such readings *could* emerge, and they released new possibilities from the classic texts, which are capacious enough in any case to be amenable to a range of readings.[2] But one way to begin – which is to make a start on responding to the tactics of Derrida and de Man since disagreement slides off the back of a deconstructive text – is to ask whether temporal distance makes these readings signify differently.

History has both changed these readings and sharpened them. There was a bleak sense of being left empty-handed, on a first encounter with these essays, once the deconstructive *jouissance* passed away. Worse than disagreeing hotly is that blank experience of feeling that a text has eliminated the terms by which one might reply to it, leaving one with the feeble recourse of 'but'. Yet they were prescient. Derrida and de Man saw that the aesthetic had become the last bastion of the private self hubristically conceived as omnipotent creator. The aesthetic harboured and justified the ultimate aggrandizement of the transcendent subject as master of its world. Aesthetic ideology was the 'pure' essence of economic individualism, which it duplicated and endorsed. So it was no coincidence that these critiques occurred just at the time when, in Europe and America, the new and violent surge of late capitalism began. Thatcher and Reagan encouraged the fantasy of free agency for an autonomous entrepreneurial subject, though simultaneously they worked to contradict autonomy by consolidating multinational capital. And the Derrida/de Man critique was timely because, throughout this time, even in orders of knowledge self-consciously recognized as organized round the 'new' twentieth-century thinking made possible by Marx and Freud and Saussure, the idea of the aesthetic was used, often in an uninvestigated way, and covertly as a criterion of value, to support conceptual systems ordinarily declaring themselves independent of the aesthetic – for instance, Marxist theory (Žižek's *sublime* object of ideology), and psychoanalysis (Christopher Bollas's self understood in terms of an *aesthetic* ordering).[3]

How do Derrida and de Man advance their anti-aesthetic? Some understanding of their positions helps to show where to go next. Meanwhile it is impossible not to be ambivalent about them. They are at once brilliant acts of undoing which attack the false consciousness of the aesthetic and the bleak critique belonging to an almost coercive scepticism.

The Anti-Aesthetic of Dd: Derrida and de Man on Kant and Hegel

Derrida continued to pursue Kant in *The Truth in Painting*, deepening and expanding what he did in the earlier essay 'Economimesis'. But much is anticipated in the shorter work. The high comedy of Derrida's ludic iconoclasm, and the pleasure to be derived from it, lies in the virtuosity with which it enacts its meaning. So his critique of Kant's 'pure judgments of taste', ('Economimesis', p. 3). playing games with the unspeakable, demands a playful response which makes my summary inappositely brusque. But to begin at the end of his essay, with *taste*: Derrida opposes Kant's 'taste' with that vulgar enjoyment of the senses from which Kant's thought withdraws, the gross olfactory processes – smell is simply taste at a remove – and the saliva of the hungry mouth. Kant's high 'taste' *seems* otherwise. Self-producing, autotelic, non-instrumental, the purposive purposelessness of the aesthetic state and the aesthetic object is created by the free unencumbered subject. The unencumbered subject comes into taste without the squalor of salary or remuneration, and is thus exempted from the processes of exchange (p. 4). This condition is achieved without entering into the instrumentality of work or labour, and so the self is exempted from nature, the body and the sordid, invidious toils of the practical (p. 5). The aesthetic state is achieved without becoming engaged with the concept of propositionality, and is thus exempted from the constraints of thought and knowledge (a characteristic he enlarges upon in the later work) (p. 5).

Remorselessly, Derrida makes the aesthetic emptier and emptier, and this is his purpose. For taste is predicated on emptying out, on the consequences of *distaste, disgust,* on vomit. Taste participates in a ghostly 'immaculate commerce', a 'pure economy' (p. 9), but its logical opposite is disgust and distaste, and thus are introduced the very coarse bodily processes which 'taste' would occlude. The logical end of disgust is violent rejection, 'expressive/emissive', or 'vomitive/emetic' (p. 16), as Derrida terms it. This is an acute move. The conventional response to the artwork which troubles, whether it is avant-garde music, lesbian poetry or rap or a dead sheep, is that it is 'disgusting'. But Derrida stresses that he means literal vomit. Vomit is not the inverse or simple opposite of art, not Yeats's place of excrement, the manure from which, in a simple inversion of romantic values, the aesthetic object grows. No, vomit is the aesthetic's absolutely hostile unassimilable other. As rejected matter, not even waste product, it constitutes an inimical heterogeneity, a limit case of the principle of difference itself, which Kantian principles cannot assimilate. 'Heteroaffection' (p. 21), the desire to master otherness, gags on what is hated and expelled, and this brute physical relief is experienced as 'disgust' – we continually remember that Kant sets pure pleasure against the vulgar enjoyment of the senses. Difference is not the negative form of a positive aesthetic but a hostile principle which simply cannot be represented. Vomit can't be put to work for you, and Derrida's point is that, covertly, the Kantian aesthetic puts everything to work.

Derrida's progressive emptying out of Kant's aesthetic is achieved by demonstrating the fallacy of a series of binary moves in which 'pure' art is marked off against its opposites. The aesthetic is first marked off against nature, work and science (or knowledge, cognition). Then 'pure' pleasure is set against enjoyment (p. 8), 'pure' spontaneous production against reproduction (p. 9). 'Pure' mimesis, the imitation of God's creative principle, is set against mere copies, and the creative principle can be iterated without recourse to mechanical repetition (p. 10). Here, pure production itself, that is, God's creation, is what is imitated rather than things in the universe simply being replicated. 'Pure' reward as against payment, pure interest, pure consumption as infinite value or pricelessness are set against exchange value (p. 12). The skill of the analysis is not simply in demonstrating that a language of transcendental value constantly collapses back into crude economic paradigms, or that art collapses back into nature, despite Kant's desire to keep them apart, as genius resembles nature's wild but innately rule-bound creativity. More important than the collapsing of oppositions is that, with each expository move, Derrida shows Kant to fold the aesthetic back into the self-same. The aesthetic depends on oneness, on self-sustaining unity, on cutting itself off from what is external to it. Excess of giving, for instance, may break with a servile, contractual economy, but it is a surplus which is given back to itself to infinity. (God in this sense plays with himself (p. 13).) Signification through analogy, in another instance of refusal of difference, signifies because the analogy is the analogy of analogy itself and does not descend to substitution (p. 14). Analogy, in other words, repeats the structure of relationship between things, rather than dealing with the deceit or at best concealment of speaking of one thing in terms of another. (Derrida returns to analogy later.)

Forced in spite of itself to find embodiment in sordid, finite signs, infinite play as Logos always attempts to find the form least likely to lead it to the play of substitution. For to be drawn into the play of substitution is to be reminded not only that the Logos loses its uniqueness but also that it is dependent on material *embodiment*. The Logos, however, depends upon orality, the mouth, for utterance. Though the mouth can be idealized, turned, through conceiving of utterance in terms of hearing, towards an interiority and autoaffection which hears oneself speak (p. 20), this cannot disguise the weak point of the Kantian system. The mouth assimilates, but it is the fatal organ of otherness. It takes things in but it also lets things out. Hence vomit. All other orifices eject matter which can be used or recycled in some way, but not the mouth. Through the orifice of the mouth Kant's aesthetic becomes the enemy of difference, of otherness, which it must violently expel. Sexual and racial otherness – the homoerotic, for instance, or the hybrid – would be the enemy of the aesthetic as Derrida here describes it.

Before turning to de Man, it is important to note a series of asides on mourning which Derrida does not develop (although he returns to this problem in *The Truth in Painting*). He speaks, for instance, of the aesthetic as the assimilation of the lost object so that there is no anxious residue of difference (p. 20). Later he says that the sublime produces the pleasure of ejaculation, and thus 'the work of mourning is consequently not absolutely blocked, impossible, excluded' (p. 22) – you can swallow it. The expelling of vomit 'burns up all work as mourning work' because, presumably, the energies used up for the act of expulsion reverse the work of assimilation: so the disgusting denominates what one cannot resign oneself to mourn (p. 23), that is, what one will not and cannot assimilate. For Derrida, Kant's aesthetic performs the perfect work of mourning, because it reappropriates the lost object so completely that the object or other virtually disappears into the unity of the same. Heteroaffection, the mastery of the other, is a paradigm of the fine art of mourning. Even where there seems to be a hitch, as in the experience of the sublime, heteroaffection succeeds in recuperating otherness. Previously he has said that mourning presupposes sight (p. 18), a statement which subsequent discussion clarifies, for he is assuming that the mourning which he identifies with the beautiful assimilates what is outside it, just as seeing something does. The beautiful has an essential relation to vision because it consumes less (p. 19), he says, meaning that seeing is the most idealizing of the senses because the eyes are furthest away from the object of perception than any other sense: you cannot *eat* a view (though you may consume it); eyes are separated from what they take in, whereas the mouth has an immediate, obscenely intimate physical relation to taste as it ingests its objects.

This all too complete mourning of the beautiful will be important to my later discussion, for an unspoken understanding of the work of art as melancholia lurks in Derrida's discourse and requires elaboration. For now, it is worth remarking that it is actually a fairly common twentieth-century move to find Kant wanting in a response to the sensuous life of the body, a taboo on the animalistic at the core of his work. From Theodor Adorno to Pierre Bourdieu, John Dewey to Henri Lefebvre, very different thinkers have seen him as the philosopher of the voided body.[4] Recently Howard Caygill has reminded readers who forget to tackle the second part of the third *Critique* that Kant puzzled over the 'vital forces' of life experienced in consciousness and through the body as an 'ambiguous site'.[5]

Kant certainly sees the body as problematic at times. He speculates on:

> what remains over when we take away from a thinking being all that is material and yet let it keep its thought. But whether, when we have taken away everything else, the thought – which we only know in man, that is in connexion with a body – would still remain, is a matter we are unable to decide. (*Critique*, para. 91, p. 141)

One could see Derrida's reading of Kant, therefore, as relatively conventional. Its innovativeness lies in the extent to which it elaborates the closed circuit of the order of the self-same, which vomits difference in the comedy of taste like a hysteric. This may be why, when he returned to Kant, it is less the body that preoccupied him than questions of knowledge and the epistemology of the frame or *parergon* which purports to surround the specially reserved space of the aesthetic.

To turn now to de Man: for him the aesthetic constructs a false unity which derives from the nature of the Hegelian symbol. A certain unintelligence and obtuseness of thought de Man finds in the *Lectures on Aesthetics* exposes more fully than works of literature the fallacies of the aesthetic – though de Man makes clear that both theory and literature are alike the bearers of a kind of incurable pathology endemic to the aesthetic.

Symbol, 'the sensory appearance of the idea', sums up Hegel's understanding of art, says de Man: 'the beautiful is symbolic'; symbol is the 'mediation' ('Sign and symbol', p. 763) between the mind and the physical world of which art partakes – stone, colour, sound, language, landscape. But symbol depends on the primacy of mind, which seizes possession of the world through the self-externalization and sensory embodiment enabled by symbol, and this embodiment is charged with the omnipotence and narcissism of consciousness. Hegel's definition of symbol is clumsy, confused and inadequate, according to de Man, so he turns to another Hegelian text, the *The Encyclopaedia Logic*, specifically to paragraph 20, and tackles the problem of symbol in relation to the self to elicit the meaning of 'I' and to explore in what sense 'I' could adequately be symbolized in Hegel's terms. The conclusion he arrives at is that, without wanting to, Hegel is forced into declaring implicitly that 'I cannot say I' (p. 769). And since the primacy of symbol depends on the centrality of 'I', which projects mind into the sensory external universe, de Man believes that he has undone the foundation on which Hegel makes his account of symbol rest. He has decentred what Hegel centres. The 'I' is founded on its own impossibility.

The deconstructive moves by which de Man arrives at his conclusion are important for my later arguments. This is how he frames Hegel's position. Hegel is writing of the paradox of deictic language, an argument actually repeated from the *Phenomenology*.[6] The problem with such terms as 'I', 'here' and 'now' is that they double between the immediate specificity of self and the absolute generality of self as a universal category, Hegel says. They signify a particular, irreducible entity or experience of 'I'ness, and, simultaneously, the most abstract, universal, empty category, 'I'. De Man translates thus: 'When I say "I", I *mean* myself as *this* I at the exclusion of all others; but what I say, I, is precisely anyone; any I, as that which excludes all others from itself' ('Sign and symbol', p. 769). De Man calls this statement 'astonishing', and believes that it confirms a more complex and possibly more tenuous argument he has made about Hegel's effacement of the *ego cogito* (*Phenomenology*, para. 23). This effacement is not to be confused with the philosophical decorum of the suppression of merely *personal* opinion advocated by Aristotle. The suppression of the 'I' goes much further than this. For, in paragraph 20, Hegel effectively says: ' "I cannot say what I make mine", and, since to think is fully contained in and defined by the I . . . what the sentence actually means is "I cannot say I" ' ('Sign and symbol', p. 768). De Man was aware that this argument might seem elaborately casuistical to some people, and it did, arousing considerable controversy. But he considered his fallback position strong: if, as Hegel says in paragraph 20, 'the simplest expression for the existing subject as thinker is "I" ', then how can a thinking subject, split between the irreducibly singular which falls out of representation, and the subject empty of content as a universal, be said to be capable of thought at all? For 'the position of the I, which is the condition of thought, implies its eradication . . . the erasure of any relationship, logical or otherwise, that could be conceived between what the I is and what it says it is. The very enterprise of thought seems to be paralyzed from the start' (p. 769). Thus if 'I' is by definition what 'I' cannot say in the universalizing work of language and the sign, the negotiation of self and other which precipitates knowledge is impossible. The argument that the

'I' is founded on its own impossibility is here consolidated and re-endorsed.

De Man argues that Hegel's work is founded on an act of amnesia around this central problem. That is why, despite himself, Hegel ends up with an account of consciousness which is merely the husk of memory and a theory of writing which is based on the obdurate materiality of signs. These are alike factors which doom an organic theory of the sensory manifestation of the beautiful to failure, because the ideal vanishes in the dead materiality of the medium (pp. 772–3). Compare Derrida on the aesthetic's repudiation of embodiment.

The whole essay turns on the morphology of the romantic symbol as de Man understands it. This, for him a regressive form, is derived very specifically from Hegel's account of the symbol as sensory manifestation of the idea and is not to be confused with later modernist or proto-modernist accounts of symbol such as those of the Symbolist movement. The romantic symbol has a structural affinity with, and may even be responsible for, a series of aberrations in western culture and thought, de Man implies. Though Hegel understands that the sign points to itself and to absence, and that the full presence implied by symbol points beyond itself and to the ties of affinity with that to which it assimilates itself, he confuses symbol and sign, de Man argues, preferring the narcissism of symbol. Symbol perpetrates a mystified, narcissistic culture of *identification*. And identification, founded on the mutual interpenetration of form and content, self and sensory world, is constituted by violence. It depends on a suspect epistemology of fusion, indivisibility, mirroring, matching, unity. Symbol is morphologically related to the following phenomena of romantic culture, phenomena which may all be cause and effect of one another.

First, the organicism of a coherent system in which intellect leaves a material trace upon the world as the external manifestation of the idea. This leads to a dialectic of inside and outside, a 'dialectics of internaliza-tion' or 'inner event' (p. 771), in which experience is interiorized and then reprojected and externalized as the ideal content of consciousness – the essence of expressive theory. The epistemology of organic-expressive experience posits consciousness as memory and privileges the *process* of consciousness. This in turn leads to 'subjectivism', which finds expression in the sublime; all these phenomena create the immobilizing binary world of symbol and its oppositions – self/other, art/nature, organic/mechan-istic, inside/outside. Predicated on the self-empowering 'I', these cultural forms derive, we are asked to believe, from symbol's seductions through affinity which *forces* ties, quenching difference (and here his argument converges with that of Derrida). In other words, to extrapolate from de

Man's argument here, the general being of 'I' becomes a symbol because it stands for all other 'I's, and by so doing offers us an experience of identification which precludes analysis because it precludes separation. Hence he refers, at the end of the essay, to his understanding of allegory and figure based on the bracing, astringent separation of the sign from what it signifies, as opposed to the melting affinity of symbol. He observes with some relief that Hegel says that art is a thing of the past and appears to agree with him – not because there are no longer communal structures and social networks to support it, as Hegel believed, but because the symbol is a regressive form (p. 773).

By this time in his career de Man had become so used to his deprecation of the aesthetic ideology that he had ceased to explain what is so intrinsically damaging about it. We have to extrapolate his reasons from his description of the subjectivist culture of identification. He simply presupposes that 'bad', or regressive, epistemology means bad aesthetics, bad psychology and bad politics.

What are the psychological and political results of the regressiveness and violence of the interpenetration of symbol with its object? Does it recall, on the one hand, a feminized environment which encourages the easy satisfaction of the infant and, on the other, a reflection of self into other by force? Jacques Lacan's mirror stage appears to be an analogy here. If symbol leaves no room for analytic separation, does that mean a social structure where dissent is impossible? Historically the 'organic' self generates the nation-state consolidated by memory and tradition and evolving 'naturally', abolishing agency as it imposes itself as an entity by fiat on its subjects. Is this the problem? De Man does not ask these questions, but may well expect his readers to ask them. His argument is looser, despite the almost tortuous close reading of Hegel's 'I', and his connections more casual – at times quite wilful – than those of Derrida. The structures he describes can actually contain and have contained very different forms of thought. They allowed the emergence of both a Hegel *and* a Marx, of both a Wordsworth *and* a Freud. If consciousness, as John Searle has recently defined it in deliberately commonsense terms, is an 'inner, first-person, qualitative phenomenon' ('The mystery of consciousness', p. 60), then even a comparatively sophisticated reader puzzled by de Man might well ask what we can do but internalize experience.

There is a certain lack of symmetry in my argument, perhaps represented by the upper-case and lower-case Dd, because Derrida emerges as a more searching reader than de Man. Nevertheless, they share some key arguments of the anti-aesthetic. To sum up: de Man and Derrida refuse three aspects of a traditional aesthetics of disinterestedness, claiming that disinterest is far from the case: they repudiate the work of a unique expressive subjectivity, an autonomous, unified self of the self-same existing in a binary world where the privileged term is a one-sided individualism; they deconstruct the aesthetic as a form of appropriation of the world, with its covert economics of gain; they refuse an art of reconciliation or assuaging or unifying, in which consciousness rests upon and returns to a coherent world and renounces alterity. Both leave openings for alternative readings which I shall pursue later: Derrida by not following through the implications of what he terms the mourning of the aesthetic, de Man by letting slip the implications of a term he uses only once, mediation: 'The symbol is the mediation between the mind and the physical world of which art manifestly partakes' (p. 763). They also share, seemingly, a complete lack of interest in gender: neither suggests that questions of gender might be relevant to an argument about the category of the aesthetic, and this breakdown or blind spot becomes a point at which critique begins. I do not intend to develop a specifically feminist aesthetic out of this breakdown, but it does provide a fissure in the smooth surfaces of these texts from which one might start to investigate alternatives to their conceptualization of the aesthetic.

To begin with, it is noticeable that the elements of the aesthetic deconstructed by both Derrida and de Man are the components of an archaic, individualist theory of art we associate historically with the nineteenth century. But this obsolete, subject-based bourgeois account of the aesthetic is universalized as *the* aesthetic, and thus both writers sometimes look as if they are doing more than they actually are. This aesthetic is credited with extraordinary power at the same time as its seductions are repudiated. And it *is* seduction, as both critiques implicitly gender the aesthetic: Derrida's hysteric, vomiting a repressed alterity, is figured from the Freudian hysterical woman; de Man's melting, unifying symbol is figured from primary narcissism, the primal fusion with the mother which must be resisted at all costs and which becomes antithetically associated with violence. Kristeva's concern with affect comes to mind here, and indeed, on another occasion, I consider the aesthetic possibilities of her work.[7] At present the response to the feminine in the texts of Derrida and de Man is more relevant to my present argument. The glee, the real intellectual virtuosity, of the energies which go into the deconstructive process, its exposure of the privileged concepts of the classical aesthetic, are, we are to understand, sufficient unto themselves, liberating in themselves. The possibility of alternative aesthetics is lost in the assertion of a phallic power of unmasking.

But the phallic can also be prissy. There is a certain straight-faced, self-protective insecurity generated in these two critiques, as the aesthetic seems to undermine the claims to rigour, a resistance, not to theory, but to the temptations of the affect of the beautiful. Interestingly enough, seduction is one of the deconstructive strategies of post-modern culture: Derrida himself later responds to Kant with the strategy of seduction. For Baudrillard seduction accomplishes that shift which realigns power relations and deflects discourse into ludic paths. It is identified with the uncertainty of the feminine. It seems there is a power at work in these theories of the beautiful, possibly because they harbour an alternative aesthetic which cannot be recognized, whose latent potentialities are repressed in the essays of Derrida and de Man.

The possibility for an alternative aesthetic latent in nineteenth-century texts, which can be arrived at by going round Derrida and de Man rather than confronting them, occupies the next stage of this discussion. Before leaving these critiques, however, it ought to be asked whether it is quite sufficient in itself to address the cultural and political implications of a mystified, essentially nineteenth-century aesthetic ideology with the *jouissance* of anti-aesthetic analytical toughness without seeking out alternatives. These writings stage themselves as *strategies*, technologies of analysis, manoeuvres. To engage such a discourse with dialectical argument, when it has effectively exempted itself from it, looks cumbersomely over-serious, a naïve missing of the point of the deconstructive genre, whether by thinking philosophically about a reinstated concept of the beautiful (the classical Habermasian solution), or by attempting to theorize a new understanding of the aesthetic.[8] Yet Derrida and de Man *unthink* the aesthetic and *have* it. They make just the aesthetic move – an exemption from the constraints of propositionality – which they attribute to the texts they critique. There are distinctions to be made between the strategies of de Man and Derrida, as I have said, and it is not my own belief, as I will argue later, that artwork does without propositionality. Yet both produce flagrantly aesthetic texts, at least *in their terms*, in the course of deconstructing the aesthetic. The intellectual depletions which come from not having an adequate, a thought, concept of the aesthetic are enormous. But there are other consequences. Artwork continues to be made, and though for some its continuance might comfortingly affirm the impotence of deconstruction and post-structuralist theory, this is not so. If the aesthetic is *unthought*, if there is no way of thinking about artwork concurrently with its production in contemporary culture, then what it is, why it is important, who makes it, who has access to it and how, and by whom access is granted, become a series of unanswered political questions. These have sharp social, educational and practical implications. If the imagination is cut through to the bone, a state in which to *think* the aesthetic is renounced, one is confronted with

conceptual emptiness. New histories make Adorno's notorious question –
Can there be poetry after Auchswitz? – worth repeating: can there be art,
to extend Adorno's category, after Nagasaki? After ethnic cleansing?
After mass unemployment?

Derrida and de Man have cleared the ground at least. In reaction to
them it begins to be necessary to theorize an aesthetic free from an
autotelic view of the subject and from the rage of the ego to possess the
world through symbol by rejecting alterity. What would be a radical
reading of the aesthetic appropriate to a democratic politics and responsive to questions of gender? The components of an alternative aesthetic
are the concern of what follows.

Interlude

A poem, Veronica Forrest-Thomson's 'Ducks & Rabbits' (1971),[9] and a
piece of sculpture, or rather, an installment, Antony Gormley's 'A field for
the British Isles' (1995). I want these particular examples and my general
argument to behave as mutual commentaries on one another. The poem I
use continuously, in a choric way, to punctuate a developing thesis. I turn
to Gormley to end my discussion. I will describe these artworks briefly.
But first, they were chosen because they are problematic instances of the
aesthetic. In terms of their cultural production they are examples of
Bourdieu's 'restricted' rather than 'general' works, that is, 'avant-garde'
rather than 'popular'.[10] Veronica Forrest-Thomson's poems belong to
avant-garde (and in many ways flagrantly aestheticist) writing of the
1970s, and their publication by a privately funded little press of
the 1990s meant that they could be assimilated both into post-modern
writing and into 'alternative' writing. This is, clearly, part of their
meaning.

Likewise, the assemblage created by Gormley's thousands of figurines
has to be seen as an attempt – a heroic but rather desperate attempt – to
create a community art which nourishes unemployment. They were made
by out-of-work families in St Helens after Pilkington contracted its
work-force. But in the context of the exhibition codes of the commercial
gallery, the almost inevitable result is that 'community' art is taken away
from the community that made it. It is not my intention to make the
components of a democratic aesthetic homologous with 'popular' art but
to map some core components of the aesthetic which would appear across
a field, and which would begin to render the binary, high/low, the torn
halves of cultural production, less coercive. Nor is it my intention to
register a sharp epistemological break, in which an obsolete nineteenth-

century art is superseded by other, radical forms of production. As well as extending what we mean by 'art', the hope is to make what we know already *look* different. There is something in Simmel's belief that what we decide to include within the aesthetic will become it. Here I enter into an act of redescribing which should release new possibilities rather than staying with the impasse reached by Dd. It is a matter of reconstructing terms rather than inventing a new aesthetic.

To return to a particular instance of artwork I use during this discussion: the poem starts from the playful possibility of overcoming the psychologists' perceptual test, the drawing which we can see either as a duck or a rabbit but not both (taken up by Wittgenstein in *Philosophical Investigations* (1953)). From the hybrid duck–rabbits swimming in the Mill Race at Cambridge, Forrest-Thomson moves to the structure of metaphor and then to the emotion which propels metaphor – here the sight of a photograph which can only become bearable by being transformed and distanced as art, or turned into language – or can it? There is a pun on the idea of the 'frame' of the photograph, for one of the theories of metaphor current at the time she was writing considers metaphor as a form of framing.[11] The term also catches up with Derrida's *parergon*, the surround which marks off an aesthetic space, but which is ambiguously of it and not of it. Playing as it does with the separation of art and life, the poem in some ways maintains a highly conventional aesthetic stance. On the other hand, this separation is both tragic and ludic. With footnotes drawn from Wittgenstein, the poem is a post-modern language game. It is marked by many of the intellectual concerns of that time, by Langer's theories of art, by psychological accounts of perception as 'gestalt', or a seized totality of immediate experience, as well as with Wittgenstein's preoccupations with naming.[12]

I propose to read the poem in the different context of Hegel's work, and I believe it can stand up to this transition. It is, of course, two texts, because if you interweave the seven footnotes into the text as you read them, they produce another poem, an alternative text. An edgily brilliant, hysterico-drunken poem, it is celebratory and cerebral – and intensely sad.

> Ducks & Rabbits
>
> in the stream;[1]
> look, the duck–rabbits swim between.
> The Mill Race
> at Granta Place
> tosses them from form to form,
> dissolving bodies in the spume.

Given A and see[2]
find be[3]
(look at you, don't look at me)[4]
Given B, see A and C.
that's what metaphor[5]
is for.

Date and place
in the expression of a face[6]
provides the frame
for an instinct to rename,[7]
to try to hold apart
Gestalt and Art.

[1] Of consciousness

[2] The expression of a change of aspect is the expression of a new perception.

[3] And at the same time of the perception's being unchanged.

[4] Do not ask yourself 'How does it work with me?' Ask 'What do I know about someone else?'

[5] Here it is useful to introduce the idea of a picture–object.

[6] A child can talk to picture–men or picture–animals. It can treat them as it treats dolls.

[7] Hence the flashing of an aspect on us seems half visual experience, half thought.

(Forrest-Thomson, *Collected Poems and Translations*, p. 22)

In the next section I return to Hegel and read the poem in parallel with parts of his *Encyclopaedia Logic*. These readings are in italics to designate the double form of my commentary.

Alternatives: redescribing the aesthetic

An aesthetic needs to be grounded in experience that happens to everybody. Everybody plays. The ceaseless inventiveness of play, which precludes privileged creation, makes an experimental space for living (and perhaps for dying) and this provides a fruitful possibility for exploration. The art of the past, comprehended under the categories of the 'beautiful', 'taste', 'symbol', *can* be seen as a form of play, as indeed Schiller saw it.[13] But he was limited by Kantian terminology and, to go further with the concept of play, a radical act of re-describing is necessary. Thus, as I have said, rather than contemplating an epistemological break we can elicit principles which make what we know look different. I began to explore the cognates of play and aesthetic object elsewhere (in the critique of

Eagleton already mentioned), discovering that Vygotsky's *The Psychology of Art* (1925) surprisingly early in the century recognized the importance of Freud's understanding of play (p. 82). But the elements of play need to be further understood. Unless both thought and the passions are fully engaged the energies of play recede.

This essay is concerned with how one might think about thought in artwork, but as a prerequisite for considering affect. Artwork is saturated in affect, for which we have no (or few) terms of analysis. A major consequence of abandoning the classical binaries of the aesthetic, as I should like to do, is that the traditional distinction between affect, or the emotions, and knowledge, is dissolved. Indeed, it is necessary to include affect under the sign of cognition and enable it to be comprehended in the definition of knowledge. In an alternative aesthetic, emotions should not be excluded, as they are at present, from an account of reason, which holds detachment and objectivity as its norm. Among the revivals of the discourse of affect the earliest was that of André Green, in *Le Discours vivant* (1973), and his – among other accounts of emotion and knowing – form part of a separate discussion which is the twin of this. In our culture masculine reason and feminine affect – it is almost banal to say so – have formed an implicitly or sometimes not so implicitly gendered account of reason. This opposition needs to be undone. To think of artwork as a form of thought as well as a form of feeling is to risk introducing 'work' into the 'play' of the aesthetic. But this seems no bad thing. Perhaps the aesthetic in our culture has always been a hybrid form: hence the need to limit and define it through the treatise on art.

'an instinct to rename'. Knowledge cannot be abstracted from the drives. An epistemic passion fuses emotion and cognition inseparably. Forrest-Thomson recognizes the hybridity of emotion-knowledge in her Wittgensteinian footnote: understanding is 'half visual experience, half thought'.

To go further with an account of play and thought/affect. Play and the epistemic passion which drives it are forms of mediation, with the world, with the culture to which play is a response. By mediation, I mean, briefly, the work on the world done by thought and feeling as self and other is defined and negotiated, though the rest of this essay expands on the meaning of mediation and reworks the commonly accepted understanding of mediation by removing self from the centre of this process. If we refuse to seal the artwork off into an aesthetic terrain, and regard the *artwork*, not the 'I' who supposedly made it, as a form of mediation, a transitive, interactive form, new possibilities emerge. For one thing, this will not allow the one-sided, privileged term, self or 'I', to dominate what is a process of relating, a constant negotiation of in-betweenness. Self and other are co-ordinates rather than fixed entities in the process of mediation, but mediation does not necessarily require a negotiation between *self* and world at all. For Hegel the 'I' is in any case 'what thinks', and the free-standing processes of thought in artwork could just as easily be conceptualized as mediation, which is above all about forms of knowing. Hegelian mediation has been dramatically re-read by Gillian Rose in *The Broken Middle* (1992), but it is a deeply unpopular term for post-modern theory, and requires a defence. Contra post-modern readings, artwork considered as a form of mediation tolerates difference and non-closure. It is not about reconciliation and unity. It takes the shape of, becomes a representation of, melancholy rather than of mourning, its scattering, its ungathered shards, its left-over, unassimilable split-off parts. For Derrida, Hegelian mediation takes everything into itself without residue. Not for Rose, for whom the breaking point of contradiction, or what she prefers to call diremption, and loss is a central aspect of mediation.

There is no 'I' in Veronica Forrest-Thomson's poem.

Mediation transforms categories and remakes language. This is a social, not a private act. The struggle for the sign, the negotiation of codes and signifying systems, are now familiar concepts to us. But I mean that artwork can be a space where linguistic experiment changes meaning by questioning categories, the prerequisite of knowledge.

> *You can 'see' through metaphor, that which transforms categories, new knowledge – 'The expression of a change of aspect is the expression of a new perception.'*

All these propositions are about artwork as a form of knowledge – which may involve redefining what knowing is. My next step is to consider knowing and mediation. This is a preparation, as I have said, for another essay exploring the way affect and knowledge work together.

Negotiating mediation

What happens if we consider artwork as a *representation* of mediation? For one thing, it is Hegel rather than Kant who becomes an interlocutor, since mediation is at the heart of his work. As a result I will have much less to say about Kant. But since much of Hegel's thought is an encounter with Kant, some problems of the Kantian aesthetic recur in the work I discuss. Anti-Hegelian post-modern, or post-Nietzschean, thought is hostile to an association of artwork and mediation, because it is hostile to the idea of mediation. Gillian Rose's agonistic, revisionary reading of mediation, making Hegel her interlocutor, was undertaken as a critique of this hostility. For her mediation is a vital moment of breakdown, both a diremption and a creation, an essentially triune movement which resists what she considers to be post-modern culture's peremptory and ultimately formal collapsing of experience into two terms. De Man did not expand his fleeting reference to symbol's (the duck–rabbit's?) mediation between mind and things in the world, in which he should have included ideas, cultural practice and ideology as well as stone, colour and sound. Yet this core of Hegel's thinking relieves experience of the subjectivism de Man deprecated, enables a rethinking of symbol and opens the way to a new understanding of knowing. Post-modernity's loving hatred of Hegel's arduous, cumbersome poetics of consciousness (his translators speak of a kind of necessary clumsiness) is almost always the Oedipal moment by which post-modernity defines itself against his thought. Anti-Hegelian readings provide the lift-off of conceptual energy necessary for redefinition, a need all the more pressing because so much of his work makes post-modernity epistemologically possible.

I will take Gilles Deleuze as a post-modern figure here, partly because he is one of the few post-modern thinkers to write, in *Difference and Repetition* (1968), with an almost old-fashioned enthusiasm for the power of art.

> For there is no other aesthetic problem than that of the insertion of art into everyday life. The more our daily life appears standardised, stereotyped and subject to an accelerated reproduction of objects of consumption, the more art must be injected into it in order to extract from it that little difference which plays simultaneously between other levels of repetition, and even in order to make the two extremes resonate – namely, the habitual series of consumption and the instinctual series of destruction and death. Art thereby connects the tableau of cruelty with that of stupidity, and discovers underneath consumption a schizophrenic clattering of jaws, and underneath the most ignoble destructions of war, still more processes of consumption. It aesthetically reproduces the illusions and mystifications which make up the real essence of this civilisation, in order that Difference may be expressed with a force of anger which is itself repetitive and capable of introducing the strangest selection, even if this is only a contraction here and there – in other words, a freedom for the end of a world. (Deleuze, *Difference and Repetition*, p. 293)

Yet Deleuze writes of the necessity of a 'non-mediated difference' (p. 25). The renunciation of mediation is essential to his ideas. True freedom lies in the repetition which reproduces or doubles itself, not with the mechanical, abstract universality of the law of recurrence, not with the circumscription of the concept, not in symmetry with pre-existing forms, or through representation made possible by the gap between subject and object. No, the very notion of pre-existing forms mediated by representation is alien to the dynamic, self-creating repetition staged as unique, dissymmetrical alterity, a radical alterity because it is made new with every repetition, and repetition is without a ground. In the pure a priori form of time, as opposed to its empirical contents, repetition is embedded because repetition itself is repeated. It does not remain 'external to something which is repeated and must be supposed primary' (p. 294): there is no first time. Christian repetition is opposed to atheist repetition, Kierkegaardian to Nietzschean, the repetition of once and for all and the repetition to infinity. And because repetition makes new it is an occasion of masking, simulacra, not copying. Twins, doubled but singular, a swimmer, matching its body to the waves but not reflecting their shape, are models of an anti-Hegelian structure which has abandoned the notion of self and world related as particular and universal, subject and object, reflection of self into other. The heartbeat itself, one assumes, possesses a kind of Heraclitean metrics, always different in a new space and time, generating a unique pulse with every movement of the blood through the valves of the heart. Deleuze's critique of Hegel is essentially that of Marx, though it substitutes *immediacy* for materiality: Hegel remains in 'the reflected element of "representation", within simple generality' (p. 10); his element is dialectical drama rather than repetitive theatre, and introduces 'mediation in a movement which is no more than that of its own thought and its generalities' (p. 10). The perverse creativity of repetition compulsion in the Freudian death wish is preferable to lumpen Hegelian sublation and its constant abstraction.

It takes some repression and selective reading of Hegel, for whom the phenomenology of experience was conceived as an eroticized bacchanalian revel of multiple agencies, to arrive at such a static understanding of his thought. But why should one prefer mediation rather than postmodern immediacy as a model of the aesthetic? Because immediacy has no way of grasping itself, no way of knowing about itself. (For Deleuze the swimmer learns the perpetuation of body strokes in an 'amorous' way, by creating and responding to repetition (p. 23).) Both the epistemology of repetition and of mediation are non-expressive forms, both refuse to put the ego at the centre of its creations, but mediation creates a space for *coming to know and knowing about that coming to know*, a space inevitably of fracture rather than connection, agonistic, but a space all the same.

Gillian Rose's reading of Hegel, one of the few to take on post-modernity with the sophistication it demands, repeatedly insists on *the broken middle*. Through mediation irreconcilables reconfigure – but not by magic. For her, too, there is no first time, but there is a third, the middle. The third, the middle, engages at the point where radical oppositions 'come into a changed relation' and is cause and effect of that changing relation.[14] 'Whereas post-modernity remains dualistic and pits its others against domination, the broken middle is triune. It will investigate the breaks between universal, particular and singular, in individuals and in institutions' (*The Broken Middle*, p. xii). Rose takes the triple terms of the Hegelian syllogism, the relation between the universal, particular and singular, in which each term moves between its contraries, and argues that equivocation, a struggle with breaks and difficulty, not an unproblematical reconciliation, is a true Hegelian response, a mode of understanding.

> They [truly post-Hegelian philosophers] configure the aporia, the difficulty, of the relation between universal, particular and singular. This difficulty is *the* political difficulty *par excellence*: the opposition between particular and general will, to use Rousseau's terms; or the struggle between particular and universal class, to use Marx's terms; and the difficulty of representing this relation in terms of political institutions and aesthetic values (Rose, *The Broken Middle*, p. 164).

Rose's final targets are post-modern theologians, from Levinas to Liberation Theology, and architectural theorists of community, with their reduction of architectural possibility to a simple opposition between sentimentalized 'community' and demonized bureaucratic planning, who become exemplary moments in post-modernity's material effect on the spiritual life of civil society, the environment and the way we live in it. But the elision of the middle, or the attempt to mend it in a premature and arbitrary way, is characteristic of figures which include Lacan, Lyotard and Foucault. The book is deliberately written against the grain of contemporary theory. For her modernity is in collusion with the violence it proposes to critique because the turn to discourse refuses to countenance a thinking through of contradiction and the anxiety of the middle. This has covertly invented new binaries: utopia and dystopia, love and violence, are the dominant oppositions for her, since she is concerned with the modern political state in post-modern writing and its refusal to recognize the intransigent relation of law and ethics: sign and simulacra, individual and panoptical power, I suggest, might be others. Rose considers 'aesthetic values' indirectly, and yet her ceaseless recourse to 'equivocation', to the trying out or working through of opposite solutions while suspending closure by returning to the middle, is an aesthetic strategy simultaneous with a mode of thought. Equivocation is a form of critique, as we move from one side of the irresolvable to the other, restructuring the problem, but not doing away with it. It does not remain suspended as ambivalence because of the ethical imperative to decide. And it is the impossibility of resolving contradiction which leads to another aesthetic stance, facetiousness, a kind of agonistic comedy rather than irony. The middle is a form of difference, as opposed to its being defined through the beginning and the end (p. 287). It can never be mended, or willed away by violence, for false syntheses and equally false oppositions arise from premature resolution of the middle. In the agon of the middle the individual confronts itself as particular and universal, but *discovers* these contradictions. Indeed, loss is the condition of the broken middle.

The example of Kierkegaard, Freud and Lacan and their conceptualizing of repetition indicates how Rose's understanding of mediation works. For both Kierkegaard and Freud, who is claimed as the psychoanalyst of the broken middle, a 'Janus-faced' anxiety is connected with repetition. Anxiety 'holds the middle' (p. 101), looking backward to the aetiology of guilt, creating sin for Kierkegaard just as for Freud guilt creates repression, by repeatedly returning to the structure of burial and reburial. Sin, repression, do not create anxiety: anxiety creates them. But anxiety is also a pivot of the movement forwards: through repetition there is always the possibility of 'recollection' of loss, as anxiety becomes a 'third', exposing the fracture of body and soul (Kierkegaard), or of internal 'neurotic' danger and external, 'real' danger (Freud). Anxiety exposes, defines the problem of contradiction between sin and faith (Kierkegaard), between blocked memory and the memory which releases a 'freely mobile ego' (Freud) (p. 104), a prerequisite for change. For Rose, Lacan does away with the creative middle of anxiety by reformulating the need for repetition in a deterministic way by making compulsion to repeat an imperative of the symbolic order, or law. An endless attempt at symbolic substitution to regain a lost pleasure is set in motion when sin, or the *non* of the symbolic order, intrudes between primal pleasure and consciousness, instantiating a chain of discourse, a closed circuit, which seeks to retrieve the lost object, in Lacan's words, through a 'conquest, the structuration of the world through an effort of labour' (p. 102). Rose makes the symbolic order eschatological in ways some Lacanians would reject, but more important are Lacanian ideas of substitution. The subject's conquest of the world is always doomed to the misrecognition of substitution. In making sin the third term, and in equating repetition with substitution, Lacan has created an essentially static world, which must reproduce the father's mistakes. Because its middle is spurious, an immobile negation, it is impossible for the self to risk its life, for Freud the register of the value of life itself, by exposing itself to the *choices* and the agonistic meanings opened up in the broken middle. The middle, 'rended not mended', makes it possible 'to know, to misknow and yet to grow', responding to the 'broken heart' of modernity by challenging post-modernity's renunciation of the law and mediation (p. 246).

How does the broken middle translate into the aesthetic?

I turn to the *Encyclopaedia Logic* for different purposes than de Man.[15] Though it will become evident that I do not believe his argument is sustainable, the point of the following discussion is not to confront him, but to think through the implications of seeing artwork as a representation of mediation, the broken middle. And it is to *Encyclopaedia Logic* that one turns for one of the sources of Rose's broken middle. This work is a logic, theology, cultural theory and implicitly a poetics. It is this not only because of the dogged rapture of its thought and the intensity of ratiocination which becomes living, creative labour: not only because of its constant marking of its logic off from the taxonomies of the empirical sciences (see, for instance, paras 7, 13, 16); it is a poetics because it is about the forms taken by knowledge, the shape of the movement and change which is the means of coming to know and the coming to know which is the source and shape of change and movement. Because form is lived it is not formalism. This is not a 'progressive' account of knowledge so much as an increasingly complex understanding of it. Throughout it one is aware of what Rose terms 'diremption', which draws attention to 'the trauma of separation of that which was, as in marriage, not originally united' (*The Broken Middle*, p. 236). The Fall for Hegel is the central diremptive moment. Here Hegel turns from the fluid, mediated subject-in-process, which is the theme of the *Phenomenology*, to the structure of mediation itself (*Encyclopaedia Logic*, 'The Fall', para. 23, pp. 60–5). He is less interested in the 'I' than in *thinking*. His *cogito* reverses the Cartesian priorities, 'I think therefore I am' (which he nevertheless respects as the founding moment of modern philosophy), in the proposal that 'I' is 'what thinks' (para. 23, p. 57).

To experiment in substituting the text or the aesthetic object for the subject as 'what thinks' is to begin to see how mediation, structuring 'what thinks' and structured by it, can address the impasse created by Derrida and de Man. Throughout this discussion, I reiterate, I regard 'what thinks' as the artwork itself, not the individual subject, self or consciousness.

Let us start with what Hegel says of an inadequate account of thinking:

> But that is not saying very much, for thinking is essentially the negation of
> something immediately given – just as we owe our eating to food because
> without it we could not eat. It is true that, in this context, eating is
> represented as ungrateful, since it is the digesting of that to which it is
> supposed to owe itself. In this sense, thinking is no less ungrateful. (Hegel
> *Encyclopaedia Logic*, para. 12, p. 36)

This slightly heavy facetiousness actually enacts the mediation being
defined. Hegel does not accept the Deleuzian antithesis between immediate and mediated experience because mediation is not something external. We are always *in* mediation: to think of it as a simple, linear,
progressive sequence in which immediacy is followed by the cancellation
of the immediate – food, eating – is simply to understand the components
of mediation without living its structure. There is no beginning in mediation. By reversing the priority of eating to food, so that *eating* defines
mere immediate matter retrospectively as food, Hegel is in the middle, not
experiencing the linearity of homogeneous empty time, but actively living
in a 'thick' or constellated temporality, calling out the cultural meanings
of what it is to consume. Here he wholly accepts the champing mouth
avoided by Kant. Consumption and thinking share the awkward characteristic of being 'ungrateful', he says ironically. They appear to demolish what brings them into being – food, immediate experience. But this
absurdity can only be imagined if you are prepared to entertain an understanding of consciousness – and Hegel does this fleetingly to inhabit the
anxiety of this state – in an external way as a mounting series of discrete,
successive experiences. In reality, eating and food are inseparable, just as
thinking and thought are inseparable. We do not come into thought from
the outside, a problem which troubles the potential philosopher
wanting to practise philosophy's forms of thought (para. 1), imagining a
pre-existing body of knowledge which has to be *entered*. There is no
beginning in this sense. Just as we *are* philosophers, already within
philosophy, when we have recognized that philosophy requires its own
intrinsic and necessary form of thought (because this is a philosophical
insight), so we are in mediation, which is not a matter of altering
immediate experience from the outside, when we know that we are in
the middle. To return to the duck–rabbits via Derrida's *The Truth in
Painting*:

> *In the stream; /look, the duck–rabbits swim between. The betweenness
> here postulated is constituted by hiatus, caesura, break. Derrida*

attributes to Hegel an organic teleology of the closed circle of know-ledge, in which experience includes everything within itself without residue. Including itself in itself so that no 'absolute beginning' (p. 28) is necessary, the circle of mind is what it is 'only by returning. Retra-cing its steps, in a circle' (p. 26). Working only from the pastness of the necessity of its own results, replete with itself, this is essentially an a posteriori philosophy (in contrast to the a priori thought of Kant) which attributes to art the same closed circle and naturalizes circumscription. But surely, in answer to this description, to be in the middle, without 'absolute beginning', is also a way of shaking free from circularity, releasing 'what thinks' from the closed circle. Faced with the naturalization of the frame or circle, Derrida says, decon-struction must neither reframe nor dream of 'the pure and simple absence of the frame' (p. 73). Isn't the self-consciousness of the middle, in the stream, the viewing of experience in terms of moments unteth-ered from the absolute beginning, a way of restating the anxiety of the enclosing circle and absence of enclosure rather than of reaffirming the circle? Perhaps aesthetic experience hovers between self-enclosed autonomy and the absence of frame? The categorical frame of either duck or rabbit and the categorical transgression of duck–rabbit?

Hegel says that mediation consists in 'a having advanced to a second', or in 'already having left a first behind to go on to a second', always already at the moment of division, of break. He means not only that the middle is a point of change and transition, but that it is a vital moment of conceptualization which requires separation from 'a first' to come into being. Here again there is that awkward poetry of thinking characteristic of Hegel. It is there to suggest we can only be grounded in the unstable middle. In *positing* the beginning, or the 'first', from the unstable middle, and the middle as a return from a point where we have never been, a point of no return – in producing these co-ordinates, 'what thinks' is able to discover a shape to experience, to separate itself out from experience, and to *think* about it at the same time as being in the middle. Thus in paragraph 12 (p. 36), he states: 'For mediation is a beginning, and a having advanced to a second, in such a way that this second is only there because one has come to it from something that is other vis à vis this second.' Derrida, working with Kant's model of the middle in *The Truth in Painting*, conceives of the middle as a detachable element, 'a separable part, a particular part' (p. 39), in a static triad. Thus reason and under-standing, theoretical and practical experience, are articulated by an aes-thetic intermediary, judgement. But the aesthetic constitutes a suspension which gives it a curious status, he says. It has neither an independent role nor is it a re-membering, connective entity. Or, like the frame or *parergon*, it both is detached, disinterested, *and* sinks its identity, loses itself either to theory or to practice.

Thus Kant's middle is always without, always associated with loss, and belongs with the displacement of the supplement. Hegel avoids this model by positing mediation as a mobile, structuring *activity*, not a separable intermediary element, a relational movement, not an entity. It is in-betweenness that keeps relations in play. Like the signifying gaps in Freudian dreamwork, it need not have a content and thus can revel in the state of being 'without' as well as creating the diremptive gaps which ask for a new content.

> *Think of the constitutive blanks that intervene between the blocks of discourse in* Ducks & Rabbits *that keep in play the Mill Race passage, the metaphor section, and the anguished memory generated by the photograph.*

Mediation has no origin. It has always left the 'first' behind; '[for] mediation consists in already having left a first behind to go on to a second, and in a going forth from moments that are distinct' (para. 86, p. 137). Beginnings are necessary fictions to think about where you are, a framing and the risk of dismantling a frame at one and the same time. Rather like Deleuze's Erewhon, or 'nowhere' (which they prefigure), the realm of pure theoretic experience, they are aesthetic constructs. The difference is that they are a mediated living-in-the-present indivisible from a contemplated past and future, whereas 'nowhere' constantly galvanizes the present into being. Mediation is a kind of three-dimensional thinking. It reconfigures experience and temporalities rather than creating an ever-new present.

> *Example of three-dimensional thinking:*
> *Given A and see*
> *Find be . . .*
> *Given B, see A and C.*
> *In the structure of metaphor it is B, in between, which gives new meaning to A and to C/See. Once a third term has been discovered it reconfigures A and C/See. But the syllogism requires a breaking apart for this to occur. B and the primal verb 'to be', the copula, are the problematic elements of analogy, or metaphor. They may be the source of new relations, but they precisely do not allow A to be identified with C, 'to be' C. They draw attention to the clash of categories which is*

metaphor as well as to the reconfiguration of singularity and universals
which occurs in the work of metaphor.

This three-dimensional thinking anticipates the three-fold syllogism which I shall discuss later. First, how and why do *knowledge* and mediation belong to one another?

Mediation is a 'thinking-over' which has thought for its content (para. 2, p. 25). As the translator's hyphen implies, it is not a thinking about, but a kind of going beyond itself which includes itself and object. But this is not a smooth incorporation of thought within thought as Derrida implies. It is more like a reworking. Hegel carefully marks off this reworking from what is sometimes assumed to be thought. It is one thing to have feelings and thoughts permeated by thought, another to have thoughts about thinking. It is not simply that thinking is the instrument of thinking (para. 7, p. 31), or that it is a fallacy to consider thinking as an instrument apart from its objects, like a swimmer who decides to learn to swim before going into the water. Some kinds of unachieved thinking make representation only a metaphor for concepts (para. 3, p. 27) and put things side by side rather than positing relationships. Thought proper reconfigures representations as thought and transforms them into concepts (para. 20, pp. 49–52). The dynamism of 'thinking-over' means that thought generates its own principles of activity from within (para. 14, pp. 38–9), and so it changes something, reworking the object by the very process of positing it, giving it a new status in consciousness and returning it to experience in a different form. It is a kind of problematization which produces a new interpretation, and a new interpretation is a transformation. It is only through the mediation of alteration that the central aspects of an object come to consciousness (para. 22, pp. 54–5). Things cannot be understood unless they are altered.

2 *The expression of a change of aspect is the expression of a new*
   perception.
3 *And at the same time of the perception's being unchanged.*

But this 'thinking-over' is not set in motion without discomfort, a frustrated awareness of the non-correspondence of consciousness and the world (para. 11, p. 35). Thinking indeed necessitates a tearing apart of thought from sensible objects, so as not to be 'stuck in its [thinking's] counterpart', the world of objects, for particulars do not lead to universals (para. 21, pp. 52–4). Grammar is not deducible by children from individual speech (if this seems grimly mechanistic and pedagogical think of 'langue' and 'parole'); nor race from individuals (this racist assumption actually proves Hegel's point that thought deals in constructs); nor are the laws of motion of the planets deducible from their presence in the sky. Such phenomena necessitate 'pure' constructs.

> *in the stream; [Of consciousness]*
> *look, the duck–rabbits swim between.*
> *The duck–rabbits, 'impure' hybrids posited in consciousness, can never exist simultaneously for perception when they are used for psychological testing. It is impossible to see a duck and a rabbit at the same time. Yet, surreally swimming, in the physical stream of the Mill Race and in the stream of consciousness, they are torn away from the empirical experience of seeing one species or the other, and the hybrid is offered as 'pure' phantasmatic construct. The hybrid monstrous births both swim 'between' categories, and between consciousness and the world of objects. Generated out of their literal impossibility (Rose would say their diremption) they are at once 'pure' construct, phantasmatic beings, thought out of thought, and creatures which return to experience as a meditation on hybridity and perception and ultimately on the epistemology of metaphor. The difficulty, the impossibility/possibility, of this return generates the rest of the poem, though at the same time, 'The expression of a change of aspect is the expression of a new perception', a footnote comments. Something has* altered *as a result of the invention of the duck–rabbit.*

Hegel was well aware that his insistence on the inner logic of thought as mediation encountered the critique of flagrant idealism. One of his defensive strategies is to argue paradoxically for the absolute banality of mediation – experience is always already mediated, whether playing the piano or intuitions of God are at issue. But this is not really the point: it is vital to bring the awareness of mediation to consciousness. And bringing to consciousness is implicitly an aesthetic act of shaping. Without this people get stuck in sterile repetition, restating rather than developing a new content to propositions. A simple, unitary subject grounded in 'naïve' immediate knowledge and believing that it understands God through immediate intuition, for instance, leads straight to an authoritarian God. 'We know *that* God exists, not *what* God is' (para. 73, p. 120). Such a subject creates an abstract God, a 'highest essence' in the beyond, a God of fear, therefore, an empty God (para. 112, p. 177). A false presumption of immediate experience may *be* false: God may not *be* like this but we will *act* as if he is. Theory, however mistaken, organizes lived experience. Hegel insists on the fallacy of immediate experience. When immediate knowing is asserted as the exclusive form of truth, consciousness only has available to itself a form of static polemic (para. 11, p. 35). It cannot go beyond itself, and the indifference of a formalism which reiterates universals as formulas is the result – the 'Being' of the Eleatic school and the 'Becoming' of Heraclitus are classical examples. Hegel also parodies the formulas of 'modern', idealist propositions here, parodies what can be taken to be his own thought – 'That in the Absolute all is one', 'The identity of the subjective and the objective'. The notion of the immediate is in any case actually a result, not a cause, of mediation. He admits that as it stands Descartes's 'I think, therefore I am' posits immediate knowledge, but regards this as a *moment* of self-consciousness which does not close down thought (para. 64, pp. 112–14). Anticipating Deleuze's turn to the singularity of experience through atomized repetition, he argues that pure singularity, logically the atom, exists in a realm of mutual externality where everything is external to everything else. 'The content in it stands at the same time in isolation': discrete and self-enclosed, atoms belong to a condition of juxtaposition and succession, not affected by time but only existing in space (para. 20, p. 50). It is a kind of associationism without association. It escapes death, but fails to live in time. It has no way of *grasping* itself as thought, itself and its other.

There is little essential difference between the analyses of Hegel and Deleuze: both offer 'aesthetic' arguments for and against an epistemology of repetition. For Hegel, atomized repetition offers no way of generating thought out of thought, which, he insists, turns thought into *experience*: 'actual', 'concrete', 'substantial', 'matter' are the terms he gives to thought which is alive. For Deleuze, on the other hand, what is important is precisely the seduction, the seizure, of repetition's sublime nature existing in disconnection as artefact, as pure construction of the will to power, or self-produced energy. Deleuze is indeed one of the most energizing of postmodern theorists, but his sense that repetition explodes uniquely into being is an ostensive definition of thought without the broken middle.

Thought enters the world as experience, Hegel insists. It does not simply convert, by means of a kind of translation, intuitions and ideas – that is, the sort of thinking everyone has experience of – into abstract (and inevitably) truistic propositions (para. 5, p. 28). Nor is it concerned with the production of dreams or the self-righteous 'phantasms' of pure ideals, an abstract mode of thinking severing actuality from the idea endemic to both ethical and political theory (para. 6, p. 30). The outer and inner world of consciousness is the element of thought. *Actuality* is its content (para. 6, p. 30). Thought is 'concrete' because out of its own resources it can generate, and continue to generate, particulars which have a structural necessity, which are capable of being developed. Reciprocally, particulars guarantee concretion (para. 14, p. 39). What is 'substantial' is only reached through the reworking of our thinking about it (para. 22, pp. 54–5). Despite the Kantian discovery of the non-correspondence between thought and matter, the mediation of thought is immersed in matter because it reaches out to the objective world and reworks both natural and spiritual. Hegel counters Aristotle's 'there is nothing in the intellect that has not been in sense experience', with 'there is nothing in sense experience that has not been in the intellect' (para. 8, p. 32). But that further leap to ethical and epistemological questions occurs because thought can work on sense experience and intellect.

> *The duck–rabbits are immersed in matter, the Mill stream as well as the stream of consciousness. They are the products of sense experience (the diagram) and of intellect. Pure artifice, a form of metaphor, they necessitate the investigation of metaphor. Not to be able to go beyond 'Given A', which can only resort to A = A, is to be caught in tautological repetition, or repetition empty of content. The more thinking changes things the more it and they belong to substantial experience, transforming material life. Therefore nothing exists only at the level of thought because thought alters experience.*

Throughout his insistence on thought as experience, on the notion of the immediate as a result, not a cause of mediation, and that 'there is nothing in sense experience that has not been in the intellect' (para. 8, p. 32), Hegel has Kant in mind. Kant did not believe that thought was an abstraction from immediate experience either, but his aesthetics create problems because one of the conditions of beauty is the disengagement of singularities from concepts. Derrida seizes on this preoccupation with uniqueness dissociated from class: 'Beauty is always beautiful *once* ... This is the paradox (the class which – immediately – sounds the death knell of uniqueness in beauty) of the third *Critique* and of any discourse on the beautiful: it must deal only with singularities which must give rise only to universalizable judgments' (*The Truth in Painting*, p. 93). We return to self-contained, narcissistic beauty here and the chiasmus which cuts off the autonomous object from thought and the world, and which therefore brings '*nothing* to knowledge' (p. 42). By making singularity the product of thought, Hegel, unlike *The Truth in Painting*, avoids this hierarchy of uniqueness and concept and the status of the singular as both bounded and free-floating.

That mind as thought grasping thought is everywhere in the universe, since all the universe becomes thought and all thought becomes experience, is often seen as one of the hubristic, even paranoid suppositions of idealism: 'and since I am at the same time in all my sensations, notions,

states etc., thought is present everywhere and pervades all these determi-
nations as [their] category' (para. 20, p. 51). It *is* paranoid in a special
sense as we shall see, but thinking is also represented as the necessary
annulment of self. True, we cannot think for other people, any more than
we can eat for them, and this is the ground of all human freedom (para.
23, p. 55), yet if the irreducible singularity of 'I' cannot be represented,
what is *left over* is that very universality of the 'I' which is actually the
ground of commonality: 'All other human beings have this in common
with me to be "I"' (para. 20, p. 51). Because 'I' can stand for all other 'I's,
because 'I' is a mediating symbol, it is possible to be released from the
singularity (or immediacy) of the ego and do what all 'I's do – think
relations, be 'what thinks'. True agency is the capacity to free thought
from the congeries of contingent, singular experience by becoming
immersed in matter, as thought displaces and doubles itself in the universe
as thought/not thought, thought which thinks the object. To constitute
the substance of external things singularity has to be distinguished from
the structural relations which can only be grasped by thought in the
medium of thought. That is why Hegel stresses the generality, the non-
immediate nature of language, in paragraph 20, just as he stresses the
non-immediate 'I', because it is only through the *mediated* nature of
language that thought can be shared. This is a social theory of language.
As a corollary, this is a social theory of 'what thinks'. Hegel concedes 'I
cannot say I' in order to open out experience which can be culturally
mediated. Nevertheless, there is loss. As always, the movement is agonistic. For the linguistic generality of 'I' does not cancel out its singularity
but actually exposes the gap between singular 'I' and general 'I'. In
romantic art (from the advent of Christianity), Hegel's *Introductory
Lectures on Aesthetics* reminds us, the one-sidedness of symbol in
which thought and sense do not adequately cohere, exposes the disjunction, the disunion, between inwardness and objective world. This dissymmetry becomes the dominant form of modernity, and it becomes the
function of the aesthetic to dramatize its culture's one-sidedness. In
other words, a unified symbol is a dream not an actuality. This is because
thought is radically 'between', moving as it were against the self. This is
actually closer than is usually realized to Lacan's decentred 'I' as subject
of the signifier and his revisionary Cartesianism in 'The insistence of the
letter in the unconscious' – '*I think where I am not*, therefore I am where I
think not' (p. 97). The difference is that thought attempts to understand
the point of aporia where things 'come into a changed relation'.

*(look at you, don't look at me): this parenthesis, picking up and
repeating the imperative 'look' of the poem's second line, intervenes*

as a pivot in the exposition of metaphor after the middle term, 'find
be', has been elicited. The gaze is transferred from the duck–rabbits
and now the imperative is for a you to look at a you and not to look at
me. But the footnote reverses this injunction: Do not ask yourself
'How does it work with me?' Ask 'What do I know about someone
else?' In this doubling you and me keep reversing, changing places,
considering each other as objects, self and other taking it in turns to be
decentred. Who is saying this? Self as subject has disappeared. An
element, B, has emerged from the relation of A and C, and B turns
on itself and redescribes that 'first' relation. Metaphor's externalizing
function seems to release one from the terrible contingencies of the self,
but at the same time it asks what grounds categories. Duck and rabbit,
A and C, come out of the conjurer's hat of metaphor as duck–rabbit, B.
Given B, we see that species categories can be shaken. The permanent
ground is the unreassuring copula, B / be, in the middle.

In an extraordinary passage (para. 24, p. 57), Hegel enunciates the 'I's
double being as absolute 'void' and 'receptacle'. Containing 'anything
and everything, that for which everything is, and which preserves everything within itself', inner and outer, figure and ground, 'what thinks' is
logically void and receptacle, empty and full, hollow and bounded, as a
bowl is concavity and matter; as a river bed is negative space and physical
channel. Both illimitable and confined, the 'I' spills out as formless dispersal or takes form upon itself. 'Everyone is a whole world of representations, which are buried in the night of the "I". Thus "I" is the universal,
in which abstraction is made from everything particular, but in which at
the same time, everything is present, though veiled'.

The night, the wild night, of the 'I' seethes with representations which
are inaccessible, potentially available for the mediation of thought, and
that which has already been transformed by it. 'What thinks' can be this
because universals and particulars co-exist without hierarchy 'in the
stream' of being: all that has been worked upon is present, even though
it is 'veiled'. It is material 'veiled' because it has been repressed in the
process of mediation, sublated by being veiled by thought itself as it
transforms the material it thinks with, 'veiled' because it takes on representation. The 'I' is a 'night' because its manifold contents move between
unconscious and conscious life in a violent, scarcely containable way and
yet these can be 'veiled' as the reconstructions of thought. This veering
movement of form / unform, shape / unshape, frame / unframe, with its
triumphalist hubris – 'everything within itself' – and tragic register – the
night of the 'I' – asserts the double nature of mediation. It looks forward
to those psychoanalytical formulations which chart the swing between

the paranoid schizoid position and the depressive position, and is perhaps most graphically understood by object-relations theory. The swirling void of the 'I'/artwork, containing everything within itself and thus nothing, offers a parallel to the multiple splittings and dispersals of the paranoid position, which cannot be organized by the ego because its fear, hate, rage, its 'night', overwhelms it, resulting in further hostile splitting of unassimilable material. The receptacle which is the 'I'/artwork corresponds to the depressive position, in which the ego begins to shape and integrate material, externalizing, objectifying and forming symbols which can be used to organize its thought. Thus one can arrive at a notion of symbol quite other than the romantic symbol of fusion and identity described by de Man.

This Hegelian movement of dispersal and consolidation is another of the forms taken by mediation. If the artwork is both void and receptacle, container and contained, dispersal and consolidation, then it becomes symbol in a new sense. It oscillates between the unassimilable and the shaped. It is a representation of this movement. It is a movement of melancholy rather than of mourning, containing within itself the absolute alterity which it struggles to assimilate.[16]

> *The Mill Race*
> *at Granta Place*
> *tosses them from form to form,*
> *dissolving bodies in the spume.*
>
> *Given A and see*
> *find be . . .*
> *that's what metaphor*
> *is for.*

The poem contains its own unassimilable materials—mental constructions tossed by the living waters of the Mill Race – and works on them, reworking the tossing forms, altering them by thinking about them. It identifies metaphor as the shaping element, and works upon that, concurrently epistemological enquiry and 'dissolving' body. But there is an infinity of ways to structure experience apart from the conventional forms of metaphor and trope. Artwork is not symbolic in the sense of being a sensory 'embodiment' of thought: but it is an embodiment of mediation in that it swings between dispersal and containment. It is thus always in excess, working on its own unassimilable materials, in the same state of anxiety as a reader. Metaphor, in this poem, is never wholly adequate to the bodies in the spume, but it is an

*attempt to come to know: it is 'what thinks' by constructing relations
which reciprocally alter one another. 'Given A and see . . . '. Seeking the
relations between A and C / see – 'see' suggests a speculative seeking for
C – discovers B, and the discovery of B enables a re-seeing of A and C,
a process which is never complete. This leads us to the three-fold
nature of mediation.*

The 'paranoid' paragraph 24 is the first to introduce the three fold nature
of syllogism, another rehearsal of mediation – 'the particular is the middle
that con-cludes the extremes of the universal and the singular' (p. 59).
Paragraph 187 provides a more complete formulation of the threefold
syllogism which moves between singular, particular and universal: 'each
of its members occupies the position both of an extreme and a mediating
middle' (p. 263). The swing between dispersed and contained experience
which constitutes the 'I' is a swing between two polarities, but this must
finally be understood as three movements when the fact of mediation is
raised to consciousness. It is not possible to think one without two, 'a
beginning and a having advanced to a second' (para. 12, p. 36). If the
beginning is actually an a posteriori construction, a fiction, then the
second is a middle, for it is not possible to think two without three: a
middle asks for the construction of what comes after. What is the middle
is always shifting, since we live in time: the third term might become the
moment of a postulated starting point for another middle. Hegel is less
interested in this permanent instability, however, than in the strenuous
energy of equivocation, which tries out opposite solutions, by occupying
each of three positions from *each of three positions*, singular, particular
and universal, positions which are perceived as positive and negative,
void and receptacle. Thus each creates uncertain grounds for the other,
and this is exactly what shifts thought. Of course, this is a relativistic
strategy, but, as Rose comments: 'There is no rationality without *uncertain* grounds, without relativism of authority. Relativism of authority
does not establish the authority of relativism' (*Love's Work*, pp. 129–30).

What precludes the authority of relativism is the necessity for an
enactment of contradictions through a serious engagement with them
such that thought becomes experience, capable of occupying positions,
and altering and abstracting them in a way that makes them luminous
with new meaning. Hegel thinks of concepts as shining in the way that the
physics of light makes reflective material flash out. This multiple saturation in extremes and mediating middle makes for a dense, intellectually
imagined group of concrete possibilities, carried out not on analogy with
the aesthetic but as an aesthetic strategy which provisionally inhabits
hostile positions, the only way the 'what thinks' can think sufficiently

richly. Of course, though it is possible to occupy all positions, it is impossible to occupy them simultaneously, or to ground oneself in mutually exclusive positions. Thus 'what thinks' is committed to choosing, which presupposes negation. A tearing apart, a moment of schism, is intrinsic to mediation and generates the anxiety which produces it. The alteration it achieves is reached with difficulty. These are the ultimately ethical grounds of mediation.

Lastly, let us see, though in a necessarily abbreviated form, some of the ways 'an instinct to rename' tries out each of three positions from each of three positions: to rename is to change things from one category to another. In a process of renaming the specificity of perception is seized as a whole, the painful convergence of date (an anniversary?), place and the features in a framed photograph. So 'Gestalt', becomes its opposite, 'Art', pure artefact dredged of specificity and possibly even of pain. An ideal time and space, perhaps, framed by renaming. The changed status of the ideal comes about through the particular need to structure and order, the need for 'thinking-over', which is called out by the specific, the moment of recognition and pain which asks for transformation. Hence associated with the particular need to mediate by renaming are the warning footnotes which point to the confusion of categories, or their reconstruction, the picture treated as a living being. But artefacts belong to both sides of the antithesis, photograph and poem, Gestalt and Art. The irreducible singularity of experience unique to the individual, the 'I' which drops out of representation, is caught by the psychological experience of Gestalt, the seized perception of a total impression in all its immediacy. The text tries to keep apart the singularity of Gestalt and the universal of Art, in which the generalized 'I' can be represented through the transformation of metaphor. But the two terms are diremptive moments of the broken middle, strange doubles of one another, since both Gestalt and Art involve shaping, yet irreconcilable because subjective experience is generalized in Art. The 'frame' suggests that the project of a pure aesthetic may be a fake. For after all art does have a content – it frames experience. This is to move the universal of art to its opposite and to reverse its significance as the singularity *of art comes to the fore, constructed from irreducible, specific time, space and photographed face, picture man you can talk to. Here the mediating particular is Gestalt itself, which has seized the specificity of experience, seized it in its hybridity (half thought and visual experience, the footnote warns), and mediated it as* perception. *This opens the way for new categories, and renaming becomes the new universal. But are things changed by renaming? What do names alter? Renaming is returned to the order of singularity by these questions, as the signifier becomes immersed in the specific referents it offers to rename – photograph, poem, pain. Art becomes the mediating particular now, restructuring language to transform it into a universal, a Gestalt, a total impression. Gestalt has become the opposite of its original singularity as raw experience. To keep apart Gestalt and Art seems harder than ever. As each term moves to extreme and mediating middle, becoming 'a/part' of one another and yet 'apart', the pain of the poem increases. But it has not only gone through the arduous process of renaming, it has used renaming to think with.*

Finally, lest this avant-garde poem seems to match accounts of mediation too easily, let us try out the broken middle on a visual experience. Antony Gormley's extraordinary assemblage, 'A field for the British Isles', was exhibited in a number of galleries in England and Wales in the summer of 1995. The exhibition rooms are filled with thousands upon thousands of clay stumps 8–10 inches high. These are almost identical and were roughly made to a simple, but rigorously consistent and exact formula which shapes a recognizably human form from minimal elements. The sheer number of figures and the infinity of repetition is at first almost traumatizing, annihilating. This post-modern mathematical sublime was achieved because each family made a commitment to complete a number of figures or stumps.

The clay components seem minimally human. But this is one of the many visual peripeteia of the construction. The almost deadening replication moves towards a sickening ideological nihilism as the minimal *elements* of the figures trap one into thinking of the minimally *human*. This is one of the first shocks of the work.

The stumps are fashioned with a suggestion of shoulders, which in turn suggest rudimentary arms, a base, a 'head' in which two eye-holes have been gouged, rather as children gouge out eyes with the end of a pencil in plasticine. The huge eyes have been pierced virtually on the top of the heads of the figures, thus making them the focal point of each figure, and they look out importunately, almost imploringly, from every one of the thousands of figurines. Yet their disempowerment slowly reverses on to the beholder. The onlooker, huge and gigantesque by comparison with these thousands of tiny figures, is forced into impotence. Helpless before this mass, which suggests the horror of fleeing thousands – refugees, the Holocaust, the Apocalypse – the huge onlooker can only watch, eyes carried to the ever-receding horizon of the room, which the multitudes of figures make distant, capable of imposing *their* proportions, *their* horizon, on the environment even as they seem in a state of terrible distress. They make the onlooker conscious of sheer mass and dispersal, but incapable of assimilating either. Here superior size disables rather than empowers. Towering helplessly over them like a colossus, the importunateness of these thousands becomes the beholder's. There is no bridge to them. Who are they? A group? A tribe? Does anything bond them? What holds these beings together beyond their physical shape? Perhaps only their suffering? Perhaps nothing?

But this sense of dispersal is not the only one. Gradually, individual stumps or figurines become differentiated. Interestingly, they are not gendered, but every single one stands and gazes differently, becomes unique. The temptation to gender follows upon the individuation of the gaze. The huge onlooker becomes aware of infinite ways of *looking*. It is their looking, not the onlooker's looking, which dominates the mind and takes over. And the figurines look in innumerable ways – jaunty, meditative, passionate, serene, moody, thoughtful, tense, eager, in reverie, attentive, intense, malevolent...It may well be that the insistent spell of anthropomorphism is taking over, but whether this is the case or not, one is released from the tyranny of anthropomorphism because it is impossible to encompass or exhaust the multiplicity, the singularity, of the gaze, which, with a curiously naïve simplicity, turns every stump into a unique, creative, perceiving being. These stumps are genuinely other, and for a moment the onlooker is lost in the other. There is an oscillation between the alienating experience of mass and the experience of individuation, so the effect of this work is complex. It is an experiment in repetition and difference. The figurines draw the beholder into their crowds. One is in several places at once – inside, outside, gazing at, gazing from, fleeing, looking helplessly at the crowds. The initial blankness is akin to the sublime, yet, unlike the sublime, it is a reverse sublime: one is not overcome by size but by smallness; and this is not an unrepresentable experience, but one which ceaselessly importunes the passions and the mind. These are fetish-like objects, but they are not fetishes. They pass Kristeva's 'test' for artwork rather than fetish by going beyond the literal and continuing to signify, whereas the mark of the fetish is its incapacity to 'mean' more than its being as a physical object. Indeed, they solicit interpretation.

To conclude: I have argued that the deconstruction of the classical aesthetic texts of Kant and Hegel should prompt us to redescribe the aesthetic rather than giving up on it as an obsolete hierarchical category expressive of the bourgeois individual self. I have suggested that the artwork be embedded in the ordinary processes of being alive, and viewed as a representation of mediation, a form of thinking, a request for knowledge, rather than as a privileged kind of creativity cut off from experiences everyone goes through. The scattering and splitting of melancholia, and the pulling apart of the broken middle, I see as moments in the mediating process peculiarly important to aesthetic work because these rendings, in Rose's terms, make it possible 'to know, to misknow, and yet to grow' (*The Broken Middle*, p. 264), a possibility not gender-exclusive but open to women and men. Rose does not gender the broken middle. She was sceptical of feminism's claims. But one might argue that because of their place in our culture the broken middle is where women tend to be.

Why see artwork in terms of an analytic? Because, rather than Deleuze's stereotypes, our society's danger seems to be that of acting out, with the violence and abuse this entails. Keeping a hold on a form of thinking is to begin to find resources for dealing with the political and cultural unconscious. Finally, predicting and prescribing are equally futile, but to ask questions can help. What would today's aesthetic education look like? And what kind of society would it be that valued aesthetic education among its projects?

NOTES

I am grateful to Dominick LaCapra for allowing me to begin exploring this work by inviting me to take up a short-term visiting fellowship at the Society for the Humanities at Cornell University, and to Mary Jacobus for hosting me.

1　Paul de Man, 'Sign and symbol in Hegel's *Aesthetics*', p. 762. This essay is republished in *Aesthetic Ideology*, ed. Andrzej Warminski, a post-humous collection of de Man's essays which extensively critiques the philosophical category of the aesthetic. See also the rejoinder by Raymond Geuss, *Critical Inquiry* 10 (1983), pp. 375–82 and de Man's reply, pp. 383–90.
2　Stuart Sim, *Beyond Aesthetics: Confrontations with Poststructuralism and Postmodernism*, p. 1.
3　Christopher Bollas, *The Shadow of the Object*, pp. 34–7; 80–1, adds the idea of *style* to psychoanalytic vocabulary. For instance, the internalization of the style of the mother's aesthetic of care by the infant; the creativity of the dream as a style of dramaturgy. Slavoj Žižek, it could be argued, reworks phenomenology and psychoanalysis by saturating his discourse in aesthetic terms – sublime, bliss, form, 'pure' fantasy – particularly in *Tarrying with the Negative*, where film, opera and fiction are invoked to explicate an epistemology: see, for instance, pp. 117–19.

4 Theodor W. Adorno, *Aesthetic Theory*, Hans. Robert Hullot-Kentor, p. 11; Pierre Bourdieu, Postscript to *Distinction*; John Dewey, *Art as Experience*, p. 252; Henri Lefebvre, *Critique of Everyday Life*, pp. 138–9.

5 Howard Caygill, 'Stelarc and the Chimera', pp. 46–51. See also Caygill's *The Art of Judgement* and *A Kant Dictionary*.

6 Hegel, *The Phenomenology of Spirit*, paras. 95–109, on Sense–Certainty.

7 Julia Kristeva's classic essays, 'Stabat Mater' and 'Women's time', both of which put value on affect, and her later work on abjection and depression, form a running dialogue with Derrida. It may even be that she represents the kind of destabilizing 'seduction' which for Baudrillard is a way of undermining the fixity of the text (see Jean Baudrillard, *Seduction*).

8 See the attack on Habermas by Jean-François Lyotard, *The Postmodern Condition*, p. 72.

9 Veronica Forrest-Thomson, *Collected Poems and Translations*, p. 22. 'Ducks & Rabbits' first appeared in 1971 in *Language-Games*, a prize-winning volume published by the University of Leeds.

10 See Pierre Bourdieu, 'The market of symbolic goods' (1971).

11 Notably Max Black, 'Metaphor'. For Jacques Derrida's interpretation of the frame, see 'Parergon', *The Truth in Painting*, Section I, pp. 15–147.

12 Susanne K. Langer, *Feeling and Form*; Ludwig Wittgenstein, *Philosophical Investigations*. Footnotes 2 and 3 in the poem quote p. 196 of Wittgenstein; footnote 4, p. 206; footnotes 5 and 6, p. 194; footnote 7, p. 197. Thanks to Alison Mark for these details.

13 Friedrich Schiller, *On the Aesthetic Education of Man in a Series of Letters*; see in particular Letter XXVII, p. 4.

14 Gillian Rose, *The Broken Middle*, p. xi. Other relevant works are *Hegel Contra Sociology*; *Dialectic of Nihilism*.

15 G. W. F. Hegel, *The Encyclopaedia Logic*, p. 198. Žižek, relying on the *Phenomenology* rather than on the *Encyclopaedia Logic*, defends the Hegelian subject and the mediation of dialectic in a way which often coincides with Rose. His framework is Lacanian and post-structuralist, but his sense of the centrality of 'what thinks' to Hegel's thought does not lead him to oversimplification; see *Tarrying with the Negative*, pp. 27–39, 120–4.

16 For a fuller account of an aesthetics of object relations see Hanna Segal, 'A psychoanalytic approach to aesthetics', *The Work of Hanna Segal*, pp. 185–206. Though she emphasizes the power of the death instinct in her model of aesthetic experience, I feel that she overstates the consolidation of the symbol-making power of the depressive position: 'my contention has been that a satisfactory work of art is achieved by a realization and sublimation of the depressive position, and that the effect on the audience is that they unconsciously relive the artist's experience and share his triumph of achievement and his final detachment' (p. 203).

Part II

The Poetics of Emotion

3

Textual Harassment: The Ideology of Close Reading, or How Close is Close?

Whole poem silly.
Who has ever seen *a 'green' house, or seen the sun shine shadily?*
Green houses are not usually cool, though I suppose they might be if anyone was foolish enough to erect them under arches of budding boughs.
Though no ornithologist, do robins sing? . . .
This is first rate. Why? [in order].
(1) Curious way it suggests immediately great intimacy with the author. FRIENDSHIP. A room at night, curtains drawn, roaring log fire, chimney corner, author musing, old inns, you and him alone . . . Topping condensation of language. No vapid and ineffectual adjectives.

Comments on Christina Rossetti's 'Gone were but Winter' and an extract from P. J. Bailey's *Festus*, in I. A. Richards, *Practical Criticism*

I do it because I like the way I feel when I'm doing it. I like being brought up short by an effect I have experienced but do not yet understand analytically . . . I like savouring the physical 'taste' of language at the same time that I work to lay bare its physics. I like uncovering the incredibly dense pyrotechnics of a master artificer, not least because in praising artifice I can claim a share in it. And when those pleasures have been (temporarily) exhausted, I like linking one moment in a poem to others . . . It doesn't finally matter which so long as I can keep going.

Stanley Fish, 'Why literary criticism is like virtue'

Close reading and the discourse of seduction

These quotations, the early struggles of I. A. Richards's sample of readers, used for his experiments with practical criticism, and its decadence, perhaps, in Stanley Fish, are a reminder that 'close reading' is about sixty years old. Is it ready for retirement? John Barrell's cultural materialist critique of the ideology of close reading in the late 1980s seemed to be fighting an old-fashioned battle.[1] Practical criticism had already retired, superseded by critical practice, both in the classroom and in writing outside it, seemingly a much more sophisticated form of analysis in which Julia Kristeva's 'shattered' subject could 'speak' to literature differently.[2] Textual practice refused the naturalization of reading as unmediated experience and the universal, depoliticized reading subject, male and bourgeois, which goes with it – or so it said.

Only Fish, returning nostalgically to the interpretative 'community' of the cold war, seems to want to retain an unreconstructed form of close reading. His deliberately onanistic textual erotics – the text in black lace underwear approach – using a knowing language of jouissance which actually has one eye on soft porn and one eye on the hard sciences where power really resides, invokes the language of seduction. Its happy shamelessness – 'savouring the *physical "taste" of language* at the same time that I work to *lay bare its physics*' – is calculated to be offensive to kinds of criticism which otherwise share little. It is antipathetic to cultural materialism's seriousness about power, 'the power of a specific political interest', which, in Barrell's Foucauldian terms, always tempts to a reading for mastery.[3] It is equally unacceptable to the post-structuralist critique which resists what de Man called the 'aesthetic ideology' and the 'mirror-like structure' of reading, with its 'seductive powers of identification', which makes us fatally prone to take prosopopeia for propositionality.[4] De Man habitually spoke of 'aesthetic ideology', meaning a consent to nineteenth-century 'Romantic' definitions of aesthetic experience as transcendence through the fusion or identity of subject and object. Such an account, he believed, is in itself an ideological definition and *leads* to ideology by abandoning rational analysis.

And yet Fish at least serves to remind us that everyone has problems with textual harassment, including him. Why? In the rest of this essay I shall argue that the discourse of seduction, present even in the very earliest attempts to theorize close reading, is created by the very means which would expel it. A rationalist poetics, founded on the antithesis between thought and feeling which still goes largely uninvestigated in our culture, refusing the importunities of the desire of the text, acts as a screen for a more difficult and subtle problem. Sexuality, feeling and emotion are associated with a language of *affect* which is deemed to be non-cognitive and non-rational. Affect falls outside what is legitimately discussable. It is merely a textual *effect*, and a persistent erotic language returns to describe it and thus intensify it even as it is banished, expelled for its blandishment, flattery, deception, 'soft' somatic and seductive power. This effort to resist desire, a refusal to be overpowered by affect, manifests itself in particular in Barrell's discussion of Wordsworth's *Tintern Abbey*, to which I shall return, but a dislike of aesthetic ideology is everywhere powerful. Even Barthes's 'jouissance' is a kind of add-on to his understanding of text, an unpredictable and uncontrollable occurrence which has no dialectical relation to the network of codes we enter.[5] So whether you welcome or expel affect it is an inessential, extraneous element. A refusal to consent to it is actually a collusive fear-fulness. Just as a response to the sublime appropriates the power that is feared, so a response to seduction appropriates the power of seduction, converting the energies of seduction into mastery: 'I can claim a share', Fish declares, in artifice (p. 15).

The task of a new definition of close reading is to rethink the power of affect, feeling and emotion in a *cognitive* space. The power of affect needs to be included within a definition of thought and knowledge rather than theorized as outside them, excluded from the rational. The solution is not to celebrate the power of the semiotic, as some feminists do, for that is to confirm the one-sidedness on which the non-cognitive understanding of affect is based.[6] The rest of this essay will develop another paradigm of reading, refusing that most fundamental of all post-Enlightenment binaries, feeling and thought. Critique supported by the feeling/thought dichotomy actually rests on an account of the text as *outside*, something external which has to be grasped – or warded off. Despite the anti-positivist language of so much modern criticism and theory, the text is seen as *other*: it is object to a Kantian subject who stands over against the world in a position of power. This is distance reading, not close reading.

What did close reading's two major theorists, I. A. Richards and William Empson, have to say about affect? Unlike their followers, neither Richards nor Empson were blind to gender and class, a blindness often foisted upon close reading by subsequent critics. In fact, Richards's 'practical criticism' and Empson's 'verbal analysis' were responses to specific political crises. *Practical Criticism* and *Seven Types of Ambiguity* appeared in 1929 and 1930, respectively, when the increasingly managed and commodified society and the threat of fascism dramatized the cultural importance of language and communications. Richards called his study an exercise in 'comparative ideology' and pointed out that, despite their problems with 'making out the plain sense' of poems, 'with few exceptions', the men and women who supplied the 'protocols' were 'the products of the most expensive kind of education' (p. 310). He was one of the first writers to stress that 'he' meant 'he/she' in his text. He affirmed that 'the women writers were of higher average discernment than the men', and included in his texts for discussion Christina Rossetti and Edna St Vincent Millay (p. 311). Empson considered the work of Gertrude Stein and Edith Sitwell and insisted that the proponents of an irrationalist aesthetics of 'sound' and 'atmosphere' not only undermined any defence against dogma but derived their values from an upper-class education. 'Pure' sound in poetry actually demands a smattering of public school reading.

Practical Criticism is just that – pragmatic – a text in the great tradition of utilitarian thought. Richards believed that he had found a technique for achieving absolutely undistorted communication. Reader and text can be brought into a perfect, stable, isomorphic relation. We only begin to judge a poem 'when we have solved completely, the communication problem, when we have got, perfectly, the experience, the *mental condition* relevant to the poem' (p. 11). But there are no fewer than nine interfering factors, from 'stock responses' to 'doctrinal adhesions', which mean that readers 'fail to construe it [the text] just as a schoolboy fails to construe a piece of Caesar' (p. 14).

But there is a further snag. Even when all these irrelevancies, intrusions, adhesions and excesses have been eradicated by the reader, the poem itself is a limit case of affective language. It is a 'pseudo-statement' and not a propositional, scientific statement: it admits 'strange material' from the unconscious (Richards quotes from Freud's *Beyond the Pleasure Principle*); it requires surveillance of the most rigorous kind (p. 205). Richards's distinction between meaning and expression, and his discrimination between sense, feeling, tone and intention, the time-honoured categories of practical criticism, were intended not to be tools for *recognizing* affect and responding to it but for *controlling* it. Feeling must be under surveillance because the fundamental experiences of our lives – ethics, metaphysics, morals, religion, aesthetics – are saturated in affect. 'Questions of liberty, nationality, justice, love, truth, faith, knowledge', are all 'matters of feeling' (p. 6). To read a poem 'perfectly' is to solve the 'communication problem' and to fend off a world where affect runs riot.

Richards's utilitarian Utopia is different from Empson's wary Benthamite rationalism, though Empson, one of whose favourite words was 'sensible', was equally aware that close reading, or 'verbal analysis', as he called it, was a defence against dogma under the control of sensibility. Unlike Richards, a poem for him was in some sense knowledge, and we could have recourse to truth value, to rational argument, to semantic explication, to the resources of anthropology, psychology and history, in order to explore the moral, political and social meanings of the text. As Christopher Norris puts it, he believed that there was something 'there' *in* the text, which could be discovered by the rational reading subject and clarified by him.[7] This is so even in the brilliant exposition of the most famous of his ambiguities, the seventh ambiguity in which two opposite meanings struggle within the same word: he sees in Hopkins 'a clear case of the Freudian use of opposites, where two things thought of as incompatible, but desired intensely by different systems of judgments, are spoken of simultaneously by words applying to both' (Empson, *Seven Types of Ambiguity*, p. 226). Rationality confronts the desire which is 'juggling with contradiction' and offers a 'sensible' explanation of it.

Empson has a much harder time than Richards with affect and feeling, which he sexualizes and genders remorselessly. Verbal analysis undoes the protective stabilizing of dogma and the defensive, reconciling strategies of ideology, and is figured as the assault of reason on the sexually timid text (or reader), who stands as 'maiden aunt' to the critic's penetration. 'And it is not only maiden aunts who are placed like this', he writes, in a gesture which intends to include in this defensiveness even those who think of themselves as sexually uninhibited or ideologically open but who are 'really' maiden aunts. 'The object of life, after all, is not to understand things, but to maintain one's defences and equilibrium and live as well as one can; it is not only maiden aunts who are placed like this. And one must remember (since I am saying the best I can for the enemy) that, as a first approximation, or a general direction, to people who really do not know how to read poetry, the dogma of Pure Sound often acts as a recipe for aesthetic receptiveness, and may be necessary' (p. 247). But the generosity is to the reader or text rather than to the maiden aunt. This is of a piece with two sets of distinctions he makes in order to clarify the function of verbal analysis. The first is between 'analytic' and 'appreciative' criticism ('one may call that feminine') and, a distinction which follows on the first, between reading for meaning and reading for the suasive, somatic elements of a text. This is on analogy with a differentiation between the 'Character' and the mere 'Looks' of a person (pp. 249, 245).

Analytic criticism (by implication masculine) explains textual meaning and in doing so undoes the 'strong [hymenal?] defences' of habit. 'Feminine' appreciative criticism 'produces literary effects similar to the one he [*sic*] is appreciating' because it aims to recreate the art object or poem and its affect in alternative form (p. 247). Appreciative criticism thus *fixes* and confirms an uninterrogated reading, conservative because it is in the text's own terms. Analytic criticism explains, but does not reproduce, a text, demystifying, defamiliarizing and questioning. By the same token, those paramount aspects of a text concerned with meaning can be thought of as 'Character', whereas the seductive aspects of the text concerned with 'sound', and 'atmosphere', feeling and emotion arising from the somatic experience of the body, are designated as 'Looks'. Sexually egalitarian and enlightened for his time in so many ways, Empson nevertheless becomes hopelessly embroiled in simplistic sexist metaphors. Perhaps Character and Looks are simply different ways of conveying meaning so that 'Looks' are a form of 'Character'. A tired business man's metaphor emerges which twists and turns in the attempt to be fair:

> A business man engaging a secretary may feel a distinction between Looks and Character, but he would not find it absurd to call this a distinction between two sorts of character estimated in terms of Looks. (Empson, *Seven Types of Ambiguity*, p. 246)

But you would not 'mix up' the two kinds of character, either, Empson ends, defensively, digging the hole he has attempted to fill up all over again. The acute discomfort is evident.

Appreciative, feminine criticism is like the seductive 'Looks' of the secretary: it flatters text and reader, and is flattered in turn. Analytical, masculine criticism resists flattery and masters the maiden aunt timidity of text and reader. Empson claims that the text harasses him, and responds with a sterner form of counter-harassment. Because affect has to be expelled as irrational and seductive (the two are conflated), these are the straits to which even so self-conscious and revolutionary a critic as Empson is reduced.

Empson saw his own revolutionary thinking co-opted by the conservative neo-formalism of Cleanth Brooks and W. K. Wimsatt after the Second World War. He never liked the theoretical, post-semiotic critique he was to live to see later, persisting in speaking of 'Nerrida', but like de Man, whose rhetorical exegesis has affinities with his thought, he distrusted the narcissism of the 'mirror-like structure' of reading. But Empson's essentially empirical demythologizing is not deconstruction. For de Man the blandishments of the text co-operate with the narcissistic desires of the reader in a way which requires an even bleaker, sterner check on desire than Empson ever envisaged. Once we recognize the substitutive textual erotics of figure, a world stripped down to figuration is paradoxically not disguised by it. Once figure is *exposed* as figure, the game of seduction is up. Yet it is one we compulsively want to play, de Man knows. These somatic metaphors of bodily exposure, threatening to get out of control, but disavowed, hover in his discourse of ghostly prosopopeia. On the one hand, figure is strangely dematerialized to unmask the beckoning fullness of the language of bourgeois reconciliation as an idealist illusionistic phantom: on the other hand, figure is just that, the stark materiality of the sign and no more. The narcissistic consolations of the aesthetic ideology reduplicate the commodified seductions of the society of simulacra and spectacle: it is as if de Man sees this, and decides to lay bare the dynamic of this deceptive consolation through his inverse but parallel world of ever disfigured figuration. A kind of ineffability comes in at the back door through the aporias such disruption creates.

Having considered responses to the suasive power of the text, I turn to the task of *including* affect within a definition of the rational, including what we describe as feeling and emotion within knowledge rather than placing them outside it. As a corollary, how do we go about forming another paradigm of reading which does not construct the text as one of the *objects* of our knowledge?

Levinas and the cancellation of the thought–feeling binary

The simplest way of finding a cognitive space for affect is to refuse the classical binary, thought/feeling. This binary needs to be dissolved in what Kristeva called a 'new discourse' which evolves as a 'new apportionment of relationships between the symbolic and the real, the subjective and the objective' (*Desire in Language*, p. 93). She claimed this discourse produces the shattering of society and subject. Three more modest questions arise from her proposition. First, how would close reading function, if at all, in this 'new discourse' where there is no subject of knowledge and where things are not 'objects' of knowledge? Second, how would claims for the cognitive value of affect relate to this discourse? Third, how would a politics belong to a new discourse? Emmanuel Levinas, whose fascination with 'closeness' is of general relevance to this argument, addressed the thought/feeling binary, creating a space for these three questions. I will look at his arguments before exploring what they would mean for reading Wordsworth's *Tintern Abbey*, always a problematic text for anti-affective critique.

In his brief essay of 1949, 'The transcendence of words', a discussion of the ideas and texts of the Surrealist writer, Michel Leiris, Levinas began by refusing the barrier between conscious and unconscious. This was not to liberate unrepressed semiotic material into the conscious but precisely to effect the reverse – to carry the principles of thought into the unconscious itself. The slash, conscious/unconscious, maintained and theorized by Surrealists such as André Breton, is for Levinas unacceptable. His whole essay is predicated on the primacy of *thought*; for him Surrealism represents the pure paradigm of thought in action, its supreme principle, and so becomes a limit case of knowledge. In his reading of Leiris, Levinas deliberately reverses the usual account of Surrealism. Dreams, at the centre of Surrealist aesthetic, are emancipatory, comic and democratic, for Leiris, not because they release the irrational into the world, thus maintaining the rational/irrational binary, but *because they refuse* the irrationalist dichotomy constituted by the opposites, rational conscious/non-rational unconscious; coherent/incoherent; repressed/ unrepressed material. Creative dream-*thought* belongs to a continuum of experience which stretches from night to day. The corollary must be that the conscious is not structured differently from the unconscious. Thus Leiris 'finds reason for his dreams in the conscious world' (p. 145), both an explanation of and justification for dreams. 'Surrealist freedom is not opposed to other mechanisms of thought – it is their supreme principle' (p. 146).

What is meant by thought can be understood when we grasp two principles underlying Leiris's conception of the structure of language. These account both for the creation of new categories and classifications, which are fundamental to thought, and for the mobility by which knowledge changes. These structural principles Leiris terms Bifurcation and Erasure. Punningly alike in French (*bifur* and *biffure*, respectively), each does something different, but they work together rather as syntax and sign work together. And they are both essentially analytical. Bifurcation works through an associational system of networks, crossings and pathways, created out of alternative pathways, deflected routes, distractions and splittings. These are connective systems based on the lateral movement or splitting inherent in a choice of pathway, for to choose *one* possibility always makes *two*. One choice makes its other: the route we have not chosen, the connection we have not made, comes into being simultaneously with that we have made. This fertile spatial model is not to be reductively confused with Bergsonian linearity in time, with chains of displacement and substitution (the whole point is that something non-substitutive is made) or with semantic fields. We make space, do not occupy it.

Erasure springs from the inherent multi-accentuality of the sign, because to isolate one meaning means the cancelling of another. The coming into being of meaning *is* an act of cancellation, a reflexive remarking, crossing out, writing over, alteration. Meaning is the history of erasure, of cancelled meanings, which condition the present meaning, because unrepressed cancelled meanings interact with successive erasures. Repression can never be wholly successful simply because Erasure is part of thought and has its logic. Again it would be easy to confuse this palimpsest, which fruitfully multiplies possible categories, with classical 'ambiguity' or with de Manian dis-figuration and displacement. But for Empson ambiguity is much more like the accidental Freudian slip than a purposive analytical invention of categories. For de Man, the figures of rhetoric undermine propositionality, whereas for Levinas they would make it possible.

Thought is Erasure and cancellation is the principle of all symbol. Levinas points to the co-existence of meaning and its representation in allegory as an example. Moreover, Bifurcation and Erasure can capture thought 'at that special moment when it turns into something other than itself' (p. 146): that is, when thought others itself to create a new thought. Category-making is at the heart of the process. What we term affect, I would suggest, is the cathecting or build-up and release of energies in this intense analytic process, as well as the process itself.

According to Levinas, the thought process inherent in language-making is not completed until there is an unbroken continuum between text and critic. Text and reader together produce a reciprocal network without being involved in subject/object positions which are relations of power. Levinas makes this move by contrasting the conditions of production under which classical art or representation was conceived, with its almost exclusive emphasis on time and vision, with a new aesthetic which depends on space and sound. In doing so he edges towards a celebration of identification by redefining narcissism. Primordially reflexive and ambiguous, consciousness cannot help but partly become the content of the text because its analysis is made from and shaped out of the same materials and emotions.

Levinas insists that classical models of the aesthetic are not based on Bifurcation and Erasure but on the organizing relationship of vision, in which an all-powerful Cartesian subject penetrates the world of appearance, and masters it from where he stands, stripping and unveiling its essence. To see is to exist in a self-sufficient world. Because what you see is co-present with seeing and closes on the signified without a space in which the infinity of the signifier can be released, seeing closes down possibility and silences the universe. Modern art belongs to the 'scandal'

(p. 147) of sound, which breaks in upon the closure of self-sufficient aesthetic space and its deadly quiet. Sound always disrupts, is always in excess, because sound, even verbal sound, never matches with and is never contained by the signified. Sound is a failed word, or the word is an inadequate sound, because of this excess of meaning, when the word is *not* made flesh and is in this sense transcendent. But sound needs another to hear it, and to perpetuate the infinite play of the signifier, which cannot be done unless sound rends aesthetic self-sufficiency and calls forth the 'need to enter into a relationship with someone' (p. 147). The aesthetic is actually brought about through the breaking of silence and through the desire of the other.

The one who makes and the one who hears sound are both in a condition of desire for 'a relation with someone', and because each is displaced by the desire of the other as well as desire for the other, a reciprocal dependency (not a changing of places) occurs. This reciprocity creates a new cognitive space in which the signifier's possibilities, the infinite process of Bifurcation and Erasure, can be perpetuated. The interactive network which is text and reader is creating new possibilities of meaning. More strangely, what makes the 'relation with someone' neither narcissistic nor power-laden is the *violence* of sound. Sound and its excess are deeply erotic and irreducibly violent, as the mismatch of sound and signified, aural sound and meaning, opens up need. That need, which is also a responsibility, for the other is paradoxically created by an assault, a breaking in upon the self.

This ethical paradox will deter some people. Levinas's model of absolute recognition of alterity is not the mediated master/slave, subject/object relationships of the Hegelian dialectic, which he explicitly repudiates, but the disintegrating, unmediated experience of persecution, obsession and paranoia. The power-ridden subject/object division only breaks down in the extremity of persecution: the perpetrator, consumed by the image of the other, lives in violent identity with the persecuted; the experience of persecution is to be forced to replicate the structure of paranoia unavoidably and without remission. Both live off each other's experience to the death, a limit case of absolute understanding, absolute responsibility, a shocking kind of love, but where knowledge begins because of the closeness of exchange and identification. There are many problems with Levinas's thought, which consciously invokes the Holocaust, not least in today's world of ethnic cleansing. I am not proposing a paranoid model of reader and text, but I do believe that all reading that is not reading for mastery necessarily gets caught up with, imbricated in, the structure of the text's processes, and that this is where thought begins. The intensity of this experience can be renamed as affect and consigned to the non-rational, but this is an impoverishment. Arguably, close reading has never been close enough. It has always been the rationalist's defence against the shattering of the subject. It has always been engaged with mastery, and the erotics of the text have been invoked to endorse the reader's power over it.

A reading of Levinas suggests that to respond to a text's coercions, to participate in its desires or its panic, is to begin to see how it thinks. A politics of reading is implicit in the work of Levinas, but there is another thinker who is even more aware of the politics of reading, and that is V. N. Volosinov, whose *Marxism and the Philosophy of Language* foregrounds a struggle for the sign. Volosinov develops a frankly Marxist model of power relations which is alien to Levinas's anti-Hegelian stance, yet insofar as Volosinov is concerned with *struggle*, his thought exists at least in some relation to the politics of persecution explored by Levinas. It brings into prominence, theorizes and makes visible ideological conflict. We need to reactivate and explore more deeply the notion of the struggle for the sign. Raymond Williams's interest in Volosinov has not been followed by western criticism, which has preferred to stay with the friendlier Bakhtinian heteroglossia of what it presumes to be Volosinov's other persona, the play of languages in a text rather than their struggle. Reading from the desire of the other involves us in coercion, persecution, struggle, and in the coercions which have produced this struggle, and Volosinov has things to say about this.

He refuses the bourgeois subject/object relation which participates in mastery. Volosinov recognizes that the socially made sign is a two-sided act, that two spheres are encountered in it, and that it occupies the borderline between world and self. The sign is constantly remade at the borderline of the outside world and the psyche. The semiotic and ideological content of consciousness means that without the sign consciousness would not *be*. The sign is always determined by *whose* word it is and for *whom* it is meant. It is multi-accentual because it will have different and antagonistic meanings depending on where you are in any hierarchy, and thus it can never be stabilized. These reminders of the politics of the inter-individual sign stiffen Levinas's sense of the necessary imbrication of text and reader with a reminder that the sign is always a contested area. Like Levinas, Volosinov believed that language could never be sealed within the consciousness of the speaking subject. It is essentially relational, made 'by the one' in relation to the 'other': a relation with 'someone' is its essence.

> I give myself verbal shape from another's point of view, ultimately, from the point of view of the community to which I belong. A word is a bridge thrown between myself and another. If one end of the bridge depends on

me, then the other depends on my addressee. A word is a territory shared
by addresser and addressee. (Volosinov, *Marxism*, p. 86)

However, even as it pulls the interlocutor into the orbit of its passions,
anxieties and desires, this is no private, non-conflictual relation.

Seducers and seduced: the case of *Tintern Abbey*

Two of the critics I have discussed, Empson and Barrell, have found
Tintern Abbey (see appendix to this chapter) particularly exasperating,
and there have been many others, though recently some less abrasive
readings have emerged. Empson, testing the poem against truth value
and logical coherence, 'grudges' Wordsworth his emotional, mystified
bad faith. He concluded the poet was 'just muddled' by a 'creed by
which his half statements might be reconciled'.[8] His exasperation seems
to arise from a need not to let the poem take hold of him. Witness his
compulsive repetition of the 'something' of line 97 ('something far more
deeply interfused'), a word which takes on more rather than less
coercive power as he worries at its meaning, and comes to have the
almost sinister erotic power of the disavowed. Barrell presupposes a
lack of sense in the poem (though he does make remarkably good sense
of 'sense'), and sees the poem in terms of 'fiduciary' language, the empty,
contentless symbol we take on trust, believing where we cannot understand, allowing it to manipulate affect in a simulacrum of sense.[9] He
points to a highly class-bound and gendered language of masculine
power which culminates in a monstrous condescension in which the
fully differentiated masculine subject refuses Dorothy access to the symbolic order.
    This is a massively anxious text and seems to make its readers anxious:
it is anxious about the politics of its precursor poem, *Frost at Midnight*,
about paternity (Coleridge's 'babe' is with him, Wordsworth's is not),
about the not quite anniversary of Bastille Day and the five years which
have passed since Annette Vallon was deserted – the revisit is dated 13
July 1798. It is a poem flying from 'something' (l. 72) that it dreads. It
flaunts its psychic erasures and bifurcations even as it asserts a closed
aesthetic 'quiet' (ll. 8, 47). What happens to this psychic and political
experience when the poem's verbal erasures and bifurcations are looked
at more closely? In what follows I shall consider one of the key areas of
the poem, the 'mystical experience' of lines 89–112. These are the lines
which have preoccupied so many readers. They also constitute a structural erasure: they are another go at, a correction, alteration, re-marking,

of the first moment of transcendence (ll. 23–49), when we become a 'living soul' (l. 46). The poem might be seen as an unsolved space of bifurcation and erasure.

The second moment of transcendence – if that is what it really is – is far more stressful than the first. Indeed the first passage, prefaced as it is with the authoritative verbs of the prospect poem – 'I behold ... view ... see' – asserts the dominance of the eye which made Levinas argue (an argument shared with phenomenologists such as Merleau Ponty): 'Western civilisation ultimately reduces all spiritual life' to the visual.[10] The visionary eye unveils, strips and penetrates so that it sees 'into the life of things' (l. 49). Barrell sees this passage as a fraudulent, auto-aesthetic screen for reneging radicalism which hierarchizes experience, ascending from sense to the pure thought which confirms masculine rationality. 'Sensations sweet' (l. 28), passing into the 'purer mind' (l. 30), are eventually transcended, so that the body (to which, of course, the feminine is confined) can be repudiated. Along with this goes an economics of aesthetic pay-off – 'I have owed to them' (l. 27). With masterly scholarship Barrell shows how Lockian accounts of language repudiate 'sense', and so he fills the empty 'fiduciary' word with content. He points to the fiduciary nature of 'unremembered' (how *can* you have an experience which cannot be remembered?) with which Wordsworth uncertainly pairs the 'pleasure' of sense experience.

There is a way in which Wordsworth agrees with him, for in engaging with a second attempt at redefining the sublime, he is surely uncertain about the first, and, indeed, addresses some of its problems. I turn to the efforts of definition in the second 'visionary' passage, though in a more extended discussion of this theme one might contest the concept of the 'fiduciary': one might point out that in writing 'unremembered', Wordsworth was thinking of the experience remembered and then forgotten again: that he relativizes both sense and mind with the comparative adjective 'purer' – purer than sense, but not pure of it, not pure mind. It would also be necessary to suggest that the text is troubled by what seeing is, and what the relation between sense and language is: one of the anxious intertextual references is to Burke's discussion (in his *Enquiry* into the sublime) of the blind poet, Blacklock, who managed to write visual descriptions without having seen anything, thus proving Burke's point that words and things are not tethered.[11]

The revisionary passage moves from sight to sound, 'The still, sad music of humanity' (l. 92). Sound is one of the keys to the erasures of this text, recalling the very beginning of the poem, which refers to the 'inland murmur' of the River Wye, which can be heard but not seen, and which elicits the strangely redundant footnote, to which I shall return,

'The river is not affected by the tides a few miles above Tintern.' The structure of the sad music line, which belongs to a serial aggregation of no fewer than eight 'of' adjuncts, allows 'of' to perform the work of erasure. The syntax is organized round 'of': the hour of thoughtless youth; the still, sad music of humanity; of ample power to chasten and subdue; the joy of elevated thoughts; a sense / Of something; the light of setting suns; all objects of all thought. The structure returns to the visual experience at the beginning of the poem and revises it: thoughts of more deep seclusion; the quiet of the sky; plots of cottage ground; little lines of sportive wood; wreathes of smoke; With some uncertain notice, as might seem / Of vagrant dwellers in the houseless woods; Or of some hermit's cave.

There is a major disruption at the very beginning of the poem as the syntax of erasure repeatedly corrects itself in 'impress / Thoughts of more deep seclusion' (ll. 6–7) and proffers successive notions of 'of': thoughts 'about' a deeper physical seclusion still (which looks forward to the *Lear*-like secluded dwellers in the houseless woods); or 'of' is virtually verbal – thoughts possessing, or being of a more secluded aspect, here meaning less accessible or hidden thoughts, not hidden places. Or 'of' suggests 'made out of, constructed out of', in which case these thoughts are constructed out of deeply hidden 'thoughts', or repressed material. These are also overwritten by the vertiginous syntax of the 'steep and lofty cliffs' which have confounded by seizing control and appropriating power of thought from the gazing subject as agent, short-circuiting consciousness, and impressing thoughts directly on the landscape, rather than impressing themselves on the mind. The mind is deprived even of being the *tabula rasa* of traditional associative epistemology. This power reversal deprives the agent of interaction with another. It short-circuits the subject, rather as Burke's sublime language leaps violently from signifier to signifier, and cuts out the intermediary referent. Language does not work to a naïve word–thing relationship, but Burke's celebration of this is about the despotism of an autonomous language of power, acting coercively and without mediation, on consciousness. That is why Wordsworth does not want to see as Burke's blind man 'sees'. There is a struggle with a threatened erasure here which can only be countered by a further erasure. Levinas writes of 'an infinite number of possible connections' and co-present 'variations' occupying the same space synchronically in the painting of Charles Lapicque.[12] The same thing is happening verbally in Wordsworth's text.

Almost every 'of' adjunct questions visual perception and a simple subject/object relationship simultaneously with the social order by exploring the corrections or remarking of 'of'. A questioning of categories opens up which prepares for the later visions and revisions. As it cannot be the object of this discussion to explore the full text of the poem, a simple spatial example will suffice. The 'plots of cottage-ground' (l. 11) seem innocuous enough; 'of' here begins as 'attached to', is erased to 'made out of', 'constructed out of' – that is to say, made out of the ground, the material earth, around the cottages – and is further erased to 'belonging to', 'owned by'. But why is the earth, the means of livelihood (because you grow the produce which supports you) *plotted*, and on what principles? If the land is owned by the *cottages*, does it *go* with the cottages as tied property, or is it owned by the *cottager*? The principle of erasure begins to question the socially created landscape and its demarcations.

If the first sublime moment is in danger of endorsing the categories questioned in the prospect proem by re-establishing hierarchical relations, the second struggles to undo this by erasing hierarchy with an interactive model, however tautologous this turns out to be. To suggest how this works I will concentrate on three 'of' adjuncts – 'of ample power' (l. 93), 'a sense sublime / Of something far more deeply interfused' (ll. 96–7), 'the light of setting suns' (l. 98). 'Of ample power / To chasten and subdue' is verbal. 'Of' here is erased to possessing, as an attribute, owning, as property is owned, and wielding, as power is wielded. That is to say, the music of humanity – expressed by it, *constitutive* of the human – does not even need to be harsh or grating to be oppressive, for it has the inherent power to chasten and subdue – purify and limit, or, more harshly, *punish and oppress*. 'Of ample power' imposes an erasure on the 'music' of humanity by suggesting that this music can be violent. Gentler and violent meaning struggle. When we come to the much disputed 'sense sublime / Of something far more deeply interfused', Wordsworth has built up so many appositional phrases that the lines of erasure form 'an infinite number of possible connections', and that is partly the point. I will deal with a few. 'Of' is generally taken, as by Empson, to mean 'about', and hence 'Of something' is seen as a kind of *thing* – a sense of apprehension about something. This is why Empson keeps asking what the 'something' is. This is why Barrell would see this as a dishonest, evasive, fiduciary word because it does not seem to have a content. But 'Of' as 'about' is erased by 'Of' as 'made out of, constructed'. One of the things the text is saying is that the 'something' is made out of something: it is deeply interfused with and made out of the light of setting suns and the mind of man. This 'something' is made out of the light (physical light and intellectual illumination), shed by or belonging to dying matter. It comprehends the space and time of a dying universe: it is *made out of*, constituted by, the categories of space and time, matter, mind. The categories of sense and thought are constructed out of one another as the subsuming of thought by matter by thought creates an interactive universe. Thus the sense sublime is not about being overpowered, as in Burke, or about the despotic subject/object relationship, but about the possibility of the transformation of categories, new knowledges. The processes of erasure make cognitive space.

There is no mystery about the erasures of this passage. The excess of the signifier is not about the unrepresentable but about the creation of further meaning. However, the poem struggles with an undoing made by that very excess. The word 'impels' ('impels / All thinking things' (ll. 101–2)) recalls the violence of 'impress' in the proem, and picks up the flight of the boy; like a *'man'* (l. 71; emphasis added) 'Flying from something that he dreads' (l. 72). This temporal trick is typical of the embedded anniversaries in the title: 1798 looks back to 1793, the year Wordsworth was in England again, after leaving France in December 1792, and the erased reference to Bastille Day is a thought of more deep seclusion, going back from 1793 to the Revolution of 1789. The cluster of anxious erasures round 'impress' suggests that the sense sublime made out of 'something' is impelled by, made out of, persecutory violence. The philosophical meaning of 'impress' is, to begin with, deeply conflicted. The associationist *tabula rasa*, sense data impressed on the passive mind, and the theory of language derived from it – that we start with sense and move beyond it to abstraction – was both a conservative and a radical model. Locke and Hartley share the same epistemology: Burke speaks approvingly of Locke's 'general words', and, as we have seen, these are coloured by violence.[13]

But as well as the political struggle going on here, there is a more brutal, military sense of 'impress'. In 1793, 'five years ago', the war occasioned by the French Revolution was under way and new impressment orders came into force. Impressment, the legal capture of men for military service, perpetrated state violence and legitimized it. This was the way the law worked in a non-republican society, and, as Nigel Leask reminds us, Wordsworth and Coleridge were still republicans at this time.[14] During this year, man-hunts in coastal towns provoked riots and violence as experienced seamen were seized when they came ashore, often from long voyages, and snatched from wives and unseen children born while they were at sea. Even inland able-bodied males were not safe, seized at fairs, sales and public gatherings. That oddly redundant footnote – 'The river is not affected by the tides a few miles above Tintern' – comes to have an over-wrought/erased meaning: the poet is 'inland', away from the impressment gangs, but still not safe, haunted by guilt for not being in France, and for the violence of a society he was complicit with. The text erases and adds another meaning of 'seclusion', that which is separated out, as impressed men were, hidden away, closed in. To be secluded was to be the subject of oppression in a way that the middle-class Wordsworth was not. The text flies from the impressment gangs in sympathetic identification and flies from the guilt of not needing to flee.

Nevertheless, despite its problematical nature, 'impress' does seize an associative bifurcation, and suggests an alternative it does not take. This is the word 'mould', used by Coleridge in *Frost at Mid-night*, from whom Wordsworth was reclaiming his child, his own boyhood, and a teleology less authoritarian than that Coleridge was exploring. In Coleridge's world of appearances, increasingly transcendental, the clouds 'image in their bulk' the world below, and the language of correspondences sanctioned by natural forms is the teaching of a God who 'shall mould / Thy spirit'. 'Impress', for all its problems, problematizes 'mould' by erasure. This leads us to a further erasure: 'Nature' will never 'betray' and can 'inform' and 'impress / With quietness and beauty' (ll. 127–8), the heart, Dorothy's, that loves her. Bad faith, of course. But desperation too. Dorothy stands in for, erases, the woman the poet, not Nature, did betray. 'Former pleasures' (l. 119) are indeed incestuously seen in those 'wild eyes' (l. 120). The poet contemplates a woman / women he has driven mad but tries to 'quiet' her and himself, returning them both to the self-contained aesthetic state. It doesn't work, partly because the scandal of sound, the sound of the Wye, the sound of human violence, keeps breaking in: but the intensity with which a language of worship keeps being displaced by a kinaesthetic, bodily language of sexual love suggests a text written to ward off madness rather than complacency. Perhaps both *Frost at Midnight* and *Tintern Abbey* are doing this. Veering between triumphalism and desperation, the text pins its hopes to the possibility of change, of categories remade, even in a dying universe. Its fears set in motion an epistephemilia which drives, or impels, thought and the process of erasure by which it thinks.

To recapitulate, I am suggesting, first, that we can claim poetry as thought, and that what has been described as the seductive power of affect – by the behaviourist positivism of Richards, by the empiricist Empson, by the deconstructionist de Man, the cultural materialist Barrell – is actually the limit case of thought in erasure. Second, therefore, we look to the text for what thought does – to examine and create categories. Third, this thought will be involved in a political struggle for the sign, as erasure suggests and contends with new possibilities: to belong to this struggle is one of the ways we speak to literature. Last – and this follows from a struggle for the sign – to see how the text thinks it is important to read in the desire of the other. This is not an ethical imperative for a gluey empathy but a *fact* of reading. As the text calls out its need to 'enter into a relationship with someone', the answering need to understand accepts the displacement understanding requires. This is much more like the rigours of transference than empathy.

It may seem that *Tintern Abbey* works suspiciously well for this argument. My discussion is in the nature of a prolegomenon: an extended argument would be obliged to explore the possibilities of erasure further and in new contexts. I am convinced, however, that these can be explored both in extended texts such as the novel and in the briefest poem.

Literary texts – at any rate in our culture – are driven by a linguistic intensity, which is bound to mean that they call up powerful contradictions, psychic and political. Like the Kleinian subject, readers are likely to find in the 'body' of the text what they fear, hate and desire. Perhaps a fear of the vengeance of the text and our own creates a need for a 'dry' rationalism which keeps this at bay. But my point is that such rationalism can actually fail to see the textual strategies by which thought works. It expels 'semiotic' material, reinforcing a thought / feeling binary which limits our definitions of the rational. A more expanded notion of what thinking is would enable one to accept that a 'narcissistic' moment of identification may be an essential response to texts and a prerequisite of critical reading. To belong to the structure of another experience, stronger than seduction, more like paranoia, may be an essential *phase* in the reading process, because it escapes from the master / slave model of reading which is the dominant model in our culture. We may not, as critics do not, remain with the terrors of closeness, but it may be that only a closeness to a text's terrors keeps one sane. A refusal to consent to closeness may produce a traumatized reading, rather as, in early life, a failure of active relationship inhibits growth in both parent and child. I am not here recommending a 'mother / child' relationship between text and reader – rather using it as an analogy, a paradigm, for the structure of relationship open to all of us. A student's definition of what reading means to her ends my piece, because it sums up what I have been driving at.

A written voice is heard distinctly, and twice: twice to begin with, then the hearing can expand. First the voice is heard distinctly with the reader's voice, the reader's perceptions. Then the voice becomes more distinctly that of the speaker's character, and then, if we are lucky, the voice of the character begins to resonate fully and loudly with the many voices it carries in its narrative, in its song. What we can *learn* from this voice becomes an individual lesson. What we can *know* is that we have heard its song. That we have read its song.[15]

APPENDIX

LINES

WRITTEN A FEW MILES ABOVE TINTERN ABBEY,

ON REVISITING THE BANKS OF THE WYE DURING A TOUR,

JULY 13, 1798[16]

Five years have passed; five summers, with the length
Of five long winters! and again I hear
These waters, rolling from their mountain-springs
With a sweet inland murmur.* – Once again
Do I behold these steep and lofty cliffs,
Which on a wild secluded scene impress
Thoughts of more deep seclusion; and connect
The landscape with the quiet of the sky.
The day is come when I again repose
Here, under this dark sycamore, and view   10
These plots of cottage-ground, these orchard-tufts,
Which, at this season, with their unripe fruits,
Among the woods and copses lose themselves,
Nor, with their green and simple hue, disturb
The wild green landscape. Once again I see
These hedge-rows, hardly hedge-rows, little lines
Of sportive wood run wild; these pastoral farms
Green to the very door; and wreathes of smoke
Sent up, in silence, from among the trees,
With some uncertain notice, as might seem,   20
Of vagrant dwellers in the houseless woods,
Or of some hermit's cave, where by his fire
The hermit sits alone.

                        Though absent long,
These forms of beauty have not been to me,
As is a landscape to a blind man's eye:
But oft, in lonely rooms, and mid the din
Of towns and cities, I have owed to them,
In hours of weariness, sensations sweet,
Felt in the blood, and felt along the heart,
And passing even into my purer mind   30
With tranquil restoration: – feelings too
Of unremembered pleasure; such, perhaps,

---

* The river is not affected by the tides a few miles above Tintern.

As may have had no trivial influence
On that best portion of a good man's life;
His little, nameless, unremembered acts
Of kindness and of love. Nor less, I trust,
To them I may have owed another gift,
Of aspect more sublime; that blessed mood,
In which the burthen of the mystery,
In which the heavy and the weary weight   40
Of all this unintelligible world
Is lighten'd: – that serene and blessed mood,
In which the affections gently lead us on,
Until, the breath of this corporeal frame,
And even the motion of our human blood
Almost suspended, we are laid asleep
In body, and become a living soul:
While with an eye made quiet by the power
Of harmony, and the deep power of joy,
We see into the life of things.

                        If this   50
Be but a vain belief, yet, oh! how oft,
In darkness, and amid the many shapes
Of joyless day-light; when the fretful stir
Unprofitable, and the fever of the world,
Have hung upon the beatings of my heart,
How oft, in spirit, have I turned to thee
O sylvan Wye! Thou wanderer through the woods,
How often has my spirit turned to thee!

And now, with gleams of half-extinguish'd thought,
With many recognitions dim and faint,   60
And somewhat of a sad perplexity,
The picture of the mind revives again:
While here I stand, not only with the sense
Of present pleasure, but with pleasing thoughts
That in this moment there is life and food
For future years. And so I dare to hope
Though changed, no doubt, from what I was, when first
I came among these hills; when like a roe
I bounded o'er the mountains, by the sides
Of the deep rivers, and the lonely streams,   70
Wherever nature led; more like a man
Flying from something that he dreads, than one
Who sought the thing he loved. For nature then
(The coarser pleasures of my boyish days,

And their glad animal movements all gone by,)
To me was all in all. – I cannot paint
What then I was. The sounding cataract
Haunted me like a passion: the tall rock,
The mountain, and the deep and gloomy wood,
Their colours and their forms, were then to me 80
An appetite: a feeling and a love,
That had no need of a remoter charm,
By thought supplied, or any interest
Unborrowed from the eye. – That time is past,
And all its aching joys are now no more,
And all its dizzy raptures. Not for this
Faint I, nor mourn nor murmur: other gifts
Have followed, for such loss, I would believe,
Abundant recompence. For I have learned
To look on nature, not as in the hour 90
Of thoughtless youth, but hearing oftentimes
The still, sad music of humanity,
Not harsh nor grating, though of ample power
To chasten and subdue. And I have felt
A presence that disturbs me with the joy
Of elevated thoughts; a sense sublime
Of something far more deeply interfused,
Whose dwelling is the light of setting suns,
And the round ocean, and the living air,
And the blue sky, and in the mind of man, 100
A motion and a spirit, that impels
All thinking things, all objects of all thought,
And rolls through all things. Therefore am I still
A lover of the meadows and the woods,
And mountains; and of all that we behold
From this green earth; of all the mighty world
Of eye and ear, both what they half-create,*
And what perceive; well pleased to recognize
In nature and the language of the sense,
The anchor of my purest thoughts, the nurse, 110
The guide, the guardian of my heart, and soul
Of all my moral being.

                    Nor, perchance,
If I were not thus taught, should I the more
Suffer my genial spirits to decay:
For thou art with me, here, upon the banks

* This line has a close resemblance to an admirable line of Young, the exact expression of which I cannot recollect.

Of this fair river; thou, my dearest Friend,
My dear, dear Friend, and in thy voice I catch
The language of my former heart, and read
My former pleasures in the shooting lights
Of thy wild eyes. Oh! yet a little while   120
May I behold in thee what I was once,
My dear, dear Sister! And this prayer I make,
Knowing that Nature never did betray
The heart that loved her; 'tis her privilege,
Through all the years of this our life, to lead
From joy to joy: for she can so inform
The mind that is within us, so impress
With quietness and beauty, and so feed
With lofty thoughts, that neither evil tongues,
Rash judgments, nor the sneers of selfish men,   130
Nor greetings where no kindness is, nor all
The dreary intercourse of daily life,
Shall e'er prevail against us, or disturb
Our chearful faith that all which we behold
Is full of blessings. Therefore let the moon
Shine on thee in thy solitary walk;
And let the misty mountain winds be free
To blow against thee: and in after years,
When these wild ecstasies shall be matured
Into a sober pleasure, when thy mind   140
Shall be a mansion for all lovely forms,
Thy memory be as a dwelling-place
For all sweet sounds and harmonies; Oh! then,
If solitude, or fear, or pain, or grief,
Should be thy portion, with what healing thoughts
Of tender joy wilt thou remember me,
And these my exhortations! Nor, perchance,
If I should be, where I no more can hear
Thy voice, nor catch from thy wild eyes these gleams
Of past existence, wilt thou then forget   150
That on the banks of this delightful stream
We stood together; and that I, so long
A worshipper of Nature, hither came,
Unwearied in that service: rather say
With warmer love, oh! with far deeper zeal
Of holier love. Nor wilt thou then forget,
That after many wanderings, many years
Of absence, these steep woods and lofty cliffs,
And this green pastoral landscape, were to me
More dear, both for themselves, and for thy sake.   160

NOTES

1   John Barrell, 'Introduction', *Poetry, Language and Politics*, pp. 1–2.
2   Such a shattering of subject and society has as its corollary 'a new apportion-ment of relationships between the symbolic and the real, the subjective and the objective' (Julia Kristeva, 'How does one speak to literature?', *Desire in Language*, p. 93).
3   Barrell, *Poetry, Language and Politics*, p. 9.
4   Paul de Man, *The Rhetoric of Romanticism*, p. 252; *Allegories of Reading*, p. ix. See also the post-humous collection, *Aesthetic Ideology*.
5   In the seminal textual strategies outlined in the codes of *S/Z* (1970), where 'everything signifies ceaselessly and several times', Roland Barthes allows no space for the 'jouissance' which appears almost as an afterthought in the final section of the essay 'From work to text' (see *S/Z*, p. 12; *Image, Music, Text*, pp. 155–64).
6   The work of Hélène Cixous, in famous essays such as 'The laugh of the Medusa', would be an example of an 'expressive' or semiotic reading of the feminine: though Cixous would not call her work anti-rational because she claims to dissolve binary opposition, she can slip into the one-sidedness of 'feminine' affect, where 'writing the body' appears to exclude writing the mind, thus reintroducing the binary she repudiates (*New French Feminisms*, pp. 245–67).
7   Christopher Norris, 'Introduction: Empson as literary theorist', *William Empson: The Critical Achievement*, pp. 1–20, 47. This is the best recent discussion of Empson.
8   Empson, *Seven Types of Ambiguity*, p. 154.
9   Barrell, *Poetry, Language and Politics*, pp. 145–6. See also Marjorie Levin-son's powerful *Wordsworth's Great Period Poems*, pp. 37–53.
10   Levinas, 'The transcendence of words', p. 147.
11   Edmund Burke, *A Philosophical Enquiry*, part V, section v, 'Examples that WORDS may affect without raising IMAGES', p. 168.
12   Levinas, 'The transcendence of words', p. 147.
13   Burke, *A Philosophical Enquiry*, p. 165.
14   Nigel Leask, *The Politics of Imagination*.
15   Thanks to Kimberly Kubik, Bread Loaf School of English, 1993.
16   First published in *Wordsworth and Coleridge, Lyrical Ballads* (1798); quoted from the 2nd edition of R. L. Brett and A. R. Jones.

4

Thinking Affect

...a hatred of emotion, and therefore, by a short extension, of life itself.

Wilfred Bion, *Second Thoughts*

The success of the symbol, the defeat of affect

Emotions, feelings, passions, moods, anxiety, discharge of psychic energy, motor innervation, pleasure, pain, joy and sorrow, rapture, depression. For the moment I shall include all these under the general rubric of affect, even though it will become apparent in the course of this discussion that they are differentiated and, rightly, delicately distinguished in discussions of affective experience by philosophers and psychologists. That affects cross categories, experienced in consciousness and registered by the body, that they belong to mind and soma, straddling conscious and unconscious just as they straddle mind and physiology, is the single most important axiom to bear in mind. The inclusiveness of the rubric of affect here arises from the presupposition of this chapter, as in the epigraph from Bion, that life is fed by the emotions, the cluster of experiences, both obvious and mysterious, that are summoned by the semantic fields of the words with which I begin. How it is possible to dissolve the customary binary, emotion/thought, and where this would take us in a democratic 'aesthetic education', is my concern here. I begin with the emotions, and with the discipline which has taken them most seriously in twentieth-century culture – psychoanalysis – though I shall not remain with this discipline alone. Here, to make a start, are two examples of affective experience from a Blake poem and a Clint Eastwood movie. Lyric and film will appear again in this discussion.

Words: 'My mother groand! my father wept./Into the dangerous world I leapt:/Helpless, naked, piping loud:/Like a fiend hid in a cloud.' These are the first four lines of William Blake's *Infant Sorrow* (*Songs of Innocence*, plate 48). Gunfire: gunfire without warning and seemingly without a target, is a common tactical shock of the Western. In *Unforgiven* (Clint Eastwood, Warner, 1992) it bursts upon two riders as they encounter the gun-obsessed Kid. What could an utterance and a burst of gunfire share? Most obviously, they temporarily alter breathing patterns, the gasp prompted by the assault of unexpected gunfire, the effort of responding to the aggressive speech patterns of the poem. And such vascular alteration and physiological change, however fleeting, is a reminder that Freud, puzzled by the nature of affect, attributed it to the anxiety generated by the toxic restriction in breathing which occurred in the separation from the mother in the birth act. In the lecture on 'Anxiety' in *Introductory Lectures on Psychoanalysis* (1916–17) Freud assimilated 'normal' affect to the model of a hysterical attack. It was derived from a collective prehistory and is 'the expression of a general hysteria which has become a heritage'. Reminding us that the same roots in German provide the words for anxiety and 'narrow place', he speculates that hysteria, the precipitate of a reminiscence, repeats the 'immense increase of stimulation' occurring in the interruption of the blood supply at birth and reinstates in the affect the 'restriction in breathing' intrinsic to the 'real situation' (p. 445).

Interestingly, in his notorious 'The name and nature of poetry' – an essay that was given as a lecture in 1933 (the year Freud returned to the theme of affect in *New Introductory Lectures*) – and is often regarded as a hopelessly old-fashioned product of expressive theory – A. E. Housman used the language of symptom and pathology to describe poetry. Poetry's 'symptoms' were gooseflesh, 'precipitation of water to the eyes' and 'a constriction of the throat', the same breathing problem mentioned by Freud. Housman retrieved this feminized experience for the male body by remarking that bristling skin impeded shaving, but at the same time made himself extraordinarily vulnerable. This kind of poetics was, of course, the target of Wimsatt and Beardsley's essay of 1954, 'The affective fallacy'. But perhaps unexpectedly, Housman shares other assumptions with the Freud of the earlier lectures. For him poetry does not 'transmit thought' but does 'transfuse emotion'. What one might call a reverse transmission theory emerges. A poet experiences affect and transfuses it into the poem: the reader encounters the poem and through it traces back to the author's original affective state, sensing a 'vibration corresponding to what was felt by the writer' (p. 12). Affect precedes representation in creation: it follows representation in reception,

Housman assumes, a reverse creative process. Nevertheless, in the transit
to 'vibration', words take a subordinate place. For the problem is that
feeling cannot represent itself. Although by 1933 Freud had moved away
from the metaphorical nature of the symptom and had become more
interested in the structure of repression rather than in describing affect
– he had arrived at the crucial understanding that anxiety created repression, and not the other way round – his earlier attempts to think how
affect might be verbalized are important. He struggled with the enigma of
the relationship between affect and meaning in a structure which did not
offer a content to affect, stressing the ambiguity and indeterminacy of
Angst.

> By anxiety we usually understand the subjective state into which we are
> put by perceiving the 'generation of anxiety' and we call this an affect. And
> what is an affect in the dynamic sense? It is in any case something highly
> composite. An affect includes in the first place particular motor innerva-
> tions or discharges and secondly certain feelings; the latter are of two kinds
> – perception of the feelings that have occurred and the direct feelings of
> pleasure and unpleasure which, as we say, give the affect its keynote. But
> I do not think that with this enumeration we have arrived at the essence of
> affect. We seem to see deeper in the case of some affects and to recognise
> that the core which holds the combination we have described together is
> the repetition of some particular significant experience. (Freud, 'Anxiety',
> *Introductory Lectures*, p. 443)

Affect is a triple 'combination', bodily discharge, perception of that
motor action and a qualitative assessment of pleasure or pain, held
together by an indefineable 'core' experience. Only a musical term, 'key-
note', will do to convey it because it has no ideational significance. Where
is feeling, or affect, when it comes to language, or representation, then?
Much later, analysing the nature of fear in a whispered anticipation of an
explosion (we think of the trauma of gunfire again), Wittgenstein said,
scrupulously, 'his words do not describe a feeling; although they and their
tone may be a manifestation of feeling'.[1] Freud presupposes the same
radical disengagement of affect from language, yet seeks a correspondence, despite his belief that 'anxiety is therefore the universally current
coin for which *any* affective impulse is or can be exchanged if the ideational content is subjected to repression' (p. 452). Indeterminate anxiety
stands in for a lost idea. We may try to reconstruct the situation as if there
had been no repression, but:

> We have always left on one side the question of what happens to the affect
> that was attached to the repressed idea; and it is only now that we learn

that the immediate vicissitude of that affect is to be transformed into anxiety, whatever quality it may have exhibited apart from this in the normal course of events. This transformation into affect, however, is by far the more important part of the process of repression. It is not easy to speak of this, since we cannot assert the existence of unconscious affects in the same sense as that of unconscious ideas. An idea remains the same, except for the one difference, whether it is conscious or unconscious. We can state what it is that corresponds to an unconscious idea. But an affect is a process of discharge and must be judged quite differently from an idea; what corresponds to it in the unconscious cannot be declared without deeper reflection and clarification of our hypotheses about psychical processes. And that we cannot undertake here. (Freud, 'Anxiety', pp. 458–9)

And he might have added that what 'corresponds' to affect in the conscious is also obscure when it comes to representation. A process of substitution has placed affect not in language but out of it, beyond its reach. Must we then assume that affect is the kind of undecipherable psychic 'accident' Sartre hoped it would turn out not to be – self-consuming gunfire, shock, catastrophe?

If one turns for help to the semiotics of sadness in Julia Kristeva's *Black Sun: Depression and Melancholia* (1987), the inhibition of symbol-making and the retarding of energy that is the work of depression, allied with another variant of the disjunction between affect and representation, offers us only the mutism of grief. Kristeva reaches back to the problems of the early Freud. What stamps our entire behaviour and our reponse to sign systems, mood, is nevertheless insufficiently stabilized to coalesce as verbal or other signs. Like Freud she sees affect as an archaic energy signal, a phylogenetic inheritance which has to be described in terms of stimulation, tension, energy conflict or fluctuating energy cathexes that cannot be reduced to verbal expression:

Sadness leads us into the enigmatic realm of *affects* – anguish, fear or joy. Irreducible to its verbal or semiological expressions, sadness (like all affect) is the *psychic representation of energy displacements* caused by external or internal traumas. The exact status of such psychic representations of energy displacments remains, in the present state of psychoanalytical and semiological theories, very vague. (Kristeva, *Black Sun*, p. 21)

If lack, or separation from the mother, makes symbol formation possible by detaching an other whose being we have to represent, sadness makes us the prisoner of affect, of the archaic 'Thing' or primal mother, source of the primary inscriptions of affects and emotions, but now retarding energy in the atrophy of grief as the subject refuses to let go of the archaic maternal union (p. 58). The fully fledged translation or correspondence of symbol can about only come with matricide, when the father enters the psychic world – both the imaginary father that guarantees primary identification and the Oedipal father of the Law – so that symbol formation can occur when the release from the object guaranteed by castration brings language, the substitutive signs for the absent object, into being. But in depression the subject's battle with symbolic collapse is in the throes of an archaic affectivity struggling with signs. A flattening of the voice itself registers this retreat from language.

Such a subject, caught in the void of affect, nevertheless has some means of expression open to it. And here a quasi-representational theory emerges. Moods do find inscriptions of energy through the process of condensation and displacement, in threshold states, in homeostatic recourse to the frontier between animality or nescience and symbol formation. Thus 'moods are *inscriptions*, energy disruptions and not simply raw energies' (p. 22). Perhaps this makes them a kind of protolanguage? If or when moods take and give the imprint of separation which is the beginning of the symbol's sway, she says, they are transposed into material entirely different from what constituted the mood – rhythms, signs, and forms which are indicators of mood on the one hand and suppressants of it on the other. Perhaps reciprocally for both writer and reader (Kristeva does not say) poetry provides a temporary respite from the failure to control affect because through it semiotic inscriptions can be made known. One can track them as an index of the death drive, when form is abstracted, distorted or hollowed out. One can track them through phases of narcissism when affect either becomes an object in itself, fills the void and evicts death (p. 48), or, as pure mood without an object, flows into psychic emptiness (p. 49). Such inscriptions leave only traces of themselves.

And yet these semiotic traces – slips, parapraxes, puns, formal disruption, distortion, deformations and disfigurations – which counter the repression of language and the symbolic order are subject to a kind of paradox. Successful symbol-making vanquishes affect. The poem as successful triumph over depression is the defeat of affect. (And presumably the poem as successful expression of love suffers a like fate.) Achieved language, betokening separation from the mother, the matricide which summons language because separation enables language to stand in for the lost object, engenders symbol-making but represses affect as a necessary outcome of its success. It has achieved the work of full representation rather than what Hanna Segal called the search for a primitive *equivalent* of experience, an equivalent which would be a kind of quasi-object, not a symbol.[2]

It seems we are at an impasse. Feeling, that which supports life itself, appears to hide from representation. Does it help to turn to poetry, which for Kristeva offers a temporary respite for the inscription of affect to manifest itself? Blake's poem, *Infant Sorrow*, may well signal the preverbal condition of affect through the meaning of *infans*, 'without a language'. This sorrow without language may be the sorrow possessed of or ascribed to the young or newborn child or the very origin and genesis of sorrow itself, the 'infancy' of sorrow's formation. But in either case Sorrow is made to speak *through* language even though the *infans* is without it, a paradox which might lead us to the heart of the problem. And the illustration may help. There are three people – a community, the Oedipal community perhaps, in the poem: the groaning mother, the weeping father and the defensively tense 'piping' infant in its 'dangerous' primordial world of the family triad. In the illustration there are only two people, the mother and the child, who is not in swaddling bands but is almost leaping off its bed, arms flung out in uncontrolled paroxysm as the mother faces it. It is unclear whether or not each is appealing to or rejecting the other, retreating or attacking, but the alienation suggests a terrible, helpless dyadic separation, the moment of frustrated matricide, maybe. The illustration offers us a rare, or rare for these poems, literal domestic interior, Freud's 'narrow place' perhaps, with an even narrower place behind the mother, the padded, curtained marriage bed of bourgeois union. It recalls the 'marriage hearse' of 'London' which blights the newborn infant's tear.

> My mother groan'd! my father wept.
> Into the dangerous world I leapt:
> Helpless, naked, piping loud:
> Like a fiend hid in a cloud.
> Struggling in my father's hands:
> Striving against my swaddling bands:
> Bound and weary I thought best
> To sulk upon my mother's breast.
> William Blake, *Infant Sorrow*

Do the parents groan and weep at the birth trauma or is this an unwanted child? The respiratory gasps and aggressive stresses suggest violence, but who originally figures the child as a fiend? The child, construing itself as helpless and violent, alone yet powerful, omnipotently leaping into the world and yet terrifyingly on its guard, encounters the failure of the parents to contain its passions with a terrorizing and terrified combination of blocking and splitting, noise and hallucinatory projection. The

infinite pathos of the oxymoron held in its loud but reedy piping is superseded by the violence of the child's comparison of itself to a fiend, taking
on the characteristics of an evil being, 'Like a fiend hid in a cloud'. Clouds
for Blake signify inert matter, pure materiality: here a kind of aggressive
obstruction directed against the parents. It seems the child attempts
empowerment by concealing itself, losing itself in an infinity of split-off
parts of its being, as the droplets of a cloud multiply to infinity – though
the effect must be to multiply and conglomerate its fiendishness as hatred
is directed both to the father and the mother. Perhaps this is why the fury
directed to the father as the child struggles and strives against violation
has the unexpected result not of violence but of appalling passivity.
'Weary': the exhaustion of depression and affective death supervenes on
struggle as the child's matricidal drive, ever more violent and ever more
terrifying to itself, returns upon itself as sullen aggression. This is the
deadened negation of a despair which would rather destroy the self than
give way to matricidal fury, 'To sulk upon my mother's breast'. A fate of
the rhyme scheme which offers 'breast' in the singular would enable a
Kleinian to think of the bad breast. The child, at any rate, seems to know
only one breast, for which the cloud is perhaps also a metonymy, sucking
the child into it, consuming its vitality rather than providing food, reversing the process of nurture with torture. The cloud, not a symbol so much
as the quasi-object of equivalence to experience which has not been fully
separated out from its object, is used brilliantly by Blake to indicate the
tragic early breakdown of child and parental love.

But have we been talking about affect or simply the manifestations of
language which signal – albeit without articulating – its presence? It is
surely the case that we have not been talking about affect, not even the
'psychic representations of energy displacements' that Kristeva describes.
We may feel anguish and terror while we describe the structures in which
they inhere. But rather, psychoanalytic language has interpreted the psychic events, the drama of violence, around anguish and fury while presupposing a kind of a priori of the emotions – that we already know what
they are. Psychoanalytic language is likely to be the nearest one can get to
affect, and I will not abandon it, though as this chapter will demonstrate,
it is not the only language one can speak. Some critics, such as, we shall
later see, Eve Kosofsky Sedgwick, impatient both with reified accounts of
feeling as cultural construction and with Freudian accounts of affect,
have turned to theories, specifically those of Silvan Tomkins, which reject
what they see as the mystifications of the unconscious. It is not necessary
to make this an issue here, but if we are to go further with what Peter
Middleton has termed the 'lost language of emotion'[3], it might be best to
abandon a theory of representation or rather turn it on its head. It might

be more productive to ask if the non-correspondence, the gap, between affect and representation, the disengagement of language and affect, might be important. In other words, one would be investigating the broken middle, staying with contradiction. For the movement of affect, we shall see shortly, depends on its capacity to work with negation, to accomplish the labour of the negative.

It is perhaps the uncertain status of the representational theory of affect which accounts for the late twentieth-century's fascination with the ana-chronistic shock of the sublime, a residual element of the nineteenth-century aesthetic which has clung to theoretical discourse, particularly in the work of Jean-François Lyotard and Paul de Man.[4] For the sublime is a supreme moment of aporia, the breakdown of representation when emotional shock and language do not match. It appears to be a perverse demonstration of correspondence or equivalence by default. And yet the breakdown of representation seems to guarantee a separating out of the unknowable logic of feeling – a prelinguistic, masochistic pathology mistakenly yearning for sign and inner feeling to coalesce – from ration-ality. The meaning of the sublime is remade for the twentieth century as that which cannot come into any system of exchange and circulation through representation. Thus, in the work of writers such as Bataille and Blanchôt, feeling is driven to incremental extremities of orgiastic irrationalism, to the dionysian ecstasy of pain and violence, secretions of the mind which return to the body's flows and fluids, a suffering with heroic, agonistic agency.[5] This is partly a result of the conviction that emotion and reason can never belong to one another and partly the result of a mistaken understanding of emotion as that which *belongs* to the individual subject like a possession or its own body, and which cannot be a *relational* experience *between* subjects.

Two desiderata, then, become clear: first, to reconnect emotion and reason and to affirm the epistemic status of emotion and knowledge; second, to reclaim the social function of emotion. Emotion, L. S. Vygotsky thought, *begins* by being social. The disengagement of affect from lan-guage opens the way to a relational understanding of emotion as media-tion which is a prerequisite for both an epistemic and social reading of the passions. My primary interest is in a cognitive reading of emotion, though I will suggest how a social reading might be taken up in the conclusion to this chapter. As in my earlier discussion, in which the artwork, not the self, became 'what thinks', so here the artwork, not the self, is regarded as the 'what feels' in mediation. I continue to use the language of psycho-analysis. The work of the revisionary Hegelian and anti-Lacanian analyst, André Green, to which I now turn, offers parallels with the revisionary Hegelianism of Gillian Rose explored in chapter 2. Green offers another re-reading of mediation which is in reciprocal relation with hers, although there are important differences, and the two readings are not identical. I am well aware that these companion essays, in separating out 'what thinks' from 'what feels', appear to confirm the very division of thought from emotion which I wish to refuse. However, the diremption of affect and thinking belongs to modernity's broken middle: we are all caught in this, and to start with modernity's formulation offers the opportunity of critique from where modernity stands. It is not easy to mend what culture has rent over hundreds of years, and to elide the difficulty would create more problems than it solves. Affect and thought are the theme of the following section. In the conclusion I consider briefly how social readings of feeling can be extrapolated from the reciprocity of thought and emotion and turn to discourses other than psychoanalysis, recognizing that these problematize psychoanalytical language.

Surges of affect: the Id and the mirror

Affect erupts from the interior of the body...without the help of representation. (André Green, *Le Discours vivant*, p. 224)[6]

Thinking has to be called into existence to cope with thoughts. (Wilfred Bion, 'A theory of thinking', *Second Thoughts*, p. 111)

Our culture separates 'feeling and thinking from each other in such a way that they are supposedly opposed to each other', Hegel says. Religious feeling (but try substituting aesthetic feeling) is the most protected of all from thought, because it is assumed to be 'contaminated, perverted, or even totally destroyed by thinking' (*Encyclopaedia Logic*, para. 2, p. 25) – again, the facetious irony, here challenging the thought/feeling binary. But he did not undervalue emotion either: in the lectures on aesthetics he contemplated the storm of grief in mourning which required the supplement of weepers in order to be externalized and understood.

The paradox of André Green's work is that to challenge the thought/feeling binary he deliberately uncoupled affect and representation, intellect and the drives, following Bion, who, he said, had added the vital category of knowledge to Klein's Manichean drama of love and hate. In a sustained dialogue with Jacques Lacan's theory, he rejected what he took to be Lacan's undervaluing of affect. Affect for Green is epistemic in its motivation: it is not simply the prerequisite of thought. Thought and affect are indivisibly part of one another, though they become so as a polarity created through violent displacement and rupture in consciousness, through constitutive gaps which signal unconscious activity. Thus Green's *Discours* evolves a psychoanalytic model of the broken middle which is not Lacan's *mise en abyme* but a form of mediation.

Green is not perpetrating a new irrationalism. Affect need be neither mystified as an idealized state nor occulted as the savage mind, he says; it is assumed to be beyond representation in both cases. No, affect belongs to an economic principle of energy and discharge with a drive to kidnap representation. It is forever seeking representation. *Affect makes us feel alive*. This is a fundamental axiom for Green. Affect moves between the visceral body and consciousness. The body is the spectator of affect. A noticing of affect is a noticing of the body which *speaks*, both confirming ownership of the body by consciousness and disowning consciousness – *my* body: *it* speaks. But a silent body is psychic death, and the invading terrors of dissolution arise from the silent body. Psychic life, on the other hand, depends on the *surprise element* of affect. Affect tears the barrier of repression, seizes, assaults and subjugates the subject. Affect rises, erupts, from the interior of the body *without the help of representation*. Representation is always secondary, always follows upon the blank, the astonishment of affect. Thus Green emphasizes his fundamental principle – the uncoupling of affect and representation. The two have to be rent in order for epistemic change to occur (*Le Discours vivant*, pp. 220–3).

When representation comes, Green says, it is *not* the orderly linear chain of signification valued by Lacan, whose reliance not on an economic model of the psyche but on the excessive prestige of the symbolic order, of memory, and of desire, persuades him to bring all material under the same lucid linguistic taxonomy according to homogeneous principles of concatenation. Consequently, Lacan creates a 'pure', idealist psychic syntax out of the structural principles of the phoneme, morpheme, word and syntagm. In other words, all material is subsumed under the order of the sign and the principles of displacement and condensation. A certain satire on Lacan's thought is actually a way of taking it all the more seriously. His is an elegant, rigorously coherent system, Green says, which values the intellectual structure of the symbolic order above all, enthralled with the beauty of its logic. In Lacan's work the Id is in eclipse, the imaginary subordinated. At best it emerges as the semiotic, waste product of the unconscious, which requires further repression. Affect for Lacan is an excrescence in the system. The unconscious, structured like a language, constituted by the effects of the sign, is organized as 'langue' and behaves almost like a platonic syntactical abstraction. The sign arrives through the menace of death. It is the mark of absence, setting in chain the pure logic of substitution as castration and language alike allow the process of 'standing in for' the lost or absent object to be set in motion as a sophisticated, svelte metonymy of signifiers. Affect for Lacan is simply an *effect*, dissipating like smoke or breath, or gunfire. It is the offspring of the play of the signifier, but it has no independent or prior life even though the Id belongs to Lacan's syntax in so far as it belongs to the Imaginary. Covertly, Green is arguing that Lacan's system is idealist in its homogeneity and perfection, cleansing itself of the squalor of affect, a kind of ascetic aestheticism. His constant subtext: *Lacan's system possesses the rinsed, Appollonian purity of 'fine art' dredged of affect. Maybe it is pure teleology.*

Claiming that he is returning to Freud, and taunting Lacan with this authenticity, Green insists that language does not possess this 'pure' functional property, and neither does the unconscious. It roughly sutures thought, representation, affect, acts and bodily states and is structured as a series of co-existing but discontinuous dialects. It can come perilously near to Babel. It stretches out along an axis which has abstraction at one end and the archaic forms and somatic dialects of the hysteric (vomiting) or the obsessional neurotic (the discourse of cleanliness) at the other. These dialects interrupt one another, not articulated but hooked together from essentially heterogeneous and incompatible orders of the self. '*Affect is the flesh of the sign and the sign of the flesh*' (p. 239). In a single session an analysand can move through a series of discontinuous languages, with different functional properties:

> I have thought over my conversation with my friend Pierre which opened up horizons concerning the reasons for my attraction for A ... I imagined that you [the analyst] would have spent your holidays surrounded by your family and playing with your children, as I always longed that my father would have done with me and I awaited your return impatiently. ... The moment I speak to you I experience an overwhelming hostility for which I can find no explanation. I'm suddenly in a state of tension – I feel that I would like to smash the trivial ornaments on your mantelpiece. Now I have difficulty in speaking, it's difficult to explain what I feel, I feel a change in my body, it seems as if my hands have separated from my arms and I can't feel them any more. The things in this room are becoming hazy, I feel that the noises in the street are deadened, I can't hear you breathe any more ... are you there? ... my body is like a deadweight, lifeless; everything is turning strange, my legs are extending themselves and there is a black veil before my eyes. (Green, *Le Discours vivant*, p. 238).

The fiend in the cloud is not out of place here. Pauses, a choking voice, physical movements, panting, all these are part of the prosody of affect, the return of primal bodily material to language from the unsayable. In saying that affect is the sign of the flesh and the flesh of the sign, Green means that affect materializes itself in the signifier, which in turn signifies the body. A breach opens up between Lacan and Green here. For Lacan a symptom is effectively a metaphor in which the flesh functions as a signifying element. To take the famous example of Dora's cough (not quoted by Green or Lacan but taken here as an example because it is a familiar symptom for most readers): Lacan would accept a metonymic explanation that the throat, a signifying element in the upper body, is displacing the lower body and substituting, a paroxysm in the throat for the sexual trauma which afflicted the genital zone, Herr K's sudden and unwanted embrace. There is an element of abstraction here, in which the body as signifier points away from itself to the *idea of symptom*, to a new conceptual signified which represses the body, forgetting genital experience as the metaphor represses the object it stands in for, the displaced signified, which disappears into the unconscious as if into a void.[7] This is effectively Freud's explanation rendered in semiotic terms, but Green would claim a more atavistic Freud. Green's sign as flesh and flesh as sign turns back towards the body. The element of substitution and displacement, so important for Lacan, is not so powerful. The cough as sign is more like a grimace which is both cause and effect of a discharge of psychic energy. The anguish and shock of the encounter with Herr K is realized in the spasm of the cough, which, one might say, is attempting to *cough up* the sexual trauma. It is the body speaking to the body, the Other speaking to the Other, unconscious to unconscious, as Green expresses it. Rather than the purity of substitution and abstraction there is almost a mixed metaphor as cough and trauma attempt to live in the same space. Freud's rebus-like dream would be seen strikingly differently by Lacan and Green. One would bring the components of the rebus under a single explanatory principle of systematic translation, the other would attend to the component parts of the rebus and their heterogeneity – the boat on the roof, the man with a comma on his head.[8]

Does Green's affect look like an exorbitantly expressive theory of emotion, re-described in psychoanalytic language, which is simply reduced to inhabiting the literalness of the body? No. Though the body is where the drives find expression, this is neither a somatic theory of the body nor a theory of the play of feeling. Affect is not hostile to intellect but simultaneously feeds it and feeds on it. This is a theory of 'travail', of the work or labour of affect which brings epistemic questioning into being. Affect can do this because it is *mobile*. Green needs to establish a model of the co-existing, heterogeneous orders of the self in order to develop a theory of dynamic intrasystematic transformation in which the unbound, disengaged energy of the drives breaches different orders of the self and brings them into new relations to one another. For that is how affect drives intellect into relation with it.

Affect is an aspect of the drives. Green locates it unequivocally in the violent storms of energy which are the life of the Id. It hooks on to things and hallucination alike, indiscriminately. Unlike the reality principle, it does not have to abandon the hallucinated object or deconstruct it, a renunciation forced upon psychic life as soon as the idealization of language calls for the discovery of the relations of words to the world and the correlation of words and images with the absence or presence of the object. Primal Id language never takes the great leap into the mental constructs which can forego both hallucination and presence, and which make autonomous mental life possible. Instead, it throws up barely 'domesticated' parts of the Id, somatic memory, trauma 'and the affect which accompanied it and whose return is dreaded' (p. 241). Id energies are constantly issuing as quasi-direct expressions of the drives in forms which require new hybrids and linguistic compounds to describe them: 'affect/representation', 'symbol/affect', are two forms. Green settles on the term 'representant' (an infant leaping in a cloud? a dissociated breast?) to distinguish the primal, rudimentary forms of organization available to the Id. Drawing freely upon late Freud and Kleinian psycho-analysis, he reminds us of the chaos of the destructive drive, where 'memories-in-feelings' occupy the perpetual dispersal of the paranoid-schizoid position and accomplish the splittings and dismemberments which fight violence with violence – the primal horror of the bad breast. He does not invoke Bion's beta-elements, those unassimilable materials which can neither be repressed nor transformed and which occupy the threshold of the unconscious, but he could well have done so. For his argument depends on an understanding that the Id never can transform the raging storms of psychic energy of which it is both depository and principle.

And yet there is a paradox: at the threshold of the Id, affect is unrep-resentable, but it is perpetually in quest of representation, searching for what Green calls 'economo-traumatic signification'. For the Id's charge of energy does make psychic and *intellectual* change possible, not because it transforms itself but because, like a current which activates an object not itself, it generates reactive change in other orders of the consciousness. Not only does it provoke reaction, it appropriates the representational possibilities of different orders of the self and displaces them. The turn of the argument occurs here. In this negation is possibility. We can already see the possibility of a poetics of affect in the exposition so far. We would search for the rebus embedded in the artwork, the disruptive affect/representation, the inscription of the psychic equivalent for experience which would co-exist with the symbol, with abstraction and the rationality of metonymy. But we would also need to search for the way 'what feels' becomes knowledge as the Id steals ideational experience. In his adaptation of the mirror stage, to which I now move, Green opens the way for a cognitive poetics and an aesthetic which harbours epistemic possibility.

How does epistemic possibility emerge out of the theft of representation? In two key moments of his penultimate chapter, strategically placed at its beginning and conclusion, Green first reworks the infant's mirror stage and then turns to the phenomenon of *adult* 'negative hallucination'. Together these constitute the moments of possibility in his psychic model – though they may be the moments of greatest anguish – and illustrate how thought comes about.

The infant's misprision of a reflected completeness, which it understands to be its own body, is as much the jouissance of the infant in love with affect as a narcissism incapable of escaping from the Imaginary (as for Lacan). Image and pleasure principle are interdependent for Green. Affect may mislead, but it is nevertheless the instigator of change. First, it invokes the dual principle of pleasure/pain, for pleasure must operate according to a rule of polarity, like an alternating current. Jouissance cannot remain as a static condition: if it is dynamic it must change. To register change is to be handed the possibility of reflecting into it. Second, affect introduces another dual structure, the body/consciousness split, the independent body which 'speaks' it and the consciousness which owns the body: *it* speaks; *my* body. The *dynamism* (an economic principle) of the double pleasure/pain principle and the dualistic *structure* (a formal principle) of body/self work together and are mutually constitutive (pp. 220–1). The different orders of consciousness are split, uncoupled, but as a result can interact. For once psychic change occurs through pleasure/pain, the divided body/self can register and interrogate change by responding to the living charge of affect uttered by the speaking body. Neither pole of each polarity can exist without the other, and neither of these polarities can exist without the other. In the mirror stage the infant has its earliest opportunity for mental life, as the body speaking can be questioned in 'a weighty presence' to the self (pp. 225). The mirror stage also occasions one of the earliest dramas of change, which liberates the infant into the autonomy of thought. Unlike Lacan's Imaginary, to which the mirror stage irremediably belongs, opposed to the symbolic where thought is possible, Green's mirror stage already harbours intellectual experience.

'Negative hallucination' is at the psychic opposite of the infant's mirror stage. Here the life of the Id, which Green claims, displaces the unconscious in Freud's late work as the centre of his system, transgresses its own space and penetrates to the core of the Ego's idealizations, occupying the site of mental life to which it is essentially alien. 'Negative hallucination' is a phenomenon of the murderous Superego and a consequence of its merciless drive to idealization. And, importantly, because it is a phenomenon of mature experience, 'negative hallucination' is a post-infantile, estranging double of the mirror stage, occasioning deep anguish in the life of the adult. Nevertheless, it can occasion a cognitive transformation in *adult* experience, and this is what makes it so important for a cognitive poetics. The Superego's repression of pleasure reaches an asceticism which asks for total deliverance from the object of pleasure. But *that deliverance* in turn becomes a source of pleasure and even the renunciation of *that* narcissistic pleasure. The result is a psychic void produced by a succession of self-suppressions: 'The Ego Ideal gains satisfaction from negative narcissism which dissolves the image of the subject in an affective void' (p. 267). This mirror stage is a reversal of the earlier position. It is 'the ultimate absence of the self', abolishing the image. Nothing appears in the mirror. 'Only the frame of the mirror is visible – not a trace is inscribed in it' (p. 274). There is an analogy here between the melancholic condition prompted by the lost object and the loss of representation of the subject itself. The self is afflicted with a mounting intensity of anguish as it seeks and cannot find its image, the specular proof of its existence. For it is the power of representation and the power of seeing which confirms existence, not the mere feeling of existence. Affect and representation are severed here, and in proportion to the loss of representation, so the terrors of affect increase with all the power of the repetition compulsion. The intensity of affect, unsupported by any representation, grows ever more violent as the mirror only reflects itself. 'The other that I am cannot appear' (p. 275). Thus this empty space evokes the space of the Other, the unconscious. The loss of the mother or mourning and the negation of death might account for the agony of affect, but Green gives precedence to negative hallucination. And negative hallucination differs from these forms of loss because it is not 'pure' absence but, all the worse for this, a *'hallucination of absence'* (p. 275). It is because the image is overlaid with this absence that the self seeks so desperately, beyond, behind, the mirror, and affect wells up because the self cannot reunite the two parts of itself, self and image, internal self and projected self. Green points to the centrality of Freud's understanding of the real, in which the self can distinguish between the compensatory hallucination of an object and its real absence. But negative hallucination seizes the power of representation and represents not a compensatory hallucinatory object but *lack*, the self as pure lack without compensation. Where it forces an image upon the mirror's surface, this confirms lack, because it can only logically figure the unrecognizable Other, the return of the repressed, or else a simulacrum of the subject which is no more than a shadowy half, a persecutory double from hell, a split representation of exactly the negative self it dreads, a representation of the not-self which takes the place of the Ego.

How does this anguish have epistemic possibility and what is the way back from it? One answer is that there is no way back: we live with the Furies (p. 287). On the other hand, Green quotes Goya: 'The sleep of reason engenders monsters' (p. 289). There *is* a way back from the horrors of negative hallucination. The explanation depends partly on a dynamic model of the psyche as circuit in which affect drives a series of constantly modified relations between different orders of the self. This is a direct rebuke to Lacan, and depends upon a heterogeneous organization of psychic material and a redistribution of psychoanalytical categories which I shall discuss at a later stage. What matters now are the principles which operate in the transformation of negative hallucination.

Affect is the pivot of a dynamic system of mediation which depends on the elements of detour and conflict – mediation conceived as means and obstacle, middle term and blockage. The structural principles of alternating system and uncoupling of polarities underlie mediation and, indeed, bring it into being, as in the early example of the mirror stage, which depended on the alternation of pleasure/pain and on the uncoupling of body/self. Affect itself is an ambiguous, alternating force. It moves between the destruction of representation, opening up an abyss in consciousness by violently breaking the barrier of repression, and appropriating, thieving, representation. It belongs to a chain of discourse and breaks it: it alternates between being bound and unbound, attached to signification and rupturing it. It is essentially an energy of the 'between' (p. 301), as Freud pointed out. Thus it has the role of conjoining and disjoining, making and unmaking. Its 'pulsion' or drive becomes 'the punctuation of the signifier', constitutive gaps which break and make, make and break relations, but through which alone meaning can come into being. The concealing and revealing, exposing and masking process which belongs to affect is structurally tied to the possibility of meaning.

Negative hallucination is centrally important in this structure. For it is not wholly a univocally negative state, conjuring loss, depletion and absence. Because it is not the absence of representation but the *'representation of the absence of representation'* (p. 302); it cannot constitute the *end* of representation. Paradoxically, it offers more potential for representation than representation itself. One reason for this is that the subject, who is by definition absent, is forced into a distance from hallucination, which can become the space of interrogation. As in the first mirror stage, the psychic void of affect, speaking through the body, can be captured and conceptualized by the self. A more fundamental reason is that negative hallucination and the compensatory hallucinatory transformations ('realization') of desire are reverse and obverse to one another, recto and verso of the same condition, each open to inspection by the reality principle (pp. 285–6). The alternating current of anguish and desire creates the possibility of movement. Negation turns on its axis and creates the conditions of change. The erased subject becomes an object to itself, an object which causes desire, and desire lives with possibility and lives *on* it, conjuring the images which fuel further desire. The Id kidnaps mental life and yet is the condition of its existence. Negative hallucination is at once blockage and the medium of knowledge, barrier and opening, detour and conflict. Affect is not left to Kristeva's void. Affect is a *discours vivant* because the drives create and are themselves the principle of alternation which brings about conflict and mediation.

Green extrapolated a social model from his psychic model of mediation, to which I will return briefly in the last section of this chapter. But first, how would these models of knowledge, drawn from the mirror stages, work in a poetics of epistemic affect? As I have said, we should be thinking of the rebus and its capacity for suturing disparate languages or dialects from different orders of the self as 'representant' and hybrid symbol/affects. We should be thinking not only of the prosody of the body – the grimace, the shudder, and their somatic inscriptions in language – but also of the prosody of the gap, the blank space, articulation through the pause, the moment of void. More important, we should be thinking less of the representation of these elements in the text in terms of substitution of symbol for originary affect; thinking more *of the reproduction of the conditions of affective life within the text itself*. If affect is untranslatable, and cannot be *in* language, cannot have a content, we might seek for devious evidences of its inscription and consider the way it cheats itself into language or inhibits symbol-making, but in the last analysis the idea of substitution has to be abandoned and replaced by a dynamic understanding of the text as generating new affect patterns and thought structures.

Triumph of an empty space

One might think of the text as a space for the creation of the conditions of 'epistemophilia', (Klein's term), a longing to know and discover, a primal curiosity which is both a drive and a mental experience, where learning is indivisible from the passions. Formal devices and linguistic strategies provide the incitement to learn, the need to interrogate. If the text reproduces the conditions of affective life, this will come into being neither through the inhibition of symbol (as in Kristeva) nor through the new representation spurred into being by the punctuation of the signifier achieved by the Id and its unnamable energies (as in Green) but through a process by which we witness different moments of language-making coming into being through constitutive gaps. A struggle between the inhibition of symbol and realized signification is a conflictual condition which reproduces the intense struggle occurring in the swing between paranoid-schizoid and depressive positions, between fragmentation and consolidation. Thus the text would not be creating an originary affect either through semiotic traces or rebus-like representants. It would be generating new, unique affect patterns through its struggle for form, which would not be recognized through their residues or absences but as dynamic shifters of meaning.

These conditions of arousal, of course, become a source of anxiety, the broken middle, because wanting to know, epistemophilia, *is* an anxious state. For Bion, the crucial moment of thinking occurs through negation at charged affective moments, the gap between a wish and fulfillment. An infant 'matches' its pre-conception of breast with an achieved concept of the breast when that expectation is met with satisfaction, and thus brings together thoughts and thinking in a way which makes affect instrumental in achieved thought. More testing, and essential for the life of thought, is the gap between wish and experience when the 'no-breast' has to be formulated. For this negative realization can be recognized and 'thought' as an abstraction, a not-thing, which enables the toleration of lack and frustration (and thus the perpetuation of thought) (Bion, *Second Thoughts*, pp. 111–12). And here anxiety is crucial. The failure to tolerate anxiety results in a parallel failure to match and abstract, and can issue in the disaster which formulates the no-breast as a *thing*, a bad object to be expelled and ejected. All thought can take on the quality of a thing of which the psyche rids itself. Here Bion establishes the primal moment of thought in the uncoupling of affect and representation, at the same time establishing that thinking is mediated by frustration. Bion, perhaps, is more interested in abstraction than Green, but his understanding of thought is bound up with affect in a way that Lacan's is not.

One might do worse than think of a text as a space for the arousal of frustration (*reproducing*, that is, affect and its mediation as well as being formed by them), remembering that Bion thought of texts as requests for knowledge. The reader, in turn, is required to mediate that mediation. The reproduction of frustration is surely at work in *Infant Sorrow*. Bodily spasm – 'leapt', 'Struggling', 'Striving' – and grimace – 'sulk' – soma and sign interlinked as the body 'speaks' to the infant consciousness, physical pain and desperation inscribed in the reading process, all mark Blake's poem. But there are also frustrating causal gaps in the poem. There is a strange causal gap as the weeping father and not the mother seems to precipitate the baby's birth, mourning before the event as well as after it. And, 'struggling in my father's hands', why does the father dominate the child's nurture, imprisoning the infant like Tom Thumb in the palms of two hands and cutting it off from the maternal body? There is the same gap between helplessness and fiend, or the Id energies which, sustained in the womb-like-breast-like cloud, seem to be birthed/fed by the child itself? And there is the enigmatic relation between cloud and breast. Is the breast a thing? As the child, choosing inertia, sulks against an inexpressive, unyielding body, what is the status of the infant's 'thought'? Is there only 'one' breast which cannot enable a move to thought? The death of the infant's epistemophilia through trauma is the birth of the reader's. These questions lead to speculation which moves out into culture and history, not back into the text.

These observations, to be valid, should work for other art forms than print culture. What kind of request for knowledge lives in the evanescent simulacra of cinematic images? How does affect precipitate a 'wanting to know'? How is affect recognized and aroused in cinema? Gilles Deleuze thinks of film as an art that consumes itself in the moment of the image, rather than being consumed, and which thus sidesteps the consumer society (*Cinema 1 / and Cinema 2*). The flash of an explosion (hinting at post-atomic art) is the model of film's mode of being – which is why the type of cinema is the gunfight, punning on the camera shot and the pistol shot, consuming itself in its own smoke. Film and psychoanalytic language also share some punning homonyms – projection, screen – which I shall make use of.

Unforgiven: A labouring figure by a single tree in silhouette during the credits, elegiac melody. William Munny is burying the wife who reformed him. (A single, bare tree will appear again much later when Will discovers that his 'brother' figure, Ned, has been flogged to death, credited with a killing Will committed.)

Sound and fury, screams, gunshots. In the brothel at Big Whiskey, Delilah's face has been slashed. Cut and cut again in a succession of confused movement and body parts; the technique of cutting in this episode reproduces the slashes made on the woman's body. She has laughed at the small penis of one of the customers.

We elide Sheriff Little Bill's rough justice, the arrangement for the brothel keeper to be paid in ponies for his damaged goods (pony/penis, is this an incomplete symbol, an affect/representant for the primitive exchange value at work in this legal 'system'?), the whores' plan, because the men 'ride us like horses' and the compensation is irrelevant to the crime, for the offer of a reward for the killing of the slasher. But a persistently repeated filming pattern, deliberately rather obvious, should be noticed. Power relationships are visually rendered through confrontations in which one person is shot from above, another from below, so that the camera's gaze can organize conflict in terms of those figures it can look down upon and those it can look up to, enlarge or reduce, see against the sky or against the ground. The ultimate shot from above, of course, where gun and camera converge, is the shooting of the enemy cowboy in the shithouse by the Kid – his first killing, contrary to his boasts. The Kid. Will's 'son'/apprentice, who has instigated Will's mission to avenge Delilah, for money.

Frames in the frame. Chiaroscuro faces in household door and window frames, or penned by palings into the filth of a hog pound. Will is either abject, on the ground, or to the side of one of these domestic frames, occupying space at the margins, as if the frame imprisons, or as if he does not quite belong there. (His 'brother', Ned, will be flogged against prison bars.)

The silhouette, lyrical, distant, of two men on horses, rhythmically in unison against a liquid orange sunset sky, the liquid elegiac melody welling up over the scene. A rare shot where the men on horses are visually on a level, are equals. Love between men. Ned, a black man domesticated with a native American wife, has consented to join Will, to break out of the household frame, and they are journeying to kill, to claim the reward. But, as the screen holds the shot, this *is* a screen. Will has used the need for money as a screen to persuade Ned to return to the old masculine fellowship, and the male bonding itself is a screen for – what?

A repetition of the failure to shoot in a Western could be logically followed by a blank screen, for the failure to shoot implicitly holds up the shooting of the film as the narrative of aim and target comes to a halt. In *Unforgiven* the failure to shoot occurs three times, almost as if handed on from person to person, like the symptom of a trauma or its feared repetition. What traumatic moment precipitates these refusals to shoot, evasive actions which almost terminate the movie? Let us look at these episodes. Most dramatically, at the film's climax, Ned, companion of Will Munny, cannot bring himself to shoot Delilah's attacker, who is cornered in a ravine. Will takes over the killing – 'got him in the gut' – and watches from above in a silence which is punctuated by the astonished victim's periodic cries: 'He's shot me, boys'. All this is watched by the half-blind Kid, who has anxiously incited them to shoot.

This scene between two men and a voyeur apprentice is pre-figured in Big Whiskey, in the sheriff's leaky house, which is also a gaol. To mark the relationship, the triangulated scene between three men in the gaol cuts several times to the stages by which the three avenging cowboys approach the town. Guns are forbidden in the town. The sheriff, Little Bill, has gaoled English Bob, an adventurer and con man, after first viciously kicking him in the street, forcing him to crawl along the ground. As rain drips into the room and Bob is almost unconscious behind the gaol bars, another powerplay develops. Little Bill taunts the bespectacled sycophant journalist, another blind son-figure who is rapidly adopting him as father, with the untruthful mediations of print journalism. He deconstructs a romantic story of English Bob's heroic honour, persistently reading the 'Duke of Death' as the 'Duck', and is nervously corrected by the writer. He, Little Bill, was there. He can even measure the size of the killed man's dick. The gun blew up in the guy's hands. English Bob ignominiously shot him through the liver (the lower body – 'Got him in the gut'). Then he teases the terrified journalist with a gun: shoot me; let English Bob, behind the bars, shoot me; give him the gun. The journalist can't shoot. Bob can't shoot. Later, Will himself can't shoot. Little Bill extracts his gun from him, arrives in the Big Whiskey saloon, and kicks him almost to death, repeating his assault on Bob. Will crawls out of the saloon, as Bob crawled in the street and as his victim is later to crawl in the ravine, chained to the lower body. And later, in the third episode, the Kid can't shoot. He can't see to hit the pursuing friends of the man he has shot in the gut and genitals, and he abandons guns after the trauma of his first shooting, by the tree where Ned's death is disclosed. (When the companions first come upon him in his frenzy of shooting, on the way to kill, he is seen as from Ned's horse, from above, his face appearing grotesquely out of Ned's knee, as if being birthed.)

Will, Bill, Bob, Ned, Kid, the Duke, the Duck, the journalist, the gun, the pen, the dick, the phallus. It is tempting to read this as if the phallus or its substitutes (pony/penis) passes from one to the other of these male figures or their substitutes in a perpetual struggle to make the phallus and the law converge; to read the failure to shoot as the moment of castration. But isn't this rather obvious? As the master/slave strategies of shooting from below and above are obvious? Another blind, another screen? The stammer of the film around guns, the blank spaces which the failure to shoot opens up might become clearer by turning to one last gun scene.

Faces of the women outraged by the 'compensation' of the ponies cut to another woman, a framed photograph of Will's wife, a film within a film. Suddenly there is a frenzy of gunfire. Will is practising his shooting. His target is a tin, perhaps a tea caddy, a container with an image of a woman on it. (And just after this he looks out of the window to the bare tree and the grave.) Bullets, projected missiles, aimed at the image of a woman.

Could we see this as projection of another kind? Split-off parts of himself, the parts he hates, objects directed towards the container, imaging the dead woman/wife/mother who can no longer deal with those parts and return them in a way they can be assimilated? If so, what kind of request for knowledge is this film making? Is it trying to find an alternative to an insistent pattern of wounding women and being wounded back? Is the failure to shoot the product of a nameless terror of the wounded woman?

Another scene: After Will's devastating illness (following his crawling out of the saloon) and once Ned has nursed him to virtual health, picking the dirt from his scars, Will and Delilah meet. Will has met snake eyes, the angel of death and 'Claudia's face all covered with worms' in his delirium. (Green's persecutory repressed objects?) When recovered, he meets a woman with a scarred face, another double, washing his face: 'I must look like you'; 'you've got to be the one those cowboys cut up'. The landscape is white, virginal. Fencing protrudes obliquely like a cross. The nearest thing to blanking out a screen is to shoot a snow-covered land-scape, a punning film of snow – the blanched, blank mirror of negative hallucination? This man does not drink, won't buy sex ('just use your hand?' asks Ned), and won't have it from Delilah. Will's affective impasse seems to drain him. And yet something happens. Will does not remain with an alienated asceticism and Delilah does not remain as a lyrical, idealized figure. It is through the double iconography of the scars that the film moves, almost literally, to a new ground. It moves from the image of emptiness, the wound (Green's hallucination of absence?), to the image of the scar. They sit. The camera aligns them, not quite on the level but in the same frame. She hands him his hat, she takes off her bonnet. She is offended at first when Will says he looks like her. But what they do is to exchange scars, not wounds. A scar is a healed wound, writing on the body. 'It's just we both got scars', Will says. Figure of mutilation, by castration or forced penetration, the scar becomes one of the graphics of suffering in body and mind, a memorial to violence. Yet it is also a mark with a history, a sign, a kind of language, not a substitution so much as a mark that can be recognized and interpreted, and thus used to mediate experience. Those hats, held, receptacles for the body (the upper body), offer, perhaps, a new kind of relationship to language, within and between subjects. Language, not as missile but as container, is the poss-ibility opened out. Is this new language possible, between men and men, men and women?

But the repetition compulsions of the dominant culture overtake the lyrical reveries of the snow scene. Will goes off to kill Delilah's assailant. And when Ned is unjustly killed he moves to the classic carnage of the Western's shoot-out. The sheriff's language wins out. His is a primitive language in which words are things – ponies, ducks, dicks, guns, shit. His is the language which expels, like hostile objects, what could become mediating sign or symbol. Ned's corpse, the material body, is displayed with obscene literalness as an indicator of the justice which meets the criminal in Big Whiskey. Parts of Bill's own body, the feet, become weapons. His leaky house, a rebus-like image, is an indicator of his failure to create structures to contain and nurture. It is, indeed, a kind of dream-work inversion: permeable, it is a negative form of his *impermeability*. Unable to create that permeable barrier between conscious and unconscious – which for Green makes the mobility that is a prerequisite for intrasystemic transformation, and which for Bion makes thought possible – he lives in a world where all affect is violent, enraged, furiously destructive. The film ends in paranoia: I'll kill everyone, Will says, if you try to shoot. American Will and Bill, black Ned, English Bob, French Canadian (?) Bouchon (the journalist), Native Americans, all scatter and disperse, through death or alienation. Ned's wife has successfully put the evil eye, the glance as missile, on Will – and on Ned. This film was made at a time (1992) not only of transformations in expectations of women through feminism but also of transformed perceptions of masculinity. Added to this cultural subsidence was the realization that English as America's prime language was being challenged, overtaken by Spanish. The question of the film: Is it possible to find a new language which will link obdurate cultural and gender variation? A question which causes a stammer in a typically American idiom, the Western's gunfire.[9]

Because it can register images of the body, cinema can get close to the representation of affect whereas language cannot. However, affect as thing-in-itself, as immediate experience, hides even from the visual image. It is the appearance of constitutive gaps in a medium other than language, gaps which enable the artwork to recreate the conditions for the arousal of affect, and that discovery of knowledge which is bound up with it, that I wish to foreground – and also the paradox that spaces bring knowing into being. Green insists on the uncoupling of affect and thought, the drives and intellect, '*la force et le sens*' in order to reunite them as complementary polarities. Pleasure/pain, body/self, negative hallucination/desire are like couplings which are severed to create movement. Because affect precipitates mental life in representation, it belongs to the symbolic; but because mental life is a ground of intellectual struggle, it is economic, it belongs to the order of the drives. Thus, he claims, to a purely economic structure he has returned the power of change and transformation through intellect, and to the abstract life of mental concepts in the symbolic he has returned the power of representation, fed by the living energy of the bodily drives and fused with thought and language. This fundamental redistribution has its exemplary moment in the negative hallucination, a moment of mobility in which psychic emptiness can be renamed, a moment of knowledge.

A social reading of emotion is implicit in the explorations I have undertaken. The concluding parts of this chapter outline some areas for future work.

A social nexus for affect/knowledge

Green ends *Le Discours vivant* by providing his redistributive structure of affect with an explicitly social model in which psychic and social change are interdependent. This depends on a circuit of four orders of experience, where external and inner life, the symbolic order and the drives are in a relation of constant interchange and displacement (pp. 1296–7). The four orders of experience, 'la conjoncture', 'l'événement', 'l'objet', 'la structure', are given meaning by collision or convergence in which any two cause a third to become manifest – it becomes their effect: that third will become part of a new configuration which is the condition of another order of visibility, and so on, in a series of perpetually self-modifying combinations. Each of the orders of experience changes places in this structure, all cause and effect, form and content. (This bears a relationship to Hegelian mediation, the trying out of positions from each of a number of positions.)

The four interacting psychic categories constitute a taxonomy whose classifications, though distinct, contain the mixed forms and heterogeneous material beloved of Green: 'la conjoncture' is a constellation of forces and conditions around the subject that are *not in its control* – biological, social and cultural conditions, for instance – but which constitute its specificity. Class or race, being born with spina bifida, or being involved in a car accident would all belong to 'La conjoncture'. 'L'événement' is the primal experience – seduction, castration, the primal scene – which issues in fantasy and which belongs to inner, psychic life. 'L'objet' is a plurality of constructions of the external object by the experiencing subject – the breast, desire, for instance – which may be *either* in the outside world *or* within consciousness, participating in psychic and social worlds. Finally, 'La structure' are those deep, formative structures, such as the Oedipal moment, which are only visible through their effects. The constellation of conditions round the subject (la conjoncture), for instance, is the condition of the revelation of deep psychic structures (la structure), but these cannot become visible without a convergence of trauma (événement) and an externality (l'objet), either constructed by the subject in fantasy or actuality, or perhaps partaking both of the real and the phantasmatic. By the same token, the collision of trauma and deep psychic structures are the condition of the manifestation of the object. Affect as force and as subjective experience, born of the vectors of the drive, energizes the system, existing at the point of contradiction and collision. It is the agent of change. Like the Id's work in individual consciousness, which brings different orders of the self into relation with one another, affect brings different psychic and social orders together in the larger cultural field, the symbolic order and the drives.[10]

Affect, the energy which has to be named and renamed, is for Green a guarantee of psychic and social experience. Traversing the space of the middle, occupying transitional moments, there are obvious parallels between Green's model of the mobility of affect and Hegelian mediation, particularly if one reads this mediation as a broken middle. However, I have deliberately avoided bringing Hegelian mediation and Green's model of affect into a single, 'unified' theory of the aesthetic, mapping them on to one another. Like Green, I prefer to leave these discourses, drawn from phenomenology and psychoanalysis, roughly sutured, to exhibit the richness of possibility promised by each. To 'reconcile' these discourses would be to close the agonistic 'broken middle' between conscious and unconscious. Obviously, they share some characteristics. Both refuse subject-centred theories of experience (though they are not, of course, without an account of the subject); both place value on the *play* of experience, openness; both have at their centre the creation of new relationships, the transformation of experience, new categories; both are cognitive theories. Both lead to an account of the artwork as *in-between*. They stress the melancholic moment of scattering, of unassimilated material, not the reconciled symbol of successful mourning. They allow the artwork to be theorized as travail, labour, a form of work which struggles to make something of its own material, swinging *between* dispersal and symbol formation. Green's sutured languages are less integrated than Hegel's linguistic categories: Hegel's generalized 'I' enables communication despite inability to express unique, unutterable feeling and sensation. (Though one could imagine the affective gap as a supplement to the linguistic lack in Hegel's system.) Neither Green nor Hegel favours the symbol formation of the depressive position alone, where objects with independent meaning can be detached from the agglomerated material churned by the drives. Both allow us to see the artwork as swinging between the fearful scattering of the paranoid-schizoid position and the ordering of the depressive position rather than as a manifestation of achieved order, to see the artwork as a *representation* of mediation as well as being structured by the dialectic of thought and emotion.

Of course, there have been attempts to relate the models of psycho-analysis and phenomenology. Paul Ricoeur, roughly contemporary with Green, explored the teleology in the archaeology of Freud, and the archaeology in the teleology of Hegel, in *Freud and Philosophy* (1965). His aim was to problematize Freud by moving from the timelessness of the unconscious to the temporality of Hegelian self-consciousness, with its possibilities of ethical and social growth. Though I do not fully agree with his analysis of Freud and Hegel, his earlier exploration of the social possibilities of emotion in *Fallible Man* (1965) leads us towards the social reading of cognitive affect.

I now turn to a cluster of work related to Ricoeur's project and argue that, despite its shortcomings, this body of work points us to the possibility of connecting a social reading of emotion with the transformation of categories, that is, to an account of change. But first, it is important to affirm that the texts I have chosen are to be seen in the context of a growing body of work in a number of disciplines – from moral philosophy to cognitive psychology to semiotics – which grounds the possibility of rationality and rational social experience in the emotions. I mention those works from which I have learned in an appendix to this chapter, though the list is by no means exhaustive.

For a social reading of cognitive affect the obvious direction to go is towards those Marxist theories which attempt to think through emotion and ideology. But the problem with this body of theory is the familiar one of its inability to think through change, as it seals experience in prede-termined, fixed structures. Raymond Williams's inventive 'structure of feeling', a more flexible understanding of the power of ideology, describes historically specific ideological moods which can change and be changed by cultural experience; but Williams simply accepts that this can occur, and that ideological shifts come about through *non-rational* means.[11] Since I am aiming to bring feeling within the province of the rational, this assumption is counterproductive. Similarly, Fredric Jameson's 'political unconscious', a non-rational, culturally shared return of the repressed which is manifest in aesthetic experience makes no room for the delib-erative mobilization of cultural critique, just as the inverse of his theory of emotional atrophy, 'the death of affect', in post-modern culture severs the links between thought and emotion.[12] Rom Harré's social constructivist work, mapping the semantic range and context of emotion words to discover the historical particularity of sign clusters, takes us some way, but without suggesting a dynamic of the sign.[13]

Two attempts, by Silvan Tomkins and Paul Ricoeur to think through the psychic and social worlds by bringing the category of feeling into play – written from the extremes of theology (or 'philosophical anthropology') and post-structuralist thought – are instructive in their limitations. Ricoeur's attempt to use Marxist structures in a post-Marxist way in *Fallible Man*, combining Kant and Husserl, begins with the 'reciprocal genesis of feeling and knowing' (p. 83). While knowing is founded on the cleavage of subject and object and the objectification of this detachment of knower from known, feeling at once confirms this dualism and restores the disconnection of subject and object. It becomes a counterpart to it: in the double sense that feeling is able to understand the conflictual nature of subject and object and yet is also able to confirm the *intentionality* and meaningfulness of the movement *towards* an object. Feelings have an 'openness to being' (p. 105) which may be formless and atmospheric but which creates that transitional 'between two' that gives self an idea of 'belonging to a community or to an idea' (p. 107).

From here Ricoeur goes on to develop a cultural order of interpersonal relations by revising the classic Marxist categories of property – institutional power (political and economic) – and the constitution of the subject, in terms of 'having', 'power' and 'worth' (p. 113). These, he insists, are essential to the humanly made work of societies, but they *can* be non-pathological and non-passional, at least in conception. (The passional is the destructive aspect of affect, such as Nazism.) Indeed, his humanism of the de-centred subject argues, a non-pathological conception of possession, power and the need for recognition enables us to make a critique of their degraded forms or 'fallible' manifestations in society. The reciprocity of feeling and thinking becomes merely abstract unless it is mediated through new relations with things and people. This reciprocity becomes concrete in, and through having, power and worth. Possession is paradoxically the guarantee of the 'otherness' of the 'mine' that breaches the 'I's wholeness and *confirms* the differentiation of I and you, which is actually constitutive of social relations. Similarly, power – economic, technological and biotechnological domination and power – over other human beings, in its non-violent form, releases the creative possibility for a multitude of interpersonal relations. Esteem, the recognition of worth, is the ultimate recognition of the subject's humanity. It is a way of being recognized in and through an objectivity (p. 123) which finds its correlative affective confirmation. Ricoeur's model of change is theological and therefore ontologically fragile. But even if one were to remove the theological framework it is hard to see how this affective knowing contains the possibility of change within itself.

Aware of the void in accounts of emotion in contemporary theory, Eve Kosofsky Sedgwick and Adam Frank have recently edited as *Shame and its Sisters* selections from the work of Silvan Tomkins's four-volume work of psychology, *Affect, Imagery, Consciousness* (1962–92). For Sedgwick/

Frank the glory of Tomkins's ideas is his theory of the specificity of the emotions (which releases us from the notion that emotion is 'merely' culturally constructed) combined with a freedom from the limiting notion of a 'core' self. Thus he supplies a post-modern theory of the emotions. The components of Tomkins's repertoire of affects – Interest–Excitement, Enjoyment–Joy, Surprise–Startle, Distress–Anguish, Shame–Humiliation, Contempt–Disgust, Anger and Fear–Terror – can be used in almost any combination and gradation and attached to almost any object or idea. According to Sedgwick/Frank, Tomkins escapes the digital model to which modern theory – particularly that of Lacan, with its founding binary structure – is prey. Tomkins does use an on/off, contrastive model of stimulus response where the drives are concerned, but he 'layers' it with a 'graduated or multiply differentiated' analogue representation of developmental emotion (p. 8). This means that Tomkins is hostile to the Freudian unconscious and to repression (which he calls 'sublimation' (pp. 60–1)), for his cognitive, developmental theory relies on the capacity of memory to learn itself. It is anticipatory and 'posticipatory' (p. 53), looking forwards and backwards, so that original affect becomes remembered affect and remembered affect can evoke new affect. Thus he requires memory, he thinks, and not the amnesia of the unconscious to provide this associative process.

The valuable part of Tomkins's theory (akin to that of Green) is his account of the versatility of emotion. Affect is able to invest any aspect of existence with joy or sorrow, and so it is linked by 'thinking' to objects. More insatiable and yet more casual than the drives (p. 53), to which we will come later, its versatility offers infinite ways of 'knowing' (p. 53) something.

> There is a real question whether anyone may fully grasp the nature of any object when that object has not been perceived, wished for, missed and thought about in love and hate, in excitement and apathy, in distress and joy. That is as true of our relationship with nature, as with artifacts created by man, as with other human beings and collectivities which he both inherits and transforms. (Sedgwick Frank, *Shame and its Sisters*, p. 55).

As well as doing without the unconscious, Tomkins's system refuses anything but purely biological status to the drives (such as hunger, sexual desire) and disengages them absolutely from affect. This disengagement enables him to affirm that whereas the drives operate on a feedback system of circuiting stimulus/satisfaction (the digital mode), the affects operate on a self-rewarding, self-punishing experience possessed of an independent variability which makes affect infinitely more complex (the graduated mode). There is a freedom of combination between affect and other components of the system, which allows of almost limitless possibility. At every point the freedom of affect is constrasted with the constraints of the drives. The drive system is constrained by time, is site specific and limited to particular biological needs. Affect, on the other hand, can be shifted, changed, invested in a variety of objects because it is more general in its operation and can be controlled in its intensity and duration, even if it is aroused by factors it cannot control. The contingency of affect – we cannot stop pain or generate pleasure at will – nevertheless allows degrees of freedom as we learn to manipulate, modulate, combine, suppress, amplify and thereby control it.

This technology of the feelings, into which self-punishing shame is smuggled as a quasi social experience which regulates affective behaviour almost mechanistically, is occasionally interspersed with valuable insights about passional experience. It completely misunderstands Freud, for whom affect *is* conscious: it is precisely consciously known anxiety without apparent cause that is the generative moment of Freud's thinking on repression. The literalness of the drives for Tomkins, which emerges from another naïve reading of Freud, is also a conceptual loss. 'Communion' (p. 34) rather than misguided accounts of orality arising from the 'hunger drive', is, says Tomkins, a preferable way to consider biological hunger and non-biological affect. But in dispensing with the mouth and the breast as vital physical markers which become sites of symbolic representation, Tomkins disposes of a vital element – the mouth, the breast – which is the source of symbolic meaning. The sacrifice of repression is a similar impoverishment. For repression enables the processes of condensation, displacement and inversion to take place – those formative structures which perhaps enable thought to occur by sporting with categories or by providing containers for meaning. The connection of affect and language is, we have seen, puzzling enough in psychoanalytic theory. Tomkins abolishes it altogether, while free floating emotion, in a perpetually volatile state, contains no principles of change within itself and no social and psychic nexus except a fitful changefulness.

Language, myth, and the matrix of social and cognitive emotion

It seems we are far from a dialectic in which social and psychic, affect and knowledge, can interact. But three elements have emerged: first, the constitutive blankness from which the passion for knowledge arises: for convenience, we can name this epistemophilia. The passion for knowledge belongs both to the desiring subject and to the world it wants to know, for knowing arises from the convergence of a consciousness and its objects. Second, Ricoeur's insight that emotion re-reads, as it were, the gap between subject and object, both acknowledging and assuaging the lesion between self and world by making the relation mobile and dynamic. Third, the importance of language to affect, and affect to language, is another matrix of the social and cognitive emotion, for language belongs to self and culture. This was apparent in Bion's understanding of language formation. Above all, in language formation is disclosed the moment of concept-making and the construction of new categories, the core of knowledge. In this last part of my discussion, I shall consider language formation as an exemplary case of the passion for knowledge and bring together language and myth, which is, after all, a culturally made narrative language. To do this I shall put the work of Vygotsky in *Thought and Language* (published in Russian in 1934), a reciprocal account of speech derived from the speech community – moving 'from the social to the individual' – beside Bion's account of myth as a group's request for knowledge.

It is customary at the point I have reached to turn to another between-the-wars Russian, Volosinov and his *Marxism and the Philosophy of Language*, and to theorize social language-making through the ideological struggle for the sign. In fact, the shared but very different use of a famous Dostoevsky episode dramatizes the unlikeness of the two theorists and indicates what Vygotsky contributes to this argument.

Vygotsky and Volosinov use the same passage from Dostoevsky's *The Diary of a Writer* (1873) in which a group of drunks construct a conversation entirely out of one 'unprintable word' (Volosinov, *Marxism*, p. 241), for rather different purposes. For Volosinov the repetition of the same word by six different people testifies to the almost infinite inflections of the sign and its virtuosity, a metonymic chain which enables the same word to mean quite different things in a series of different ideological positions, to be a different kind of bridge every time it is used (p. 86). For Vygotsky the passage testifies to the shared apperception of a speech community which implicitly depends on orality and presence to the extent that *abbreviation* is possible, sometimes to an extraordinary degree (*Thought and Language*, p. 235). Inner speech, the assimilated, interiorized language of the speech community, is also constructed from heavily abbreviated forms. It is conducted as monologue, and does not take the dialogue form of oral speech, for the shared apperception is that of the self. It is a form of draft, an economical mode of expression which can afford to abandon subjects and deal only in predicates. If this seems unpromisingly undialogic, the importance of Vygotsky is that he did conceptualize an interior language-maker in dynamic relation with a speech community, whereas Volosinov, in his anxiety to eradicate an expressive account of language created by thought and emotion issuing from consciousness to form, from the inside out, annihilated interiority altogether. For consciousness he substitutes a chain of ideological creativity which has its being in language independent of individuals, the culturally made two-sided sign. This is always pointing to the other and depends on the other, and then, in turn, on another other, for its existence. The sign is corroborated and disputed in the arena of social interactions constructed from language. Volosinov appears to think of consciousness as an entity whose being and borders can be defined only by the boundary of the biological body and its interface with the world of signs. Individual consciousness and agency mean so little to him that the excess of idealism is matched by another excess which abolishes the subject except as a construction of language, a point of calibration between one signifying chain and another.

Valuable as Volosinov is he drains the struggle for the sign of affect. Vygotsky does not, but the fully affective element of language-making for him is concealed in an earlier book, written in a different political climate and when Freud was acceptable in the Soviet Union, *The Psychology of Art* (completed in 1925; published 1965). At the end of *Thought and Language*, Vygotsky fleetingly speculates that verbal thought is driven by affective-volitional motivations. He reaches back to the speculation in the earlier book, where he had also stated that emotion is behind the need to think. In the following exposition of the later theory of language, it is necessary to put the unsaid of affect back into his framework. Vygotsky put enormous emphasis on the unpromising phenomenon of inner speech. It has been misunderstood both by his Russian detractors, who thought of it as a form of 'subjectivism', and by western liberals, for whom it was a treasured form of inner creativity. But it is not easy to understand the individual's slow discovery of the functional use of signs unless one restores to inner speech the mediation of emotion. In the earlier, heavily Freudian, work a text embodies a principle of 'affective contradiction' (*Psychology of Art*, p. 139). It is organized round opposing feelings and thus opposing logics, reworked as in the structure of a dream. Vygotsky argues strongly against Tolstoy's 'contamination' theory of emotion in art (he is rather less certain of this later) and thinks of art as the social technique of emotion, a way of negotiating violence. He reverses the customary Marxist formulations into paradoxes. Emotion is always social. The social exists where there is only one person (p. 246) (presumably because one cannot *think* a person without a sociality): therefore the antithesis between the private and public sphere is a false one; emotion only becomes personal when every one of us experiences it through the culturally made aesthetic work. Vygotsky literally reverses the expressive model without sacrificing interiority by working backwards, from social outside to consciousness.

Inner speech is at the interface of consciousness and world, which certainly mediate one another, and one of its functions is to enable the individual to make language its own and to use it to think with. But the process is more subtle than this. Throughout *Thought and Language*, Vygotsky's anti-paradigm of language acquisition is Jean Piaget, whose model of the child's socialization is, he thinks, a coercive one. The child has to be forced out of its self-enclosed individualism or even solipsism (for Piaget individual children don't even understand one another) into the 'reality' of adult speech and language, a model of development from inside out, individual to social. Vygotsky's model, as we have seen, is precisely the opposite. The communicative model is an interactive one, from social to individual, as the child reaches out to the signs it shares with the adult world and attempts to use them in collaboration with adults. Because child and adult share a world of signs, this is an interactive and social world from the beginning. As the sign is impossible without the concept, thought and words converge, language is born, when a qualitative leap to the recognition of concepts is achieved, and the child learns the mediation of language and its own agency simultaneously.

Vygotsky's view of the indivisibility of sign and concept and the constitutive nature of the sign/concept in language is as rigorous as that of any proponent of the symbolic order. But he argues this so insistently because thought *is* divisible from words *except* at the moment when sign and concept converge as language. They are two different systems, and the conjunction of thought and language is learned with immense laboriousness and continual experiment with classification. The child learns to prise apart words and things, moving from the sorting of 'psychic amalgams' and 'complexes' (p. 117), where things are brought together metonymically under systematic orders of similarity and difference, to the connection of things by contingent bonds of relationship of any sort, such as shape or colour, to generalized representations, and finally to the detachment of concepts and their alliance with signs. Only then is it possible to generalize the generalizations of an earlier level. If we retrieve the affective element from the earlier book, then the child's struggle with thought and language is the struggle with the 'affective contradiction' of opposing logics before it discovers what Bion would term 'thinking' to which it fits 'thoughts'. For Vygotsky there is always a crucial gap, a gap of suffering (in the strict sense of being acted upon) and labour, before the inimical relation of thought to language is overcome and concepts are interiorized. This is another space of the 'in-between', the 'in-between' of thought to language, the 'in-between' of consciousness and speech community. Such constitutive gaps are surely what drive epistemophilia, and perhaps what are created by it. It may even be that we could think of those 'psychic amalgams' with which the child struggles on analogy with that prelanguage or not quite language which issues in the representant for Green and the unassimilated thing-word, for Bion, or 'Beta elements' those elements over which abstract signs triumph if language-making is achieved.

The detachment of concepts from aggregates of things is as crucial to inner speech as it is to the formation of language. Yet inner speech is not the internal aspect of external speech; it is an entirely different phenomenon. It is an autonomous structure, a protean, delicate form, privileging semantics over phonetics, sense over meaning, sentence over word, compounds and adhesions where the senses of individual words flow into one another and, above all, shaping sense through its relation to changes of context and producing multifaceted configurations of sense which register the uniqueness of new contexts. Inner speech thinks in pure meaning. Words die out as they generate thought. The opposite is the case with external speech, where thought is embodied in words. Inner speech is a 'dynamic, shifting, unstable thing, fluttering between word and thought' (p. 249). But inner speech has to be translated *back* into external speech for the subject to belong to language and to culture. Inner speech, interiorized from the speech community and 'owned' by consciousness, has to be returned to it. I would suggest, again borrowing from the earlier book, that inner speech remakes affect patterns from the speech community and inscribes them anew as it engages with the reciprocity of interiorizing and externalizing language. And it does seem, from Vygotsky's descriptions, that inner speech is affect-dominated, driven by the need to become other in a way that outer speech is not.

And thus is re-enacted the intense labour of reconnecting thought and language. Because thought does not have its counterpart in words, the realignments of language have to reorder in serial and successive form what inner speech has experienced as abbreviated compounds. 'A thought may be compared to a cloud shedding a shower of words' (p. 251). The lesion between word and thought, the systematic non-correspondence upon which Vygotsky builds the principles of language, is here invoked to suggest how individuals of necessity remake language for the social and cultural world which has given it to them in the first place. Vygotsky's is no romantic theory of the unrepresentability of the individual's thought, though he covertly allows the speaking subject the possibility of manoeuvre, which is not available in Volosinov's system. 'Manoeuvre' is exactly what goes on. Thought *is* representable, but it is the space between thought and word, the gap in which thought and language do not *fit*, which enables a process of translation for communication. This 'translation' can register the counterpart of thought in words, but because this is not exact the subject is forced into linguistic creativity, as it attempts to seek a unique equivalent for unique inner speech. 'Experience teaches us that thought does not express itself in words, but rather realises itself in them' (p. 251). Yet this attempt is organized round strict limits: the language of external speech is not only rule-bound but also culturally worked through the operation of the functional use of signs, just as the 'contexts' to which inner speech are responsive are simultaneously psychological and social.

Despite the limits set on language-making, Vygotsky goes some way to making the inalienable split between unique experience and the universals of language, on which Hegel founded his account of the 'I', a virtue driven by necessity. For this *is* a theory of language change. There will always be a residue of meaning inexpressible in the speech community, and this Vygotsky terms the 'subtext'. 'To overcome this problem, new paths from thought to word leading through new word meanings must be cut' (p. 251), like the cutting through of new roads from one valley to another. It is impossible to communicate inner speech: those who believe that a form of art might be created out of the notation of inner speech are mistaken; inner speech *negotiates* with what we might call outer speech and this is what creates the dynamic of language. Paradoxically, language change occurs because we cannot share inner speech. But the subject is driven to do so, impelled by the need to translate, impelled, and I layer the unsaid into his work here, by the emotion of 'towards', the emotion directed to the other. Perhaps in this process of unshared speech, a process of perpetual frustration, emotion is both solvent and structuring agent. And maybe the most innovative artworks are those which manage to translate the dialect of inner speech by making another, unique, dialect of outer speech.

The combination of a rather bleak instrumentalism with genuinely imaginative thought makes Vygotsky daunting reading. But the conceptual innovativeness of his work is apparent. In thinking through a speech community and its presuppositions, Vygotsky helps as perhaps no other theorist could because of the relative independence and autonomy that he attributes to inner speech in its ordering of external speech. However, though he returns us to the subject's agency, tied to speech community, more needs to be said about groups and their relation to the making of artwork.

Bion's interest in groups is promising ground. But his interest in re-defining the work of thought and the transformation it accomplishes in individual and group is as important. He insisted that forms of processing of psychic material must be claimed as knowledge. From his earliest work, knowledge is interpersonal, whether it is the infant labouring with concepts through relating to the breast, as we have seen in 'A theory of thinking', or the mother's reverie which acts as container for the infant's thoughts. He evolved a flow of new terms to describe this proces-sing – 'modelling', the hypothesis which restores concreteness to an abstract situation; 'provisional thinking', the experiment in naming which is the result of a hypothesis; knowledge as 'getting to know' (*Learning from Experience*, 1962) – and they are all the result of colla-borative acts between analyst and analysand. Later he began to work with a psychoanalytical notion of myth, bad theory according to the scientist, but essential as a mode of processing, working over and storing psychic material (*Elements of Psychoanalysis*, 1963).

In the post-humously published *Cogitations* (1992), he extends his notion of myth to the group, particularly in an undated piece, 'Tower of Babel: possibility of using a racial myth'. A myth, he says, is society's dreaming of the environment, a way of processing and storing psychic material which is generalizable. The dream of the individual is exactly like this but is too particular for what he calls 'publication', or powerful repetition. Could we say that a myth is a cultural narrative, a form of Vygotskyan 'outer speech'? Could we say that it is a successful translation into general terms of society's 'inner speech', an inner speech which has been the response to earlier myths, given back once again to the general-izing power which enables 'publication'? A myth is the 'as if' which Freud denied to the dream state, Bion says, the stored and communicable version of an emotional experience, and can be published because it is constructed out of elements which are constantly conjoined, even when they recur in different contexts. A myth of this kind is capable of recur-ring across nations, cultures and histories: it constitutes a form of linking, but, more important, it contains 'material from which it is possible to learn; that is, material suitable for dream-thoughts (Freud's unconscious waking thoughts) or for correlation with common sense . . . which are part of the individual's endowment and equipment as a member of a group' (p. 233). For, above all, a myth is a request for knowledge, a testing out of a hypothesis, a way of negotiating a problem. Myth will change according to different historical circumstances, where it will be reordered, reap-plied, to new circumstances and psychic questions. Like the manifest dream, the external configuration of facts and images gives coherence to material which would not ordinarily possess it, but its configuration is an indicator of the problems being explored, as material which is seen but not connected until the myth organises it, begins to *mean*. But it is the process of investigation into it rather than the synthesis of the myth which is important, and thus it is mobile where constructs such as the political unconscious are not.

Bion insists that, reversing the Freudian pattern and using the unconscious to interpret the conscious, the analyst can reach the problems encoded in myth and work on them. But it appears that he believes this is also within the skills of those who publish and respond to myth. And here a democratic reading of myth brings together the social and psychic, affect and knowledge. Myths make us all interpreters. The mythic examples Bion adduces are the classical and biblical myths of Adam and Eve, Babel and Narcissus. He ends with an interpretation of Babel for his own time, the construction of an artificial breast–penis which would prevent scattering, and the repressive attack on 'the language that makes cooperation possible' (p. 241) by a hostile God. But it would not be difficult to find other meanings, nor would it be difficult to add other myths to Bion's core group – Robinson Crusoe, Frankenstein, Jane Eyre, the Western, film noir, blues, rock, Mondrian, Andy Warhol. And just as the dreamwork offers multiple and conflicting meaning, so would the dream of myth.

'Failure to interpret the dream is the most potent contribution the analyst can make towards producing acting out; failure to dream . . . is the patient's main contribution' (p. 232). Transposed to the order of culture, Bion is making immense claims for mythwork and its analysis. Answering or attempting to answer the myth's request for knowledge – and we have to assume that this is within the competence of those who circulate and audit the published myth – is a way of preventing the resort to the acting out of unresolved psychic experience, communal fantasy or misprision, the literalizing of symbol in the world of the actual.

I can root these theoretical remarks by returning to the texts I discussed earlier, Blake's *Infant Sorrow* and Clint Eastwood's *Unforgiven*.

As Blakes' infant, no longer 'piping loud', refuses communication and withdraws from affect to 'sulk [not "suck"] upon my mother's breast', the fall of the Holy family hovers over the poem as a paradigm. When Adam and Eve were banned from paradise, their exit brought not only death into the world but, as a direct consequence of the fall, *reproduction*. There are no births in paradise. Jesus, Mary and Joseph are consequences of the fall. Four years after Blake published *Songs of Experience* (1794) Malthus was to publish *An Essay on the Principles of Population* (1798), predicting death in proportion to the exponential growth of population. What happens to parents and children when there are too many children, too many unwanted children? As the mother–child dyad falls apart and the father recedes there is a frightful struggle around nurture. Each side withdraws into *possessive* ownership of the body, *my* mother: *her* breast. Breast-feeding rather than the use of a wet nurse was a progressive act at this time. But it fails. As a corollary the child gives up on both love and *thinking*. The no-breast has become a *thing*, my mother's thing, a bad object inspiring hatred. The child cannot move to the world of abstraction or symbol-making that might redeem it. Is its capacity for inner speech crippled?

A very different Adam and Eve myth hovers over *Unforgiven*. Men are forced to crawl, abjected as they drag the lower body along the ground – English Bob, Will, Will's victim, all suffer this humiliation, not to speak of the prone bodies in the final carnage who, if they remain alive, have to act from the ground. Will describes his early life of violence in terms of crawling: he dreams that his wife's face is covered in snakes. What is being asked through this overdetermination of the wounded phallic serpent? As in dreamwork, its opposite, Homo erectus, provides the answer by standing in for the crawling body and thereby insistently, anxiously, questioning the overvaluing of phallic power. The temptation to *think* through the phallus afflicts nearly every figure in the film. But what is the consequence of *undervaluing* the phallus and negating masculinity? Abjection? If men become carers, what is sacrificed? Both Will as parent and Ned as loving male nurse exemplify this role. But Will lives in poverty as a feminized single parent and Ned, abandoning violence, is killed.

There is no guarantee that myth can always be read. And it might endorse horrors rather than relieve them. The powers of horror do not disappear, but this is not a reason for refusing to contemplate what might give people the power to resist them, the means to defence. What then, would an aesthetic education consist of, and what would it achieve? To put people in possession of the passions is one answer. 'Passion', says Bion, is an essential component of the interpretative process: it is about linking minds; 'there cannot be fewer than two minds if passion is present'; it is through passion that we extend the capacity for suffering rather than assuaging it, learn *about it* (not through it) rather than repressing it. The creativity of affect and its *analytical power*, for which I have been arguing, is cognate with this project. It leads to another proposition, to put people in possession of language, the language-making power which enables naming and renaming to negotiate experience in, with, and even against a speech community. Perhaps people, perhaps societies, fall ill if they lose the instinct to rename, the mediating power of language. And finally, as a necessary corollary, people need the power to dream.

APPENDIX

There have been a number of philosophical taxonomies and codifications of emotion which suggest how emotion can be seen cognitively, claiming its status in rational life. William Lyons's *Emotion* and Ronald de Sousa's *The Rationality of Emotion* approach the problem in different ways. Lyons develops a 'causal-evaluative' theory of emotion and argues for a multidimensional reading of emotion in which three aspects interact: a cognitive aspect which involves factual judgements and from which arises belief or knowledge; an evaluative aspect from which both objective appraisals and subjective evaluation arise; and an appetitive aspect from which desire arises, a desire which stems as much from cognitive and evaluative motives as from appetite.

> It has sometimes been held that emotion is a completely non-cognitive state, that it is a matter of feelings or animal attraction or instinctual behaviour. At the opposite end of the spectrum, some philosophers have held that some emotions at any rate, such as love, involve a special some-what mysterious type of knowledge...the true picture is to be found somewhere between these two extremes, which is to say that an emotion is partly cognitive but that this is not so much a source of knowledge about the world as an evaluation or appraisal of some part of the world *in relation to oneself*. (Lyons, *Emotion*, pp. 70–1)

De Sousa's belief in the axiological nature of emotions, which tell us things about the real world (*pace* Lyons) and ground the possibility of rationality, is based on two core arguments. First, culturally learned 'paradigm scenarios' or narratives of behaviour dramatize the salience and range of emotional response possible. Emotions, though culturally trained, are not subject to cultural determinism because, second, they supplement the insufficiency of reason. They limit and organize the potentially infinite range of information and inference confronting the rational faculty at moments of choice and, in shaping principles of salience, *act* on one reason rather than another. Emotions 'take up the slack in the rational determination of judgment and desire, by adjusting salience among objects of attention, lines of enquiry, and preferred infer-ence patterns. In this way emotions remain *sui generis*: the canons of rationality that govern them are not to be identified with those that govern judgment, or perception, or functional desire. Instead, their exis-tence grounds the very possibility of rationality at those more conven-tional levels' (*The Rationality of Emotions*, 203).

Philosophers and aestheticians have continued to explore emotion and rationality (see John Deigh, 'Cognitivism in the theory of emotion'; E. M. Dadlez, 'Fiction, emotion, and rationality'). Slightly to the side of my interests, moral philosophers such as Martha Nussbaum (see *Passions and Perceptions, Studies in Hellenistic Philosophy of Mind, Proceedings of the Fifth Symposium Hellenisticum*) and Amélie Oksenberg Rorty (*Explaining Emotions*) ground ethical choices in emotional experience, exploring what de Sousa would term 'paradigm scenarios' to elicit the interrelation of ethics and feeling. Robert C. Solomon's *What is an Emotion? Classic Readings in Philosophical Psychology* is also useful.

In a recent review in the *Times Literary Supplement* (July 17, 1998), Ian Hacking remarked that 'the emotions are flourishing subject matter' (p. 11). He was reviewing a number of psychology-related studies, including a new edition of Charles Darwin's *The Expression of the Emotions in Man and Animals* and Paul E. Griffiths's, *What Emotions Really Are: The Problem of Psychological Categories*. However, recent books on emotion from a number of disciplines suggest that psychology and philosophy are not the only fields in which exploration is taking place. The semiotic work of A. J. Greimas and Jacques Fontanille, (*Sémiotique des Passions: Des États de Choses aux États d'Âme*, Éditions du Seuil, Paris, 1991) arguing the social construction of emotion, has recently been translated (*The Semiotics of Passion: From States of Affairs to States of Feeling* (1993). As is suggested by the appearance of an anthology edited by Mette Hjort and Sue Laver, *Emotion and the Arts*, the topic of emotion is beginning to attract more attention than formerly. Peter Middleton's valuable chapter, 'The lost language of emotion' in his *The Inward Gaze: Masculinity and Subjectivity in Modern Culture* is indicative of this interest. He anticipates to some extent Susan Feagin's *Reading with Feeling*. The psychoanalytical world continues to interest itself in affect: see conference papers for the conference entitled 'How do we think about feelings', (Spring 1995) organized by the British Journal of Psychotherapy and the Freud Museum, chaired by David Bell, in which André Green was a plenary speaker (*The British Journal of Psychotherapy*, Vol. 12, no. 2, 1995, pp. 208–50). Thanks to Kirsten MacLeod of the University of Alberta for many helpful bibliographical suggestions.

NOTES

1 Ludwig Wittgenstein, *Philosophical Investigations*, trans. G. E. M. Anscombe, Oxford, Blackwell, 1976, para. 582, p. 153.

2   Hanna Segal, 'A psychoanalytic approach to aesthetics', *The Work of Hanna Segal*, pp. 194–7.
3   Peter Middleton, 'The lost language of emotion', *The Inward Gaze*, pp. 166–232.
4   Most notably: Jean-François Lyotard, *The Postmodern Condition*, pp. 81–2; Paul de Man, *Aesthetic Ideology*, pp. 105–48.
5   English translators seem to select texts that emphasize this trait. See Georges Bataille, *Visions of Excess: Selected Writings, 1927–39* and *Literature and Evil*; Maurice Blanchôt, *The Siren's Song: Selected Essays* and *The Writing of the Disaster*.
6   Translated as *The Fabric of Affect in the Psychoanalytical Discourse*. As this publication became available only in late 1999, page numbers throughout this chapter refer to the original French version.
7   Jacques Lacan, The insistence of the letter in the unconscious'. For 'Dora', see Sigmund Freud, *Fragment of an Analysis of a Case of Hysteria*, pp. 58–61.
8   Sigmund Freud, *The Interpretation of Dreams*, pp. 381–2.
9   I am grateful to Pietro Cardile and members of the MA/MSc Gender, Theory and Culture Class of 1997 for illuminating discussions of this film.
10   'Thus constituted, this model will pivot around its axis in an alternating oscillation. Through the event, the conjuncture will force the structure to become manifest. Through the object, the structure will act on the conjuncture. To that outward movement will correspond a return. Through the object, the conjuncture will dislodge the structure and take its place, modified by the preceding stage. Crossing the event, the structure will find its original place.

This oscillation round its axis shows us the importance of the value of "the return" (or "turning round") in psychoanalysis, Here, as so often, the plurality of the semantic contexts shows us that the term is applied to the most primitive operations of the psychical apparatus,[*] as also to the most polished expressions of the unconscious.[†]

Now, in psychoanalytic theory and experience, the affect is the privileged place of the return: turning round against oneself and turning into its opposite in the duality of the pleasure–unpleasure principle.[‡] *On the basis of the structure, as combining a source, a thrust, an aim, an object, and of the double return (reversal into its opposite and turning round upon the subject's own self), I shall propose a theoretical model of the psychoanalytical field in which the subject is defined as process.* Process (*procès*) is to be understood both in the sense of movement, development, progress, and in the (legal) sense of an outcome to a conflict as decided by a judgement after due examination of it. I prefer this term to that of psychoanalytic process (*processus*), which renders only one of the two senses, omitting the other. Its application is not restricted, in my view, to the theorization of the analytic field, but also to one's experience through the analytic situation and the transference.

*   I have explained elsewhere the metapsychological significance of the double reversal.

†   It is by the message that 'the subject is constituted, which means that it is from the Other that the subject receives even the message that he emits' [Lacan, *Ecrits*, p. 305]. It is in the inverted form of this "sending back" that the unconscious is marked. The article in which this quotation appears, "Subversion of the subject and dialectic of desire", seems to me to be Lacan's most important one. I commented upon it in Piera Aulagnier's Saint-Anne seminar of 29 April 1968.

‡   "What a queer thing it is, my friends, this sensation which is popularly called pleasure! It is remarkable how closely it is connected with its apparent opposite, pain. They will never come to a man both at once, but if you pursue one of them and catch it, you are virtually compelled always to have the other as well; they are like two bodies attached to the same head. I am sure that if Aesop had thought of it he really would have made up a fable about them, something like this: God wanted to stop their continual quarrelling, and when he found that it was impossible, he fastened their heads together; so wherever one of them appears, the other is sure to follow after." Socrates' last words to his friends on the day of his death. Plato, *Phaedo*, in *The Last Days of Socrates*, trans. Hugh Tredennick and Harold Tarrant, London: Penguin Press, 1993, p. 112.' (Green, *The Fabric of Affect in the Psychoanalytical Discourse*, pp. 227–8)

11   Raymond Williams, *Culture and Society 1780–1950*.

12   Fredric Jameson, *The Political Unconscious*. See in particular 'Conclusion: the dialectics of utopia and ideology', pp. 281–99.

13   Rom Harré, *The Social Construction of Emotions* and *The Singular Self*.

Part III

Cultural Capital, Value and a Democratic Aesthetic

5

Beyond the Pricing Principle

Prologue

I begin with two experiences. One is Joyce's prose poem, through Stephen Daedelus in *Ulysses*, which celebrates scavenging through the eye. Through time, of course, its initial shock has been assimilated into the vocabulary of high modernism.

> Ineluctable modality of the visible: at least that if no more, thought through my eyes. Signatures of all things I am here to read, seaspawn and seawrack, the nearing tide, that rusty boot. Snotgreen, bluesilver, rust: coloured signs. Limits of the diaphane. (James Joyce, *Ulysses*, p. 31)

Stephen is composing a visual experience made up of the irreducible singularity of detritus – that's why he is reading signatures of things, because signatures guarantee uniqueness. The rusty boot, the sea, are sensory signs offered up to the workings of thought upon them. In fact, they can only be perceived as coloured 'signs' at all because they are 'thought' through the eyes. The particularity of boot and tide is 'thought' as it is perceived through sense, through the eye, a particularity which can be guaranteed because, not in spite of, thought's capacity to transfer aspects of other visible coloured phenomena to these objects – rust and snot. Thought is working upon random sensoria and making relationships out of them. The limits of this process may be the limits of the transparent lens of the eye, the diaphane. Or, the limits of the ineluctability of the visible might lie in things themselves. Stephen goes on to think of Aristotle's belief that the essence of solids is to be transparent before they are coloured. What would happen to relationships if we lived in a world of near-invisible translucent objects, like glass phantoms of themselves? The famous meditation on space and time follows this passage.

Contrast this dream vision of detritus with the experience of looking at other coloured signs, the railside graffiti which strikes a traveller when moving away from any London terminal, to Surbiton, say, from Waterloo. Gashes of red and black spray paint declare not simply the violence of an attack on the environment but the daring and risk to life this must have incurred. For rail graffiti exists in the most dangerous places, on sheer walls above the tracks, on box-like structures marooned amid meshes of steel rail. Interestingly, there are not that many obscenities. I have heard Toni Morrison describe these graffiti as writing. But they do not have the decipherability of writing. The many sets of initials tell you only that these are initials, just as the dominance of pseudo words – KOF, UURZ – tells you that you cannot read them. Or the letters, ACNE, arranged and rearranged in different configurations, will come to seem like an unknown acronym. These are anti-words. In a script of angular dashes or swollen cursives they mime the calligraphy of an illusory alphabet, a code other than the one we know. But it is more like the semblance of a code. For it constitutes an aggressive barrier to reading. Hieroglyphs I am here not to read. That is why actually *understanding* graffiti is a strangely defamiliarizing experience. The urbane message, for instance, 'Greetings from the Chicago Graffiti Association' comes as a surprise.[1]

The Joyce passage, once thought by some to be coarse and disgusting, was a test case for the novel's entry into the privileged category, art, when *Ulysses* was first published in the 1920s. Though if anything at all is meant by the word, Joyce's work falls into the category of art today, or at least into that of high culture. Some graffiti has taken on test case status, too. Deemed to possess urban aura in an age of mechanical reproduction, New York subway graffiti of the eighties was collected in artbook photographs for display, like some Kantian artefact of disinterested creation. Though unlike Joyce's detritus dream, the case for graffiti is still open.

Perhaps the designation, 'art', requires such test cases and demarcation disputes to be kept alive in our culture. I shall return to these test cases at the end of this essay. They will help me to see how far it is possible to get in re-describing this privileged category, art. I shall consider some democratic readings of the aesthetic and consider how democratic they are. Related to the problem of a radical reading of art is the question of value. Must value always be bound up with the aesthetic?

The double discourse of value

My starting point is John Guillory's impressive *Cultural Capital: The Problem of Literary Canon Formation* (1993), whose concern is actually far wider than that of the literary canon.² His diagnosis of the crisis in literary studies does not derive so much from an analysis of debates internal to the literary academy as from an understanding that the arrival of a new managerial, technocratic class with no need of the category of the aesthetic has undermined the base of literary culture. Thus he would see the questions explored in George Levine's important collection of sophisticated essays, *Aesthetics and Ideology* (1994) as questions which are slightly to the side of the ones he wants to ask. George Levine's question, 'Can, in fact, a category, literature, be meaningfully constituted?' and his belief that 'a reductive assimilation of literature to ideology' has occurred, which generates the opposing view that 'the literary and the political should have nothing to do with one another' (p. 1) are themselves part of a wider crisis for Guillory. Similarly, for him Peter Brooks's claim, in a contribution to Levine's collection, that the practice of poetics, along with other inherited traditions, has been swamped by 'an ideologization of the aesthetic' (p. 157) in which a political anthropology of culture is displacing the need for 'a more public language' (p. 166), expresses an unease more bound up with the low contemporary status of the aesthetic in the grand narratives of the dominant technocratic systems of our time than with specific debates between new historicism and formalism.

Guillory's is the most complex and ambitious attempt so far to analyse the origins of contemporary debate on the aesthetic and to remake the category. If he attempts, but fails, to remake the category of the aesthetic in a Utopian moment towards the end of his book, it is an ambitious failure. The complexity of the problems he discloses at least points up the continuing urgency of some of the questions addressed in Levine's collection. For the primary problem Guillory poses is that of value. The 'aporia between the cultural and the economic is the most fundamental problem confronted by bourgeois sociology' *(Cultural Capital*, p. 341) – he might have said 'society' or 'culture'. His attempt to think through a form of Franco-American aesthetics by exploring a 'double discourse of value' is the theme of his last chapter. The double discourse of value is both repudiated and accepted, subjected to critique and then reinstated. The dilemma of value remains unresolved, but more important is that the aesthetic gets left behind in the process. How does this come about?

The description, 'double discourse of value', is taken from Barbara Hernstein Smith's influential *Contingencies of Value: Alternative Perspectives for Critical Theory* (1988). Her widely circulated distinction between two forms of value, economic and aesthetic, which are thought to be incommensurate and yet are constantly conflated, is Guillory's text. On the one hand, she says, there is economic theory with its discourse of 'money, commerce, technology, industry, production and consumption, workers and consumers', and on the other there is 'aesthetic axiology' with its antithetical transcendence of the economic in terms such as 'culture, art, genius, creation and appreciation', supported by the explanatory machinery of 'inspiration' and 'taste' (p. 127). Some critics, including Guillory and Mary Poovey, have suggested that Smith sees this as a false and consoling opposition for which aesthetic ideology is responsible.[3] The tendency of art values to converge with economic values is only an indication of the reality of economic value which a mystified reading of the aesthetic refuses. This view of Smith rather precipitately assumes that for her the aesthetic *disappears* into the economic, extinguished by it; whereas in my reading she is more concerned with the aporias created by the conflation of two sets of values than with disavowing the category of the aesthetic. But Guillory does not seem to read her in this way. He confronts Smith by attending to the history of value. But his own commitment to Pierre Bourdieu's economic readings of culture, a commitment embodied in the title of his book, forces him to work within what he perceives as her economic terms, however much these are modified.

To digress for a moment to Guillory's allegiances: he is friendly to the Bourdieu of *Distinction* (1979) and to the essays of the 1970s and 1980s now translated and collected in *The Field of Cultural Production* (1993).[4] For Guillory, Bourdieu's work is the culmination of a double discourse of value which is at the same time recognized as such and demystified, and Bourdieu's central concept of cultural capital is fundamental to his own concept of culture. Cultural capital is the accumulation of prestige through education, family training, class status, familiarity with a hierarchy of cultural codes, and the privileged knowledge through which value is socially produced. It is related to money but not in itself money, though it is used instrumentally in symbolic struggles for distinction and power just as money is. For Bourdieu the apotheosis of cultural capital rests on 'restricted' cultural production, 'the charismatic image of artistic activity as pure, disinterested creation by an isolated artist' (*The Field of Cultural Production*, p. 34). This aesthetic of autonomous art, in which production is intended for a small elite of other producers or for an audience homologous with its producers, reaches the height of interest in disinterestedness in its disavowal of economic dependence or need. The more cultural capital, the more the disavowal of economic interests: the more interest in disinterestedness, the more restricted production actually depends on economic motives. But these, Bourdieu ironically sees, are strange, because they are represented through an 'anti economy', an 'upside-down economic world' (p. 40):

the economy of practices is based, as in a generalised game of 'loser wins', on a systematic inversion of the fundamental principles of all ordinary economies. (Bourdieu, *The Field of Cultural Production*, p. 39)

That is, autonomous art excludes the profit-making of business, abjures the power of temporal greatness and occasionally eschews even the institutional hierarchies of cultural authority which would normally confirm, or, as he terms it, 'consecrate', the artist.

Despite the consecration of symbolic value rather than economic value, the legitimation of cultural forms proceeds with Darwinian intensity, and a struggle for survival occurs which ruthlessly attempts to 'impose a legitimate definition of art and literature' (p. 41) on culture and to reproduce and perpetuate it. Struggles round the symbolic value of the fetish, art, result in fierce rules of exclusion, regulation and access which create boundaries because these are bound up with power and status. Bourdieu's great achievement is to have found a way of analysing the field of production and infrastructure in which artworks appear and by which they are supported – publishers, journalists, museums, art galleries, academies, cultural agencies, institutions. He claims to have dissolved the sterile dualism of individual creator (individualist romanticism) as against material external conditions (the Marxist view) as the 'source' of art, both essentially correspondence theories which have been the dominant model of aesthetic production. For his 'field' is a site of reflexive relations rather than correspondences, a complex configuration of conditions and institutions, in space and time, which organizes cultural struggle by defining and limiting the possibilities of change. This occurs because the number and possibility of positions which can be taken up at any historical moment are defined and limited by many factors – for instance, by the history of a discourse itself, by social class and economic conditions – which impact on one another. Generated by struggle, the field is interactive, as each position changes when others do. The 'artistic field as, inseparably, a field of positions and a field of position-takings' (p. 34) is one of multiple interactive change. Presumably both Guillory's and Levine's defensive interventions into the discourse of value, and their attempts to reclaim value by defining a new place for the aesthetic in contradistinction to the old conservative definitions of high culture, would be regarded by Bourdieu as made possible by a number of related shifts in the field, opened up by, to hypothesize, mass education, global capital, post-modern repudiations of the grand narrative, and electronic media which have displaced the centrality of what we traditionally call the humanities. On the other hand, both are strategically intervening in a hegemonic discourse, taking up new positions and attempting to legitimate them. Just as art is a fetish, debate is a matter of strategy and game-playing, rather than reason, as one utilizes cultural media in order to legitimate and perpetuate 'a definition of art and literature'.

The stakes are no different in 'general production', that is, all that does not belong to high culture, though here the dominated elements of the field rather than the dominant and empowered are actants. In *The Field of Cultural Production* (though less often in *Distinction*) Bourdieu frequently rolls up bourgeois and 'popular' culture together, because they are alike dominated elements of culture. He is hazy on the part TV, cinema, the pop music industry and virtual reality play, for instance, in the social production of value. He ignores the category of gender, failing to see that gender capital also plays a part in the struggle for meaning. If the tautology entailed in the internal analysis of works of art is only shifted to the tautology of economic explanations, this is acceptable to Bourdieu because economic complexity appears to have an explanatory function. A rigorous science of art recognizes that 'belief in the value of a work of art, which is one of the major obstacles to the constitution of a science of artistic production, is part of the full reality of the work of art' (p. 36). The ideology of the aesthetic is intrinsic to the meaning of aesthetic production, but there the matter rests. The aesthetic, that is to say, can never have an explanatory function. It *is* the problem to be explained. But how can it be explained without being explained away? This is a difficulty, I shall suggest, lurking in the work of both Bourdieu and Guillory.

The double discourse of value of which Bourdieu's work is the modern exemplar emerged, Guillory says, in the eighteenth century with the economic autonomy granted to civil society. It was then that aesthetic and economic realms became separate. Guillory traces and defends this separation because by keeping cultural capital and economic capital apart, the aesthetic can be prevented from being assimilated into the economic and so presented as merely ideology. While he insists on the convertibility of one to the other, of aesthetic to economic value, he maintains that this does not entail a *reduction* of one to the other (*Cultural Capital*, p. 327). It is on this convertibility without reduction that he founds a redefinition of the aesthetic.

Guillory's is a complex, subtle and powerful argument mounted in three stages. First, he offers a critique of Barbara Hernstein Smith's discourse of value in order to forestall the collapse of the aesthetic into the economic. Second, he engages with a history of the discourse of value in order to show how political economy and the aesthetic, commodity and the work of art, became antithetical; whereas they had formerly converged in eighteenth century economic discourse as an independent economic realm severed from ideas of the beautiful. Third, and last, he considers the aesthetic in modern culture, where 'the market is the inescapable horizon of all social life' (p. 325). A Baudrillardian 'logic of equivalence' in the modern discourse of value attempts to create the 'absolute commensurability of everything via exchange value as the result of a reifying discourse of value'. Guillory is ill at ease about this reification, but accepts that this uneasy recognition of actual incommensurability with a virtual drive to equivalence is endemic in modern culture. It is 'the social condition of modernity'. Though he sympathizes with Marx's Utopian, redefined aesthetic 'state', which breaks the mould of economism, he insists that 'any analysis of objective social relations will... reveal that both "values" and the discourse of value are historically *determined* as objective social facts' (p. 324). Crucially, he says that without the discourse of value the beautiful as we know it would be unrecognizable.

> It would be difficult if not impossible now to think of works of art as more or less "beautiful" without abstracting from the appearance of beauty a quantum of value – 'aesthetic' value; but if it were possible to think of the aesthetic without thinking of value, we would in effect have discarded the concept of the 'work of art' as we know it. For that object is by definition the embodiment of a quantum of aesthetic value. (Guillory, *Cultural Capital*, p. 322)

If we discard value, '*we would in effect have discarded the concept of the "work of art" as we know it*'. Guillory arrives at this position through his analysis of Barbara Hernstein Smith and Adam Smith. I will trace in an abbreviated way, which will not do justice to the subtleties of his analysis, the foundations he lays for his acceptance of value.

Linking Barbara Hernstein Smith with Tony Bennet, whose positions, he believes, are comparable, he shows that the argument for contingent values – set up to repudiate the universal subject, which transfers its universality without warrant to the object of beauty – arises from a naïve liberal pluralist individualism. In order to counteract what for Guillory is a travesty of Kantian aesthetics, Smith works with the notion of a *personal economy*, in which the famous formulation, 'purposefulness without purpose' is reduced to the sense that aesthetic objects have 'no purpose at all' (p. 291). The subject as consumer is a 'user' of aesthetic experience for pleasure, rather as one might 'use' drugs recreationally. The value of an artwork must be assessed, then, purely in terms of 'the value of an object *for oneself*' (p. 288). The user establishes the price or value (which must be the same) according to the extent of his or her need or desire for the object. But this, Guillory points out, is to work with the use value of the privatized individual within the terms of a primitive barter economy. It ignores our existence in a social world and the existence of the third term of exchange value which mediates worth. Aesthetic productions circulate in a world in which the social function of art inheres in the category itself, so that they necessarily belong to social discourse.

In just the same way, he believes, Smith's understanding of community is limited by her post-modern conception of community as comprised by different, shifting and overlapping, groups of individuals. If we refer the importance of artwork to anything, it is to the use value of the groups and subcultures to which we belong, she thinks. However, this does not escape the problem of community. For such a reference to separatist subcultural mores reintroduces the universalization of value all over again in the context of the subgroup. Indeed, the movement to subcultures results in a contradiction, because it treats the subcultural 'community' as a collection of individuals at one level and simultaneously universalizes the group and its collective judgement at another. For Guillory it is precisely because artworks *can* be contested in and between groups rather than consecrated by so-called 'communities' that makes them live as artefacts. The example he gives, favourite of commentators on contemporary culture, is the photography of Mapplethorpe, whose work can be read either as homoerotic 'pornography' or 'art'. He is well aware of the sterility of a critique of the category of the aesthetic which posits a choice between aesthetics and politics, for once one has set up a *choice* between aesthetics and politics there is no place for a discussion of the relation of the aesthetic to other domains of the social. The debate is foreclosed. However, I think that one of the unsolved problems of his argument, honourably unsolved but difficult, is the evolution of an idea of community which neither excludes groups from participating in aesthetic pleasure nor relativizes the pleasures and passions of those who do.

From Barbara Hernstein Smith, Guillory moves to eighteenth-century economics in the form of Adam Smith. His history of the discourse of value considers the moment when aesthetic value and economic value became disengaged from one another. Smith and other eighteenth-century economists, he argues, elaborated an 'aesthetic of the social order' (p. 311) at the point when civil society developed an independent economic sphere. The conceptualization of the fine arts emerges simultaneously with political economy, for a theory of civil society was incomplete without a theory of culture. As production and consumption became the recto and verso of civil society, a claim for their autonomy entailed a claim for a similar autonomy on the part of cultural production. In fact, the separation of material production from cultural production and the move to a vertical hierarchy of aesthetic production and consumption was slow to emerge. Cultural production was seen by David Hume, for instance, as part of a continuum of commodity production because all could be valued as forms of wealth. Consumption and contemplation were slow to be differentiated. Beauty was an aspect of utility, or took on what he terms (adopting Howard Caygill's expression) 'deferred utility' (p. 309) because it could be described in terms of fitness for its end. Thus Adam Smith was able to derive the beauty of the social order, not from the beauty of fine art but from the beauty of the commodity and 'the harmony of its unlegislated production' (p. 310) in the self-regulating movement of *laissez-faire* economics.

For Adam Smith the economy was actually driven by the surplus of beauty over use residing in the commodity. It is this that arouses desire, which is far in excess of need or mere subsistence, and drives the production of ever more differentiated and refined commodities to satisfy what is actually permanently unstaunched want. But this convenient concordance between two sets of laws, aesthetic and economic, was doomed by the market's own logic. The proportion and harmony of consumption and production covers over the violence of labour, but it is also exposed by the mechanism of exchange value. The variability of exchange value precisely opens up disharmony between the realms of production and need, for exchange value is regulated irrespective of need and varies according to principles of scarcity or glut which reflect neither labour nor demand. Thus the convergence of the aesthetic and political economy are the occasion of their separation. The artwork comes to be excluded from the discourse for which it was once a paradigm. The separation of the two discourses culminates in Kant's opposition between consumption and contemplation. Thus the double discourse of value, the discourse of modernity, is inaugurated in Enlightenment economics.

Mary Poovey has pointed out that Adam Smith's untheorized and peculiarly abstract limitless desire, which feeds on imagination or fantasy, masks a different desire altogether: an eroticized aesthetics, a desire of appetite which arises and expends itself in the body. It masks, in other words, male desire. She sees this recognition played out in Mary Wollstonecraft's relationship to Burke and Rousseau. Manifesting itself as discrimination, eroticized desire sustains and institutionalizes male power because it depends on the dissymmetry of sexual difference. Women's bodies have become the fetishized objects of the male subject. The dynamic of market society is manipulated, Wollstonecraft realized, through the apparent separation of the aesthetic and the economic and political, the economic and the erotic. But commodity culture depends on 'the persistence of aesthetic concerns within economic exchanges' (Poovey, 'Aesthetics and political economy', p. 94), as the nascent fashion industry made clear, perpetuating as it did the subordination of the female body. A compromised relation to the sensuous is the result of Wollstonecraft's understanding of the gendering of political economy, as she struggled to reclaim rationality and to extirpate those cultural meanings of women's bodies which caused them to remain in subjection.

This historical reading of sensuous experience leads us back to Guillory and Bourdieu, for it is on the irreducibility of the sensuous that both rest an argument for the ultimate importance of the category of the aesthetic. In the postcript to *Distinction* Bourdieu argues that a Kantian 'pure' aesthetic legitimizes social differences (p. 489). Kant quite directly states the social basis of the opposition between the 'taste of reflection' and the 'taste of sense'. '[A]rt and cultural consumption are predisposed, consciously and deliberately or not, to fulfil a social function of legitimating social differences' (Randal Johnson's précis). Distinction 'is a misrecognised social relationship' represented as a cultured elite's aesthetic rejection of distasteful sensuous enjoyment: 'The denial of lower, coarse, vulgar, venal, servile – in a word, natural – enjoyment, which constitutes the sacred sphere of culture, implies an affirmation of the superiority' of those who sublimate the pleasures of the senses in high art (Bourdieu, *The Field of Cultural Productions*, p. 25). Bourdieu assumes that we must know what the 'natural' pleasures of the senses are, as if they lie outside historical experience and economic necessity. But strangely, the more self-evidently literal these physical pleasures seem to be, the more *ineffable* they become. They fall outside representation because they are deemed to be undescribable except in terms of themselves, recognized in a non-verbal, at best deictic, way.

Guillory also falls into this ineffability of the sensuous. He has reminded Barbara Hernstein Smith (when she conceded that the aesthetic might derive from biophysical drives unassimilable by language) that even these are negotiated by the culturally made world. However, when he moves to reverse Bourdieu's negative conclusions he does so by making a distinction between an aesthetic *discourse* of value and aesthetic *experience* which cannot be conflated. He arrives at this proposition by considering Bourdieu's differentiation between the values of the dominant restricted economy and those of the dominated general economy, both doomed to antagonism and to a struggle for power. Restricted production values form, whereas General production values content, Bourdieu proposes. In both cases a specifically aesthetic experience escapes from language. There is a double silencing, as each mode of cultural production rejects one another's discourse (*Cultural Capital*, p. 335). This problem can be met, Guillory says, by recognizing that, though one might not have a *discourse* of aesthetic value, one might still be capable of having aesthetic *experience* which is not theorized. Both Restricted and General production have access to the sensuousness of content and the sensuousness of form, but the aesthetic *experience* enters into the discourse of neither. He admits that this aesthetic experience, because it falls out of analysis, must be hypothetical, but he wants to reverse Bourdieu's negative conclusions by presupposing access to an *undefined* aesthetic experience. For the advantage of this is that though it is undefined it is *universal* despite its fall from language into the ineffable.

Once the universality of aesthetic experience is hypothesized, it is possible to argue that, though aesthetic *value* is indeed class-related cultural capital, aesthetic *experience* is universal. Thus it falls outside the acquisition of cultural capital. For this reason we can disarticulate cultural capital from the class structure by enabling 'total democratisation of access' to cultural production, and not merely to the 'materially advantaged' (p. 339). Guillory favours democratization of access to Restricted production, on the grounds that its autonomy guarantees freedom of judgement. Since Bourdieu has approved the autonomy of intellectuals, it follows for him that the autonomy of the Restricted economy offers the greatest opportunities for 'a vast enlargement of the field of aesthetic judgement', despite being the most ironized of Bourdieu's categories and the least amenable to the pleasures of the senses (p. 339). Cultural producers will still compete to have their products read, looked at, listened to. *Judgement* would not disappear. Nor, therefore, would the disposition of value which Guillory deems indispensable to the aesthetic and the artwork as we know it in our culture. On the contrary, we would simply reform the hierarchical conditions of the practice of judgement and allow *everybody* to judge.

Guillory is worried about the Utopian implications of his proposal and calls it a thought experiment. But Utopianism is not the problem. For does he not fetishize the act of judgement rather than the art object? And isn't a democratic discourse of value a strangely abstract process in a context where aesthetic *experience* falls out of analysis? This is to mystify aesthetic experience as ineffable, unnameable.

It's possible that abandoning hierarchy might mean the abandonment of the centrality of judgement and that a complete redefinition of the field of aesthetic experience might result. That is why I turn to an unfashionable American thinker who tried to think through the aesthetic by abandoning hierarchies of experience, and who turned to an analysis of the sensuous without surrendering it to the ineffable: John Dewey.

Art as experience

When he gave the lectures comprising *Art as Experience* to a Harvard audience in 1932, John Dewey joined a powerful modern movement which repudiated Kantian aesthetics (or a version of it which has become an orthodoxy) and which sought to demonstrate Kantian ideas as one of the limiting factors of both modern knowledge and the form of civil society. Dewey's refusal of Kantian aesthetics represents a microcosm of his democratic theory of art. This is founded on a radical definition of the nature of *experience*, everybody's experience. It is an account of what Marx would term species life, that which we have to go through in order to be fully human. It is not an attempt to universalize experience or to essentialize either subject or object. By making *experience* central to his theory, Dewey deftly refuses to distribute the aesthetic across the conventionally accepted categories. He never splits up the aesthetic between producer, or artist, artwork, and consumer or audience. Experience crosses the boundaries between maker, art object and response and reconfigures them. Indeed, anyone – myself at least – trying to explicate his theory tends to flounder for terminology, because the vocabulary inherent in our culture for describing relationships is exiled – subject, object, consciousness, self, artist (along with, significantly, the vocabulary of beauty, imagination, creativity) – are all too individualist for Dewey. 'Art' is a meaningful term for him, but only because it is synonymous with 'experience'. I will consider what 'experience' means after these preliminaries. For the present it is enough to emphasize that, from the moment of birth, the aesthetic is inherent in experience, prefigured in the very process of living and inscribed in the body. Thus the potential for responding to and making the aesthetic is in everyone, possibilities held in common by the fact of being alive. *Arousal* is the cause and effect of experience and the aesthetic alike – and it occurs everywhere in our lives, in the experience of a crowd at a ball-game, for instance, in the gratuitous poking of the embers of a fire, in the surge of interest in an excavating machine at a building site. 'Experience' is *not* ineffable.

Admittedly, the heart sinks a little when Dewey writes that the sources of art are to be learned by him who 'notes the delight of the housewife in tending her plants, and the intent interest of her goodman in tending the patch of green in front of the house' (*Art as Experience*, p. 5). His aestheticization of the ordinary is often bald. There are elements of the Utopian romantic organicist in his writing: though implicitly he envisaged a new art yet to be made and repudiated the museum, he took most of his examples of pictorial art from the Barnes Foundation collection; he struggled with the meaning of collective life and community; he struggled with the contradiction of shared potential for the aesthetic and the need, as he saw it, for training in understanding artworks. Nevertheless, in the search for a democratic theory he constantly disengaged himself from the conventional positions of his class and education. He was both more and less sophisticated than those who followed him, including Adorno and Bourdieu, in his efforts to define the elements of sensuous life and to free them from a notion of 'pure' art.

Like his contemporary, Walter Benjamin, Dewey recognized that aesthetic propensity was dominated by class, by work and by the market. The 'work of art' as we know it is hardly a work of art at all. Segregated into museums as a separate realm, art is isolated in buildings which are 'memorials to the rise of nationalism and imperialism', militarism and the 'loot' of conquest (p. 8). A history of modern art could be written in terms of the rise of the museum, he wrote, a task which Bourdieu was later to undertake in 1969 in the work translated as *The Love of Art: European Art Museums and Their Public* (1991). 'Art' is fed by those who need to claim 'superior cultural status', either to screen their absorption in accumulating material wealth (modern industrial patronage, which actually shames the conduct of business rather than endowing it with status) or to aggrandize aesthetic individualism or class hegemony by 'the insignia of taste and certificate of special culture' (p. 9). Dewey insisted that the economic conditions of modern capital, which create a gulf between producer and consumer, create the 'chasm' between ordinary and aesthetic experience (p. 10) and lead to false 'contemplative' theories of art. A 'pure' theory of art could arise only because mind is given status in a society which can use other people's bodies in vicarious labour (p. 21). It was Kant who 'gave the separation of the esthetic from other modes of experience an alleged scientific basis in the constitution of human nature' (p. 252) by making contemplation 'remote from all desire, action, and stir of emotion' (p. 253), elements central to his own theory.

To this extent Dewey is at one with major post-war figures of the left such as Bourdieu and Adorno, though Adorno enquired further than Bourdieu into Kant's 'castrated hedonism', as he called it.[5] Sensuous pleasure for Adorno is at least an 'embarrassment', a puzzling aporia. The demonization of Kant in *Art as Experience* comes about because of Dewey's need to investigate the sensuous. It makes him look at situations we do not include within the aesthetic, and argue that ordinary experience is in continuity with aesthetic production. He begins with skin, the epidermis, because it participates indeterminately in self and world, less a barrier than a connective integument which registers so-called 'gross sensation' (p. 20) and 'low appetite'. Such sensations constitute a life-

giving 'primitive need' which is 'the source of attachment to objects' and
the ultimate basis of 'happiness' (p. 10). The experience which is arousal
and the arousal which is experience is cause and effect of an interactive
psychophysical drama, struggling in a world of things and events. Its basis
is biological, as organism and environment intervene in one another's
spheres. But it is inherently qualitative and cannot be directed simply
towards consumption. For the quickening of arousal is a primary condition of the aesthetic because it precipitates an active shaping of form.
Adjusting to ever-changing relations with the environment necessitates,
calls out, an ordering principle which initiates form and which becomes a
primal principle of survival. (To a limited extent the aesthetic principle of
ordering is available even to animals, Dewey allows.) Without aesthetic
form the organism dies of an inability to shape experience. The anti-
aesthetic condition is that which possesses either too little form or too
much, for both extremes make *experience* impossible by failing to allow
the change and mobility which makes form possible (p. 17). Continual flux
or absolute finitude would both preclude the rhythms of sleeping and
waking. Dreaming would be impossible. Dewey does not extrapolate the
politics of these two extremes, but clearly finitude is authoritarian while
flux is anarchic individualism. Psychoanalytically, an inability to move
between repression and the Id, or, in Kleinian terms, the paranoid-schizoid
and depressive positions, would be the result of finitude and flux. Coercion
on the one hand and incoherence on the other characterize these states.

Dewey reiterates that the artwork does not *lead* to experience but
'*constitutes* one' (p. 85). It does so because experience is interactive, the
sum of an interactivity which is always double at the same time as it
dissolves dualisms. Experience is a two-sided state because an act of
expression and the response it calls forth are a unity, just as the expressive
object and the perception which shaped it are a unity. Experience is
transitive, always *of* not *in* an environment, which must mean a two-
way movement. Thus he considers concurrently experience and what is
made of it, the art object and how it is experienced. He refuses, as I have
said, the distinctions which split experience up – subject/object, 'fine'/
practical or applied art, emotion/thought, mind/body. Such distinctions
create artificial boundaries and exclusions, made 'in fear of what life may
bring forth' (p. 22).

What he is arguing for, in fact, is a kind of aesthetic a priori (although
the Kantian structure of this thought remains unacknowledged). There is
always something of art in every experience. We can go further into the
meaning of experience for Dewey by considering how he thinks of the
three terms he repeatedly invokes, Form, Emotion and Thought, although
each term is involved in the others.

Form is with us from birth in the living physiomental conditions of awareness and arousal. Form has no origins because it is an aspect of being alive. From the beginning, the rhythm of lack and demand jolt experience into breaks, disjunctions and imbalances, which are felt as phases and discrete states. Life itself consists of phases in which the organism finds itself out of step with the environment. It lives in a state of agonistic tension as it struggles to discover a new equipoise which allays the threatened disorder. The perpetual remaking of order and stability is a condition of life, just as the threat of disorder is inherent in experience. This aspiration to form is a struggle brought to consciousness as the aesthetic powers of shaping are invoked to organize energies. Indeed, the organization of an experience *as* a phase presupposes the formal understanding which is a prerequisite for creating it. Art is 'what actual experience actually becomes when its possibilities are fully expressed' (p. 280). Art, that is, is a shaping of the *process* of shaping. It does not consist in achieved form, which would become finitude, but in the experience of making form, an experience distributed across makers and perceivers.

There is another aspect of form, temporality, which involves both emotion and thought. The aspiration to form is a *sensuous* state. Consciousness of breaks and disjunction is registered in and through emotion. The discord which generates disturbance and desire is also, however, the agent of reflection, as the transitive impulse to form responds to the sensuous with the need to shape, which is itself reflexively sensuous. Thus reflection is not separated out from the sensuous experience: 'reflection is incorporated into objects *as* their meaning' (p. 15). Reflection, one might say, belongs to Dewey's characteristically hyphenated, compound states of transitional relationship. Another hyphenated condition is the relationship of time to the aesthetic experience. Form is achieved through the use of the past and therefore through the use of remembered emotion and reflection. Remembered discomforts and disturbances, and the remembered interactions which accomplished a partial resolution of distress, are used to reinforce the new structure of shaping in the present, while the future becomes a 'quickening of what now is' (p. 18). Throughout *Art as Experience* Dewey stresses the importance of the learned past of the culture. Nothing derives wholly from unlearned experience. This appears to entertain a conservative reading of the unbroken continuity of cultural tradition and the necessity of consecrating the aesthetic objects of the past. And perhaps this is a possible reading, for undoubtedly Dewey valued the resources of what we call high culture. However, if we see his theory of art in terms of an overcoming or attempted overcoming of trauma, a description which would by no means do violence to his ideas, the emphasis becomes rather different. To be socially made experience must have a history. The memory of trauma quickens the present, precipitating new solutions to distress. It is the vital memory of *disjunction*, which is the creative agency of form. Seen in this light, cultural tradition becomes the need to remember, to reremember and perhaps to mythologize, moments of stress, breaks, shock, along with history's partial solutions to them. Consider the history of slavery and slave narratives.

Emotion is closely allied with Expression, a term Dewey uses idiosyncratically, to designate an act or object 'informed with meaning' (p. 59). Thus, in the titles of his fourth and fifth chapters, he can speak of 'The act of expression' and 'The expressive object', which constitute the meaning-charged double movement reciprocally bringing aesthetic experience into being. For Dewey it is impossible to think of emotion without its objects, so that in this transitive condition it is also impossible to split self and world. Emotion, therefore, must be always already public, never private. Emotion, indeed, is only private if it is pathological, for in the sane mind excitation is always attached to events, to something beyond itself. Emotion is a mobile component of those compound states of doing-and-undergoing or acting-and-being-acted-upon to which life commits us. Experience is intrinsically emotional but there are no separate things called emotions in it, Dewey insists (p. 42). For to classify different forms of emotion as anger or pain or fear is to misrecognize emotion as simple, violent discharge for expression (p. 62). On the contrary, emotion is a continuous process of 'Impulsion' (p. 66), a drive 'to', 'from', or 'about' something external, occurring when a being is aware of a state of 'commotion', when inner impulse and environment are thrown into a 'ferment', when something is at stake and the living creature is prompted to search for new shape, to synthesize and reorder experience. Emotion is *all* these elements together. It is not is 'content' – for emotion is not *what* is expressed (p. 69) – but it *is* an activity, an activity which permeates the material with which it works (p. 53).

Psychic energy is put out in order to receive. Thus the perceiver's or beholder's experience is incorporated into what is made by the artist, who 'embodies in himself the attitude of a perceiver while he works' (p. 48), actively trying out possible meanings a beholder might experience and building them into the artwork. This interpenetration of action–reception, outgoing–incoming is not a pre-emptive empathy, as it may seem, but a labour which creates the possibilities of a response. Perhaps curiously, Dewey offers a conversation and then an extension of conversation in the job interview as a model for this process. But this dry analogy suggests, first, that power relations are not precluded by aesthetic experience and, secondly, that the end of an outflow of psychic energy is not the satisfaction which is exhausted in consumption so much as the pursuit of an evolving activity, structured round two parties strenuously engaged with one another. A job interview is a sensuous emotional experience. Something is at stake here, after all.

Thought, as one would expect of Dewey's hyphenated epistemology, cannot be disengaged from other aspects of experience. The 'esthetic cannot be marked off from intellectual experience' (p. 38). Indeed, intellectual and aesthetic experience are indivisible. Since the classification of categories is artificial and not inherent in human nature, we must see the split between sense and knowledge as a historical dissociation, not a philosophical necessity. In truth, sense and knowledge are reflexively compounded: 'As we manipulate, we touch and feel; as we look, we see; as we listen, we hear' (pp. 49–50). The sensory provokes the cerebral, the cerebral the sensory life. The disjunction which brings about the aesthetic work of form-making puts problems and problem-solving at the heart of its activities. Therefore the surmounting of problems, apprehension of relationships and the progressive bringing of these to consciousness is an activity which permeates the aesthetic state and its objects. An example of this saturation of experience with thought is the nature of coming to a conclusion. A conclusion is never detached from a body of argument. Premises emerge as conclusions manifest themselves, so conclusions are simultaneous with the ideas from which they evolve. 'A conclusion is no separate and independent thing: it is the consummation of a movement' (p. 38). Thought permeates experience as form, the effort to shape, plan and complete an action. Here the example is deliberately sinister. The planning and completion of a battle exemplifies aesthetic power. For Dewey is at pains to point out that if the aesthetic permeates experience as a form of thinking, it is necessarily indifferent to ethics.

It is the aporia between the aesthetic and the ethical which implicitly preoccupies Dewey; the aporia between the aesthetic and the economic which so concerns Guillory. This concern returns us to the question of value. To recapitulate, it can be established that Dewey does not leave sensuous experience to the ineffable but regards it as the architect of experience. Following from the formative or constitutive nature of the sensoria, a democratic understanding of the aesthetic emerges as the common propensity we must have as species being for aesthetic experience, indeed, of the functional centrality of the aesthetic in keeping us alive. The revolutionary or emancipatory possibilities of what Dewey assumes to be empirical fact rather than theory I shall explore in a moment; for he offers a far wider definition of aesthetic work than that to which we are accustomed. But these propositions have been arrived at by seeming to put the question of value aside. In a sense Dewey does put the question aside, because his arguments have made it irrelevant. It is precisely because he has established the literal existence of inherently qualitative experience and the *necessity* of this experience to both biological and mental life that he can afford to forget both economic and transcendent value. The exercise of aesthetic faculties are both a necessity and a good. Nevertheless, he does consider the question of judgement, a function of the 'Desire for authority': 'Criticism is thought of as if its business were not explication of the content of an object as to substance and form, but a process of acquittal or condemnation on the basis of merits and demerits' (p. 299). An assessment of merits and demerits readies an art object for the market and certainly invokes the hierarchy of value which Guillory thinks of as intrinsic to aesthetic works. But Dewey replaces the legal tally of merit and demerit with the need of 'a more adequate perception' of the artwork. The aesthetic energizes us by demanding not judgement but a desire of explication, an ever more adequate understanding of its possibilities, a repeated pursuit of the meanings informing it. Such arousal of intellectual and emotional desire, which persuades us not to judge or to consume, constitutes the importance of the aesthetic for Dewey. By this he does not mean either that the artwork is valuable because it generates an infinity of meaning or that it is valuable in proportion to its complexity, thus allowing 'value' to reintroduce itself all over again. He means something both more simple and more profound: the experience which makes us pause, not because it is transcendent but because it is so close to our sensuous and intellectual life that it starts some involuntary hermeneutic and shaping process. This could be a popular song heard in a supermarket, the lyric seizure of memory Yeats describes in *Among School Children* as a 'Ledaean body' rises to the consciousness of the 'smiling public man' inspecting a schoolroom, kicking the embers of a fire, a symphony. Sometimes the reverberations of this experience quickly exhaust themselves, resonate and are gone; sometimes they do not. It is of a piece with such thinking that Dewey's definition of spontaneity is 'complete absorption in subject matter that is fresh, the freshness of which holds and sustains emotion' (p. 70). But whatever can be said of these experiences, they are not easy to incorporate in structures of economic or transcendent value. They are to the side of the double discourse of value and do not belong to it. The hyphenated, transitive experience Dewey describes is not easily amenable to fetishistic possession either, because it is on the move, a provocation to form, whereas the essence of the fetish is a holding down through repetition of the same. It is interesting that Dewey constantly alludes to Keats, who was so fascinated by the physical arousal of sensuous life and the intellectual energies released by it.

In arguing that the aesthetic is a founding moment of fully human experience and in emphasizing the centrality of pleasure and arousal, Dewey clearly believes that there are far more opportunities for aesthetic work than we are aware of because he offers a far wider definition of it. Some people might want to argue that his understanding of the artwork is so inclusive that it disappears into the experience of everyday life. Dewey, in fact, would probably have had some sympathy with those theorists, such as Henri Lefebvre and Michel de Certeau, who explore the everyday and quotidian.[6] It is likely that he would have seen the arts of ruse, trick and diversion, which de Certeau in particular associates with creative tactics of survival practised by the alienated consumer, as a poesis which restores some autonomy to individuals dominated by technocratic systems. Certainly Svetlana Boym's interest in the way aura is remade from personal bricolage in the houses of emigrants and Elaine Scarry's delicate exploration of the sensuous lyricism of the flower catalogue are ways of considering the democratic possibilities of the aesthetic which are not far from Dewey's concerns.[7] And of course, these discussions hugely expand the customary boundaries of the artwork. Nevertheless, there is a hidden hierarchy in his book, because the fully constructed artwork which becomes for him a form of interpersonal and intersocial communication is his model of the achieved aesthetic object. He is, quite deliberately, always unwilling to give a content to what is essentially an art of the future: he never stipulates or predicts what it should be *about* any more than he considers the economics of cultural production as a formative aspect of *any* artwork's existence; it is enough for him to set up the potential for aesthetic experience as a biophysical and cognitive necessity.

So in some ways the revolutionary possibilities of *Art as Experience* remain implicit. But they are there. His much earlier educational thought of the turn of the century insists on this. His belief in a universal capacity for arousal, curiosity and aesthetic shaping is consistent with a democratic educational theory which asserts as a given the child's fascination with language, with inquiry, with making and with 'artistic expression' (*The Child and the Curriculum*, p. 47). 'I am afraid we have not what you want', he quotes a school desk supplier apologizing, 'You want something at which the children will work; these are only for listening' (p. 31). Immensely subtle, but travestied as 'child-centred' because he rejected passivity in learning, Dewey insisted that to structure the dialectic of education as an opposition between the child's experience and the developed consciousness of the adult, the child against the curriculum, nature against culture, was to engage with a false opposition. He recognized that the problem of creating a democratic education in a sophisticated indus-trialized society inevitably sharpened a distinction between training, which would ultimately fit a child for labour in a mechanized culture, and the release of imagination, which would defend the child against that culture's depredations; but he thought both views were wrong. 'There are those who see no alternative between forcing the child from without, or leaving him entirely alone. Seeing no alternative, some choose one mode, some choose another. Both fall into the same fundamental error' (p. 17). The educational thought works with contradictions, struggling to think through the relation between tradition and child, the school and community. It provides dimensions not apparent in the later aesthetics, which were evolved when Dewey was in his seventies. He was certain early in the century, however, that failure to work with a child's energies and to credit it with 'large and meaningful business for the mind' led to social breakdown, just as he was certain later that anarchy and authoritarianism were twin conditions. When 'formal movements' are substituted for 'vital reality', the learner becomes, ironically, content with this denial as the only option open to it, 'save in those cases of more intense activity which cannot accommodate themselves, and that make up the unruly and *déclassé* of our school product' (p. 28).

This political argument leads back to the 'incoherence and coercion' which for Dewey inhibit aesthetic experience. These, it will be remem-bered, preclude both sleep and waking. Hyperactivity and paralysis, the extremes of unrepressed material and repression, alike impose a regime which puts conscious and unconscious so far out of touch with one another that to dream becomes impossible. 'I dream of a Ledaean body'. I close this chapter by considering the impossibility of dreaming as conjoint with the failure of aesthetic work. To do so I turn to Wilfred Bion's account of the dream.

To wake, perchance to dream

For Freud dreamwork enables the eruption of repressed material into the conscious, offering it in the psychical structures whose terms are now very familiar – condensation, displacement, inversion and juxtaposition of symbols. Some act of translation has occurred, in which latent material is coded as manifest dream. For Bion, the dream is less a code than a continuous processing, as psychic materials move to and from the perme-able barrier of the conscious and unconscious. Some elements are more assimilable than others. Bion's notation characterizing psychic material in terms of alpha elements and beta elements registers the qualitative difference between transmutable materials, which are amenable to the dreamwork's symbolizing power and can thus be stored, and intransigently resistant and intractable materials which are not. These beta elements can be dealt with, if at all, by infinite splitting and projection, desperate efforts to transmute intransigent experience. They block what Bion thinks of as linking, the reconfiguration of symbolic materials which makes them available for new groupings, new kinds of cohesion. (For Bion the trauma of separation, or what would be castration for Freud, results in the possibility of new relationships, linking.) But the most fundamental conceptual difference between Freud and Bion is that Bion believed that dreamwork is a continuous process, occurring in sleeping and waking – we fall ill if it does not. Yeats dreams of his Ledaean body wide awake and energized. It is only through the continuous process of dreamwork that we are saved from the disintegration of splitting. In the post-humously published *Cogitations* Bion radically redefined the dream, dramatizing his differences with Freud:

> But *Freud* meant by dream-work that unconscious material, which would otherwise be perfectly comprehensible, was transformed into a dream, and that the dream-work needed to be undone to make the now incomprehensible dream comprehensible . . . I mean that the conscious material has to be subjected to dream-work to render it fit for storing, selection, and suitable for transformation from paranoid-schizoid position [scattering, splitting], to depressive position [symbol], and that unconscious pre-verbal material has to be subjected to reciprocal dream-work for the same purpose. . . *Freud* states that a dream is the way the mind works in sleep: *I* say it is the way it works when awake. (Bion, *Cogitations*, p. 43)

This continuous two-way exchange, rather than the unidirectional return of repressed material, enables not just dream thoughts but transitive *thinking* to occur. To return to Stephen Daedelus, thought is coming out of his eyes in a transposition of the colloquialism, coming out of one's ears. And he is dreaming, relating, sorting, assimilating, linking. Waste products of the body, snot, and of culture, a rusty boot, ally themselves with wrack and wreckage of the sea. But there is seaspawn and seawrack. Seaspawn and snot are seminal, semen-like secretions. Sea spawn can go to waste in seawrack. Stephen himself could become a kind of waste product of his culture, a rejected boot, a snotboot, as the related sounds suggest, the careless flotsam of blind reproduction. But there is also the possibility of reproduction and dissemination. Seaspawn and sea wrack become a dialectic about the possibility of meaning. He *does* make signs of them.

And graffiti? We recognize components of the aesthetic as Dewey described it in the arousal and violence of sensuous intensity which graffiti advertise. As anti-words they are non-consumable, not incorporated into the apparatus of the consumer. There is a raw enjoyableness in the refusal of meaning. This could make them modes of protest. The fat, distended brutalism of comic strip or advertisement graphics is offered so that violence is clearly disarticulated from signification, foregrounding violence with an odd kind of purity. But incoherence, Dewey reminds us, affords neither sleep nor waking. And to see the daring of graffiti in terms of incoherence is to consign Dewey's 'unruly' and *declassé* 'school product' to a form of social waste product. Are these aborted attempts to dream? And by the same token aborted attempts to wake up? Do these non-readable signs signal that they are something like beta elements, blockages which are being manipulated with fierce energy but also attacks on linking? To wake, perchance to dream. To consider this is to reflect on the denials of our culture and social organization, which does not enable everyone to dream by day and by night.

NOTES

1 See, on the graffiti tag, Iain Sinclair in *Lights Out for the Territory.* 'Urban graffiti is all too often a signature without a document, an anonymous autograph' (p. 1).
2 Useful discussions of value are also to be found in the following: John Frow, *Cultural Studies and Cultural Value*; Arjun Appadurai, 'Introduction: Commodities and the politics of value', *The Social Life of Things: Commodities in Cultural Perspective*, pp. 3–63; Steven Connor, *Theory and Cultural Value*; James S. Hans, *The Question of Value: Thinking through Nietzsche, Heidegger, and Freud*; Gianfranco Mossetto, *Aesthetics and Economics*; Herman Parret, ed., *Peirce and Value Theory: On Peircian Ethics and Aesthetics*; Gayatri Chakravorty Spivak, '*Scattered* speculations on the question of value', *In Other Worlds: Essays in Cultural Politics*, pp. 154–75.
3 Mary Poovey, 'Aesthetics and political economy in the eighteenth century: the place of gender in the social constitution of knowledge'.
4 Bourdieu's work has attracted increasing attention in Britain and America in the 1990s. See Richard Jenkins, *Pierre Bourdieu*; *Bourdieu: Critical Perspectives*, ed. Craig Calhoun, Edward LiPuma and Moishe Postone.
5 Theodor W. Adorno, *Aesthetic Theory* (1997), trans. Robert Hullot-Kentor, p. 11. I do not want to underestimate the difficulty of speaking of the sensuous. Adorno himself is ambivalent about it. Having emancipated artwork from cuisine and pornography, bourgeois taste, he thought, falls back

into philistinism when it concretely enjoys artworks, wanting 'art voluptuous and life ascetic' (p. 13). Yet though Adorno's own high modernist asceticism makes him reluctant to concede pleasure, he admits that art would feel odd without it. The answer is a dialectic in which the Kantian 'without interest' must 'be shadowed by the wildest interest, and there is much to be said for the idea that the dignity of artworks depends on the intensity of the interest from which they are wrested': a struggle to transform the sensuous both reproduces and transforms it. In an important contribution to Levine's collection of essays, 'Justine; or, the Law of the Road' (*Aesthetics and Ideology*, pp. 106–23), Frances Ferguson explores the aporias around discussion of the sensuous in historical terms. It is the shared relativization of the body and its physical experiences, leading to what she terms 'ontological relativity' (p. 121), that puts pornography and the aesthetic, de Sade and Kant, together as formative agents of modern civil society. This relativism has been built into the law (her example is Bentham). Both de Sade and Kant exemplify a shift from intentionality to effects and consequences, de Sade in relation to actions and Kant in relation to objects. The hyperbolic frisson of the sublime comes about through the body's response to the natural world, which is peremptorily made into an aesthetic object through the mind's construction of that sensuous event, irrespective of nature's 'nature' as an object. An aesthetic effect has been imposed on the world. This finds its parallel in de Sade's conception of bodily acts, which are made to yield sensuous experience irrespective of their own wills. Ferguson sees in this a shift from meaning and intention of the individual actant to *consequences* of the bodily act. Because ethical judgement or blame enters only at this point, the sensuous is opened to a field of relativization, both by being severed from intention and because assessment of 'behaviourist' consequences is open to a variable interpretative framework. Thus in both de Sadian practice and Benthamite theory the sensuous took on a new status in civil society, both foregrounded and relativized.

6   Henri Lefebvre, *Critique of Everyday Life*; Michel de Certeau, *The Practice of Everyday Life*.

7   Svetlana Boym, unpublished lecture, 'Memory' conference, Center for Literary and Cultural Studies, Harvard University, November, 1995; Elaine Scarry, 'Imagining flowers' pp. 100–101.

6

And Beauty? A Dialogue

Scene

The musculature of Bloomsbury trees, their top branches veining the sky, can be seen through four ceiling-to-floor oblong windows at the new Institute for Research into Culture and Democracy. A discussion is about to begin before an audience.

CHAIR: Welcome to IRCD, established with the aid of the Local Governments of London Association and the Metropolitan Universities Fund, the people's ICA so to speak [*uncertain laughter*], and to this discussion, organized to mark the new translation of Theodor Adorno's great post-humous work, *Aesthetic Theory*.[1] Helena Smith-Bradley, who holds the recently founded Beautiful Soul Chair of Aesthetics at Oxbridge (funded by the Gowrie Trust and a grant from the Lottery Commission) and Tim Jones, Benjamin Reader in popular culture at the University of Milton Keynes (established with contributions from the Tesco Consortium) are with us today to initiate the debate.[2] I should say that we are unable to have coffee today because work on the Institute buildings is unfinished – we are existing in torn quarters so to speak [*slightly more reassured laughter*] – but I hope the sound of hammering is sufficiently distant not to disturb us. I call upon Tim Jones to begin.

[*She dwells with Beauty – the beauty and the wonder and the power?*]

BENJAMIN READER: Tetchily agonistic, choleric, costively aporetic, what do we do with Adorno and his discontents today, in 1997, over a decade after the 1984 translation of *Aesthetic Theory*, and over two decades after the work was first published in German, in 1970? After nearly thirty years, does his inveighing against the barbarism of the culture industry – the 'face of the most beautiful girl becomes ugly', you remember, 'by a striking resemblance to the face of a film star on whom it was carefully modeled' (p. 67) – help us to think about culture? The regression of commodified artforms, kitsch, and the 'culinary' tastes of 'philistine' consumers, the rage of the masses, who revenge themselves on high culture by blacking out the teeth of the toothpaste ads intended to seduce them with commodity culture – pearls before swine – all this is familiar stuff. How relevant to cultural analysis is it now? Arguably we are much more subtle today. We are aware of the vitality and variation in popular subcultures – in music, for instance, despite the culture industry's insistent co-option of subcultures into the mainstream, a recent occurrence being the transformation of Underground Garage into Speed Garage. We are aware of variation in the commercial mainstream itself. We have come to see that this stark opposition between the elitist isolation of high art and the culinary tastes of the masses emerges from Adorno's own sweeping categories. That is, once you have conceptualized a group monolithically as 'the masses' your own definition prevents you from perceiving anything but homogeneity in this group. By insisting on seeing cultural forms in dissociation from an analysis of social and political forms, without reference to class or hegemonic structures, he gave himself only the broadest distinctions to work with. By generalizing Marx's theory of value so that the contamination of exchange value affects everyone alike, he could not, as Gillian Rose has shown, derive an analysis of social structure from economic structure. Nor, as she says, could he distinguish the political effects of different forms of popular culture.[3] He glorified high avant-garde art, but ended up angrily impaled on the horns of one of his frequent aporias, impotent, because high art was both elitist and collusive with the very torn halves of a culture it had helped to rend apart. That is the problem we have to discuss today.

[*I died for beauty?*]

BEAUTIFUL SOUL: No, it isn't, quite. You are, of course, too complacent about the nature of commercialized culture, but the problem we have to discuss today is beauty. This is the term perpetually present in Adorno's prose. He was one of the few Marxist critics to use beauty as a viable term, and to use it consistently and seriously. You've ignored it. Terry Eagleton, in the broad lampoon of his chapter on Adorno in *The Ideology of the Aesthetic*,[4] cannot bring himself to introduce the B-word into his discussion. The truth is, Adorno was a liberal humanist struggling to get out of Marxist clothing, vainly attempting to give the old bourgeois humanist terms, the traditional nineteenth-century aesthetics, a Marxist gloss. He was, if I can put this provocatively, one of us. I am repeatedly struck, noting the interesting convergence of the publication of *Aesthetic Theory* and Iris Murdoch's essays, *Existentialists and Mystics*, this year, 1997, by how very much they share with one another.[5] Both are unembarrassed about using the term great art, which seems to trouble you, if I understand your work aright, and neither is anxious about introducing the notion of spirit. True, Adorno's touchstone for great art is Beckett, whereas Murdoch's criterion of irrefutable greatness is the work of Shakespeare and Tolstoy. Art and morality converge because beauty is one of the spiritual things, perhaps the only spiritual thing, we love by instinct. In beauty, 'the truth of the sublime', as Murdoch puts it, we find love, 'the non-violent apprehension of difference'. A 'loving respect for a reality other than oneself' (p. 218), which is also true freedom. She saw as clearly as Adorno that one person's freedom became the unfreedom of the other (p. 62). What is this if it is not Adorno's repudiation of 'domination', a repudiation of power relations, and its corollary in his striving for what he termed 'non-identity'? That is, a saving mismatching of subject and object which creates the space for critique, the motive of *Negative Dialectics*.

[*She walks in beauty – Beauty is truth, truth beauty, – that is all / Ye know on earth, and all ye need to know – I died for – the power?*]

BENJAMIN READER: I admit there's a way they share Arnoldian values (for one thing they are both totally gender blind, not to speak of race). But they don't occupy the same humanist frame. Adorno's analysis has political roots. You simply confuse matters if you subsume Adorno's antihumanist deconstruction under Murdoch's essentially religious and consolatory...

[*so inform / The mind that is within us, so impress / With quietness and beauty – she walks in?*]

BEAUTIFUL SOUL: Murdoch did not believe that art *should* be a consolation and stay. She saw that it could be *used* as one. Like Adorno (p. 61) she saw that art's degeneration into a consolatory form was correlative with the actual rise of inhumanity. That is why she insisted that 'Art and morals...are one' (p. 219). Beauty and morals are one because art is about the struggle between good and evil (p. 55). Art for her, particularly in later work, is rapture, ecstasy, mystical experience, the will to power, violence, extremes of spirituality and debasement, but it is capable of placing us under the sublime obligation of the ethical. The aesthetic transcends, ultimately, categories of politics and gender. In essence, if we *are* talking politics, her liberal critique of the unboundedly free, 'totalitarian' bourgeois subject that she discovered in Sartre's existentialism, her attack on the destructiveness of the instrumental Kantian rational being, and her analysis of late capitalism, have a striking affinity with Adorno. Listen to this, from an essay of 1958:

> There is less poverty but no more (in some ways less) true community life. Work has become less unpleasant without becoming more significant. The gulf remains between the skilled and creative few and uncreative many. What was formerly called the proletariat has lost what culture it once had, and gained no true substitute. A stream of half-baked amusements hinders thought and the enjoyment of art and even of conversation. Equality of opportunity produces, not a society of equals, but a society in which the class division is made more sinister by the removal of intelligent persons into the bureaucracy and the destruction of their roots and characteristics as members of the mass. In short, a proletariat in the fundamental sense intended by Marx still exists: a deracinate, disinherited and excluded mass of people. Only this mass is now quiescent, its manner of life largely suburban and its outlook 'petty bourgeois', and it increasingly lacks any concept of itself as deprived. (Iris Murdoch, *Existentialists and Mystics*, p. 183)

[*Where Beauty cannot keep her lustrous eyes – labour is . . . beauty born out of its own despair – The Genitals Beauty?*]

BENJAMIN READER: [*Putting aside his notes*] Well, even Adorno's fanatical bitterness about mass culture wasn't quite as eugenic as that, and I do not believe that Adorno would have wanted the revival of moral and religious vocabulary for which Murdoch was searching. *That* for him was ideology, confirming rather than deconstructing the sanctified bourgeois subject, just as simply to recognize other people in their otherness and 'contingency', as Murdoch has it, would be neither a political analysis nor a political act. Her sense that to recognize the 'messiness' (a word she uses a lot) of contingency is supremely important does not constitute a politics. And to attempt to render the richness of the other through the particularities of the realist novel is simply the other side of the coin of individualism. But still, let me try and convince you that Adorno's, I admit, passionate concern with beauty comes out of a politics quite alien to Murdoch. To begin with, why was it that, in contrast to Benjamin, Adorno did not abandon traditional aesthetic vocabulary? Benjamin invented terms adapted to the new forms of industrial and technological production: 'Aura', for instance, so familiar that it has almost become an accepted aesthetic term, with its archaic religious association of the halo, replaced what we would call unique aesthetic value, but at the same time it had the advantage of incipient resignification as the lit-up advertisement sign of the urban scene, having your name in lights; 'dialectical image' did duty for a kind of surrealist symbol embodying contradiction; 'blasted out of the continuum of history' stood for the shock of insight or defamiliarization, inevitably traumatic, as the new violence of mechanized culture was.[6] But Adorno deliberately preserved traditional terms such as beauty, or slightly adapted them, using 'transcendence' and 'enigma' alongside one another, for instance, and 'art' and 'artwork' in the same way. For him Benjamin's surrealist aesthetic broke with history, with the idea of dialectic and with mediation. The traditional terms made possible that anamnesis, a sacramental memory of the past, which acknowledged a sedimented history accumulated through time. It was vital not to let go of these cultural meanings, *not* for the sake of simple preservation or conservation of a static or hypostatized past commemorating the static qualities of the true, the good and the beautiful, but precisely because such terms registered ideological change, a history of both dispossession and emancipatory possibility. They also registered suffering. For 'the memory of accumulated suffering' (p. 261) can never be shaken off. If for Benjamin the cultural trophies of high art register exploitation and oppression, because they are appropriated by the power of the conqueror, for Adorno art is an admonitory testimony to the eloquence of suffering as well as to the powers of horror. Benjamin reminded us that every aesthetic 'achievement' was predicated on the barbarism of oppression, so much so that some Marxist critics literally cannot encounter the politically contaminated western artwork, let alone the notion of aesthetic experience, which stinks of privilege and power. One would have expected Adorno's pessimism to have made him congenitally sympathetic to such a view, and there is a crude interpretation of his work which figures him as rejecting the possibility of poetry after Auschwitz. But this is not the case. Because suffering is inscribed in art, is the very core of the aesthetic, art must be remembered rather than rejected. Art is the mnemosynistic passion of a culture.

[*Dulce it is, and decorum, no doubt, for one's country to fall* – *Brute beauty and valour and act* – *A terrible beauty is born?*]

But terms become frozen, petrified, refusing to yield up memory. This is how Adorno understood reification, the congealing of language to stone-like imperturbability, smoothed by cultural amnesia, commodification and the administered world of capitalism, so that concepts became things.[7] Thus was necessitated a Nietzschean effort of destruction – and Adorno is nothing if not a Nietzschean Marxist – of tearing up of terminology by the roots, at once to expose the genealogy, in Nietzsche's sense, of old meanings and to create the new. Aesthetic products can be given radically different meanings in different historical periods, sometimes serving conservative, sometimes emancipatory interests. The old meanings themselves will be agonistically crossed with contradiction and fissured with a history of reification and upheaval, and notions such as beauty have to be redeemed from falling into hypostatized universal concepts (p. 83), but, all the more reason in the case of beauty, is it necessary to vaunt its possibilities for modernity. Thus Adorno returns compulsively again and again to rework, tear up and lay down again the aesthetics of Kant and Hegel, like workmen who keep tearing up and relaying the same bit of pavement . . .

[*I died for beauty – brute beauty – terrible beauty – the wonder and the power?*]

BEAUTIFUL SOUL: But so far you have said little about beauty, or what I call beauty.

[*truth beauty – quietness and beauty – and the wonder?*]

BENJAMIN READER: I'm coming to that. What Adorno calls 'the unstillable longing in the face of beauty', the something, the 'what was promised' (p. 82) in the artwork, can only be got at by making it *appear* in prose criticism, manifesting itself rather than being discursively analysed. It can only appear through understanding the dense contradictions which bring it into being. So, in Adorno's complexly impacted prose, one sentence will negate another without, as it were, the argument seeming to be aware of this: because the argument doesn't describe or even enact dialectic; it becomes it. It has to *be* rather than discursively describing the aesthetic, and thus Adorno uses the paratactic method of exposition, juxtaposing contradictory ideas without telling us they are contradictory.

[*I died – where Beauty cannot keep her lustrous eyes – born out of its own despair?*]

BEAUTIFUL SOUL: And beauty?

BENJAMIN READER: Hold on. The argument also becomes, it *is* beauty. Consider how Adorno quietly reinstates aura, refuting Benjamin utterly without telling us he is doing so, affirming a telos for the artwork in history and in modernity. In the piece, 'Situation', he has already mentioned that the externalization of an image is common to both cave paintings and the multiple reproductions enabled by the camera, and that Benjamin's sharp break between auratic and mass-produced art suppresses this similarity. In another discussion, 'Art beauty', he uses a number of terms akin to 'aura' which hint at the argument at issue simply through semantics – appearance, apparition, radiance, luster [*sic*], incandescence, fireworks. His point is that aura is not a shine that can be taken off artwork, like a polish, at different

historical periods, or even in modernity when it is reproduced mechan-
ically. Lustre, incandescence, is bound up with the very nature of artwork as that which is not a substitute for anything, not a copy, not a
representation, and which therefore shines out independently, without
needing to parallel relations of economic exchange, which are all about
substitution and reproduction. He wants to retain aura because it
resists the abstraction to which modern economic conditions have
reduced exchange. At the same time the artwork's radiance *is* bound
up with mechanical reproduction and its production of spectacle. This
is how it works. Autonomous art withdraws into its own truth, affirming that it is not a copy, a substitute for, a representation of anything. It
has overcome the primordial visceral and psychic shudder of powerlessness in the face of nature (the motive of all art) and exists as an
after-image of that moment. Nevertheless it is dependent for its existence on its a priori, the mechanics of spectacle in the empirical world,
which it secretes in its being. Adorno instances the unofficial culture of
'art-alien' forms at different historical periods, such as the circus, the
modern revue or musical comedy, or the mechanical fountains of the
seventeenth century, as forms of spectacle which make themselves and
the mechanisms which produce them obvious. It is only through such
mechanisms that artwork can be consummated in objectivation as
'appearance', and only through appearance that it can take on the
nature of 'apparition' – literally a vision, a heavenly vision, radiant,
lustrous, a promise of beyond. Valéry understood and theorized artwork through the phenomenon of fireworks and their momentary
grazing of the sky with surprise and wonder, a model for what Adorno
unashamedly called the magic of the aesthetic. Appearing empirically,
yet 'liberated from the burden of the empirical' (p. 81), they are at once
artefactual, *actual* and *other* to the empirical world – a magical phenomenon which is not a 'higher truth' but an astonishment and a
wonder, intellectual delight and kinaesthetic happening.

[*What the imagination seizes as beauty must be truth, whether it existed
before or not?*]

But here the sentences begin to configure different contours as the
dialectic swings against itself. The very rapture of spirit conjures its
antithesis, a blocked corporeal experience. To be outside the empirical
world is to leave it untouched, and thus to be physical image, naïve
illusion, is art's way of belonging to the world. When 'the vagrant
fiddler disappears from the spiritual chamber musician' (p. 81), and
when clowns disappear from drama (Adorno is thinking of Beckett's
Endgame and *Happy Days*) apparition will be displaced by the dry,
transparent artwork which is essentially dead. Nevertheless, illusion,

even radiant illusion and even the illusion that refuses consolation, brings artwork into the sphere of substitution and the copy. The 'ether' of the beautiful, which resists appropriation as an entity or a concept and epitomizes that which cannot be subsumed into exchange, becomes susceptible to exchangeability, the world of 'everything-for-something else' (p. 83). It can be equated with something else. Thus appears a characteristically Adornian aporia. The beautiful moves into the sphere of ideology. It beckons to a world emancipated from exchange but in the act of doing so is betrayed into exchange. Is it capable of showing us that not everything is exchange, or of becoming a critique of exchange, and more, of exchange which has become abstract and mystified? The pure use value of the aesthetic, the expiring flare of the firework's jouissance gives up its promise. For Adorno this is a catastrophe because the beautiful is a rare apparition, perhaps a vision, of use value in a commodified world which persuades us that our experience is of use value while remorselessly subjecting us to the false consciousness of exchange value. That is why, whatever you think of his objection to jazz, he saw it as the music of exchange value because it was repeatable, copying itself as it were, and fetishizing that copying. It is hard to reproduce the density and compression of the ideas . . .

[*Dulce – what the imagination seizes must be – brute beauty?*]

BEAUTIFUL SOUL: Well, at least you do not think the beautiful is ideology, though I am uncomfortable with notions of ideology and the aesthetic. And I'm not sure in any case if the pryrotechnical model doesn't smuggle the ineffability of 'pure' art uncontaminated with the economic back on to the scene where it has been condemned as idealist. I prefer Murdoch's sense of the limits on art set by neurosis and convention. She believed that art could be taken over by the psychotic and by extreme formalism and conventional correctness. Both extremes lead to the death of art. In some ways she was bringing together psychoanalysis and culture in a very creative way. Certainly she was not the slave of a totalizing economic theory. You have persuaded me that Adorno has a rather more generous and flexible understanding of the beautiful than I had believed possible. But you have not persuaded me that he was anything like a materialist in the classic Marxist sense. I don't think he was. All his analysis is carried out at an abstract epistemological level. So the Marxism is gestural, all a matter of the perpetual choreography of subject/object relations, the dance of the non-identical. The epistemological forms have no political content, which Adorno shrugged off as mere epiphenomena. He dismissed overt Brechtian politics as mere functionalism. That's what irritates Eagleton

(I am very glad to say). What would worry me if I were a Marxist is that Adorno seems to pay exaggerated attention to the 'idealist' foundational aesthetics on which western ideas of the beautiful are grounded. Kant and Hegel are forever being invoked. That's not my problem, of course. It's yours.

[*all ye need to know?*]

BENJAMIN READER: You interrupted me. I was coming to that. Marxists have always had immense respect for their idealist predecessors. As for abstract epistemological forms: there is something pure about epistemology –

BEAUTIFUL SOUL: You said it!

BENJAMIN READER: – pure about epistemology which can *be* the sheer beauty of ideas. That's what Adorno wanted, for his exposition to expitomize the beauty of ideas themselves, almost as pure geometry does. But I'm amazed you cannot see the sense in which he was a materialist. To go back to the incandescence of the firework: as usual, Adorno works through encountering a series of intellectual impossibilities and blocks, the impediment of contradiction and irreconcilability; the firework brings into the world something that 'does not exist' (p. 82), as he puts it; a kind of miracle has occurred; and there is a real sense in which the firework, all evanescent flare, a kind of second-order thing, does not exist as things in the world do. But ultimately it never transcends empirical reality; it needs the sensuous, the brute physical existence of the material world, and depends on crude mechanism for its very nature as apparition. So the work of art is *intrinsically* material, corporeal in its essence, tied to history. It is not just a matter of the conditions of production and reproduction, as in Benjamin's essay on mechanical reproduction, although of course these always shape the attributes of the artwork. And Adorno goes further than Benjamin to the artwork's core: popular or unofficial artforms which do not trouble to conceal mechanical artifice – which indeed are predicated on exposing artifice – will, at any historical juncture in culture, *always* be absorbed into artwork in some form, demonstrating its dependence on demotic experience. Otherwise the artwork will die of its lack of the clown's red nose and grotesque devices, the fountain's upsurge, the musical comedy's svelte routine of sequin-and fish-netted legs high kicking in unison. 'The abounding glittering jet . . . Stoops', in Yeats's words, to 'a mechanical / Or servile shape'. Here the aesthetic hierarchies we associate with Adorno are not in evidence. Popular, visceral forms are 'incorporated' into the ether of art, a pun Adorno would have liked, incidentally, suggesting the aporia between the bodily and the unembodied at one and the same time. For all artwork is 'mythically' bound up with its antithesis and this cannot be explained away (p. 85).

[*what the imagination seizes as beauty must be – whether it existed before or not – wonder and – the Genitals Beauty?*]

BEAUTIFUL SOUL: Since you have forgotten Kant and Hegel I will make a start on them, or at least on Kant, for in him we encounter a major problem. Now I think in his critique of Kant Adorno again coincides with what you have chosen to call humanist criticism. I will take Murdoch as an example again. Adorno said that 'art itself thinks' (p. 99), that as a second-order thing it is the objectivation of a play of forces, which include those of thought. He was unhappy with the Kantian refusal of the concept to the aesthetic, but he was always doubtful how far thought entered into artwork, sometimes affirming the necessity of thought, sometimes that art 'lacks the concept' (p. 99). Murdoch is much clearer on all this. She brilliantly describes Kant's view that the apprehension of the sensuous object through the union of imagination and the understanding is 'not brought under any particular concept', as a 'synthesis', a 'putting together of conceptless representation', obeying Kant's dictum that the object is given but not thought (*Existertialists*, p. 207). She points out how supremely limiting and indeed trivial this account is, restricting aesthetic appreciation to form, to abstract lines such as those in wallpaper (Kant's example), to looking at a flower, to hearing wordless music (*Existentialists*, p. 209). It is all very well for the play of art to resemble morality or for the imagination to play *as if* in seriousness, but it is impossible to encompass high art, great tragedy, for example, through these criteria, and therefore she moves to a notion of the moral law derived from the imperatives of the sublime as the foundation of art. The incommensurateness of the sublime, in a virtually religious moment, imposes an obligation on the rational faculties to encompass its nature in the same way as the awesome imperatives of moral law compel assent. Insofar as Adorno is interested in the 'incommensurable' (p. 96) of the sublime (which is a pervasive concept for him) and insofar as he too constantly acknowledges the presence of great art, he, too, is moving towards an account of the sublime in 'the autonomy' of the 'spiritualized artwork' (p. 92) just as Murdoch does. Both are fascinated by form and its dangers. I think he smuggles in morality, but even if you do not agree with this, you could say that the movement of Adorno's thought through negation and aporia is just another way of speaking of the post-modern sublime. Adorno's antihumanism seems to mimic humanism closely here, how-ever much he surrounds the sublime with those wretched aporias.

[*truth – and the power – and the power – and the power – I died for?*]

BENJAMIN READER: Now that really is a travesty. I agree that Murdoch's discussion of Kant is wonderfully lucid, and that Adorno settles on the same passage that subtracts the concept from the beautiful (p. 94). But Adorno reads Kant dialectically and ideologically, and this is not simply a formal difference. Remember the reasons for the eternal return of Kant and Hegel in Adorno's writings. He wanted to demonstrate that one both can and cannot derive a materialist poetics from them, that the possibility for a materialist reading has sedimented through history, virtually *pari passu* with the dominant 'idealist' cultural meanings they accrued. In simply reversing idealism Marx failed to problematize it. Hence the turn to Kant and Hegel in Adorno's work, to a foundational aesthetics, rather than to Marx. Actually, the problem of the concept can be best approached through Hegel, and to the worrying at Hegel's analysis of natural beauty, which Adorno finds 'crass' (p. 75) but vital for an understanding of precisely the way mind has its roots in material otherness. To begin a materialist aesthetics with the 'classical' idealist topic of natural beauty seems strange, particularly as Adorno insists that mediated nature has already been ruthlessly devastated by capital, which has oppressed animals, landscape and woman (p. 63) – a rare reference to gender difference. But he begins this way precisely to invoke and lay bare the simple tourist's or landscape painter's expectations of an unmediated nature as other. For the way *culture* has always already constructed natural beauty as other and the way such physical 'immediacy' exists for us is the first test of materialist accounts of subject and object. Hegel has been taken in by culture's construction of the other or nature as external to the subject, always, in a sense, escaping from the subject but always ready to be seized by it. On the contrary, it never is. Adorno offers us a wonderfully eloquent account of the interchange of history and nature – in a Holderlin poem a stand of trees bears 'the mark of a past event' (p. 71). Hegel failed to see the vital dissonance between mind and nature, which keeps them in irresolvable tension, because he simply formulated a one- sided account of nature, locked within itself, as 'other' to mind, thus opening the way for an equally one-sided domination by mind (and by extension ruthless economic exploitation) as it seeks to penetrate the material order of things (p. 74). The irreducible independence and excess of nature can only be grasped when it is understood, in a negative recalibration of the relationship, *to* mind as other and not *for* it as other. And this is a deeply *aesthetic* perception of nature's otherness and indeterminable beauty (p. 72). Possibly the only meaningful relationships with anything or anybody are aesthetic ones, although domination is never absent from them.

Hegel's crassness is connected with a passage in which Adorno says that Hegel's epistemology, in offering a paradigm in which mind is first separate from and then united with externality, was led to mystify sheer sensuousness (p. 90), which in turn allows sensuous particulars to be indistinguishable from the details of life in an administered society (p. 84). Worse, that fusion of mind and sensuous nature invited by Hegel disallows that vital tension and negativity between consciousness and the materials it tries to penetrate. Hegel's sense that mind and its other could be fused is, of course, a response to and challenge of the Kantian idea that beauty exists for the subject without the concept, and this is the bridge to the Kantian view of beauty which you have shown Murdoch to critique.

Adorno reads Kant in much the same way as Hegel, but with a further twist. If the aesthetic were purely intuitable without concepts, then there would be no difference between it and the empirical world (p. 96). Art can be reduced neither to intuition nor the concept but exists in perpetual mediation of them (p. 97). And artwork needs the concept paradoxically, to release sensuousness into being, rather as, earlier, Adorno says art imitates not nature but natural beauty itself (p. 77). But the false dichotomy between intuitional and conceptual experience is at heart as ideological as the notion of its gapless synthesis. Intuition is another name for bourgeois freedom, the concept is another name for the work and labour from which it is alienated – 'Behind the cult of intuitability lurks the philistine convention of the body that lies stretched out on the sofa while the soul soars to the heights' (p. 98).

[*Nature . . . can . . . so impress / With quietness and beauty – what the imagination seizes as truth – labour . . . blossoming – beauty born out of its own despair?*]

BEAUTIFUL SOUL: [*yawning slightly*] But what is the beautiful? We seem to be retreating from it into abstractions or ideology. What is beauty? How are we to write about it, think about it, let it belong to our daily lives? Is the aesthetic something different from beauty? Is it an experience, a thing, or exclusively an artwork in which is comprehended our response? We've been talking very amorphously. Murdoch says aesthetic experience is a 'compound' (*Existentialists*, p. 55). Adorno says the intuitional elements in artwork are 'intermittent' (p. 98). So what is it? That poem's stand of trees against which history has brushed? Those residual swags of yellow autumn leaves one can glimpse out of the window here? The streaked, fleshy blue of a single

hyacinth bell from the reception desk over there? The surge of an aria?
The dimly transparent billows of film-covered petals which rose up on
the London pavements after Princess Diana died? In some brilliantly
original articles Elaine Scarry has argued that the vivacity and particularity of sensuous experience is only conjured under the aegis of the
imagination, 'that the imagination consists exclusively of its objects,
that it is only knowable through its object, that it is remarkable among
intentional states for not being easily separable into the double structure of state and object' ('On vivacity', p. 19). Like Kant, she considers
flowers as instances of the beautiful.[8] But presumably the same authority of the sensuous would be held by the garden catalogues she
describes, or even a cookery book. Or a collection of family photographs? Beauty is something you don't want to ingest or consume. I
wonder if that would disqualify pornography.
[*she walks in – she dwells with – lustrous eyes – imagination seizes –
Beauty?*]
BENJAMIN READER: Intentionality would certainly be characteristic
of the beautiful for Adorno. And what he called objectivation, and not
the wildly subjectivist expressive theories of bourgeois aesthetics
(which lives in the false consciousness of the aesthetic 'state'), was a
prerequisite. But beauty is not an invariant. It is anything that is pulled
away from the empirical world and which achieves aura in the process,
which lights up – it is sometimes prised gently away, sometimes torn
with traumatic violence. He does seem to think that the intentionally
made aesthetic object is the paradigm case of beauty – though I
personally can see no reason why the things around us should not
incandesce. The temptation of reification is built into the artwork,
Adorno remorselessly says, because it has gone through the processes
of domination simply to be created, but it, beauty, is not a thing, an is,
or even an ought; it is a *want*, or *wanting*. Beauty conjures wanting
because it is a promise of the as yet unsayable, a fleeting promise of
new possibilities, of scarcely envisioned openings in experience
emancipated from the world of exchange. Possibilities not actualized
vanish as memories do. That is why for Adorno beauty is the place of
unstillable yearning. Not only does it conjure the longing that does not
want to consume: it conjures longing's longing for a world where
consumption does not dominate, even if we can give this world no
content.
[*the imagination seizes?*
I died for beauty born out of its own despair
I died where Beauty cannot keep her lustrous eyes
I died for – wonder and beauty that must die]

BEAUTIFUL SOUL: Oh dear, you've spoilt it all. This looks like some Lacanian theory of beauty as lack, the void of desire which desires further desire and more lack. This, you know, can be turned into a kind of consumption in itself. Or else, together with the refusal of praxis, it looks too like the lie of the aesthetic, the idealist's sensuous vision ultimately empty and helpless before the political and cultural real, delusive magic casements opening on to the wasteland.
[*its own despair?*]

BENJAMIN READER: No. Adorno's work comes out of the Holocaust, and later out of 1968, the first time students openly condemned the elite category of the aesthetic and trashed bourgeois art. It comes out of the most terrible realism. His revision of the visionary *must* be predicated on the black modernity he conceived himself to live in – 'what after all is left to do but scream' (p. 30). We may hate its fanatical bleakness, its simplicities, its rancour, the zero world of the impoverished subject eviscerated by the 'total society' (p. 31) which finds its reduction of life to abstract social relations mirrored in the iconography of Beckett's theatre. But for Adorno only an absolutely negative analysis of modernity is the guarantee of art's emancipatory possibility, which is always in dialectic with the functional society (p. 251). The possibilities opened up in the aesthetic, however fleeting, are real. He himself answered the charge of idealism by taking over its ground and by saying, in a wonderful phrase, that the beautiful is what 'cannot possibly be thought away' (p. 77). In other words, artwork is so substantive that it enters into mind and insistently stays there. And this answers the charge of Adorno's refusal of praxis: as Rose concludes, his is a 'praxis of thought not a recipe for social and political action'.[9] If he lived with aporias that could not be explained away he did not hesitate to embark on the arduous task of explaining why they came into being.
[*Dulce – I died for – imagination – brute beauty – terrible beauty?*]

CHAIR: Well, I'd like to thank both our speakers. This has given us a lot to think about, and I will now open up the discussion. Any questions?
[*Three people speak simultaneously*]

WOMAN: You've said *nothing* about gender.

MAN IN A SUIT: You've said *nothing* about cultural value and tradition.

MAN IN A MAC: You've said *nothing* about art and democracy.

BEAUTIFUL SOUL: Gender... As I have said, the category of the aesthetic, beauty, transcends gender. I've come to this conclusion because whenever I consider a great artwork I cannot attribute anything in it specifically to gender difference – and I've often tried, because I'm not out of sympathy with feminism, as you will know from my work. Great art is above sexual difference, for the reason, I think, that it is androgynous, and I think that is why gender issues hardly ever occurred to Adorno. I think Rita Felski is right when she says there is no specifically feminist aesthetic.[10] Though there is, as she says, a feminist counterpublic sphere which has made us aware of gender issues in artworks and made it possible for women to have access to the aesthetic and gain acceptance as artists. There is equality of opportunity now for women in the arts world, and so I don't feel that gender is an issue any longer.

[*Member of audience*:   'Post-feminism, huh?']*   ['OK. So what about race?']

BENJAMIN READER: It is quite clear that Adorno thought women oppressed, but if he had addressed gender issues it would have simply given him more to complain about without altering the general picture of culture or the culture industry very much. Seriously, though, I wonder if his account of Beckett might have been rather different if he had taken gender on board. Does Beckett attack the mother's body as Roger Scruton insists,[11] or are the plays critiques of male hysteria in a reified world? Without the work of feminist criticism we would not be taking it for granted now that there are gender *issues* in texts and works, even if we cannot discover a gendered aesthetic. And more seriously, I believe that, both then, in pre-war Germany and in post-war America, and now, questions of the aesthetic were and are always haunted by the fact that to work on them in our culture is to be *feminized*. Thus male critics strive to show that they are not working in a feminized discourse and occlude gender. Or they do what I think Adorno interestingly did: reduce the feminine to stereotypes, and suppress homoerotic desire. Though *discursively* his argument with Benjamin has all the marks of homoerotic feeling, a love affair.

['Special pleading for queer theory!'] ['So feminism is displaced by cultural theory to satisfy the egos of male critics like you!']

CHAIR: Let's turn to cultural value and tradition.

BEAUTIFUL SOUL: I think I've already implied a great deal about cultural value and tradition. I do believe in the great work of art, and it may well be that our high traditions are only open to the few with cultural skills. And equality of opportunity, expansion of the universities and so on, will presumably enable some without cultural skills to gain them. However, I think that a great deal more things are eligible as aesthetic *experience* than would have been admissible in the past, and this of course is open to everyone –

'Wildly contradictory: so there is great art and then there are ordinary people with ordinary aesthetic experiences.']

– please let me continue. Iris Murdoch said we are all storytellers but some stories are high art and some are not. I'm making an aesthetic and not a class judgement here –

['Oh no you're not.']

– as for tradition I agree with Roger Scruton that tradition is a culturally sustaining, educative force – it shows people how to conduct interpersonal relations, how to express themselves, according to agreed, deeply sanctioned social principles by which they *recognize* themselves. Above all, tradition is a matter of *training*.[12] People who belong to a tradition share certain practices, and art and culture are among these. Some cultural artefacts are bonding. For instance, what Scruton sees, contra Adorno, as Beckett's rampant celebration of the Cartesian ego would not create the social adhesion he looks for. And he is trying to see how aesthetic experience could be a kind of a priori for social and cultural judgements.

['Sentimental elitism!']

Well, I'd rather Scruton's slightly supercilious elitism, if that's what you want to call it, than Eagleton's jeering intellectual's pseudopopulism any day.

['Travesty!']

BENJAMIN READER: If I could come in here. I think what Scruton has in mind is actually, rather naïvely, ritual rather than tradition. But there are real problems here. To whom does this mysteriously self-regulating tradition belong? People don't *elect* to belong to traditions. How are criteria for inclusion and exclusion arrived at? How does change occur?

['It doesn't!']

Adorno saw that access to cultural experience was a vexed problem. On the one hand he argued that in modernity avant-garde art *had* to be isolated in order to perform its function of agonistic critique. On the other he argued that 'the elitist isolation of advanced art is less its doing than society's' (p. 254), which is really the topic I came here to talk about. The binary high/low creates the problems it seeks to resolve. Nevertheless, in spite of high culture's grotesque irrelevance he believed that 'Culture checks barbarism' (p. 252). Now –

['Antihumanist elitism!']

– today, I think, we can see that a monolithic culture split down the middle is not what has actually happened. People don't work in this binary way. They shift from one cultural idiom to another, from watching sports on Sky to listening to a CD of *Traviata* to going to a movie to *Only Fools and Horses* on BBC TV. Look how popular public readings of poetry are, whereas ten, fifteen years ago poetry was a dying minority interest. Nicholas Cook has shown that we don't require special technical expertise to appreciate music.[13] They...

['Post-modern relativism!']

– As to value, Adorno held two views. One was that the aesthetic must be self-evidently *important* because whatever falls into the category of use value declares itself as a special experience separated out from exchange value. In that way it was transcendent, though works of art that strove for the effect of transcendence were doomed. I know that he talks exclusively of the western tradition, as does Murdoch, but I think he would say that non-western artworks still belong to a culture of ritual. Once their context is transformed by western capitalism, the criteria of use value holds for these as well, wherever in the world they are made. The second criterion, following from the status of the work of art as use value, was that it was logically impossible to value artworks *against* one another because 'genuine' aesthetic products all fall outside consumerism and into the sphere of culture, which is precisely not about comparing value. Only philistines did this. There's a kind of backhanded democracy of the beautiful in all this.

['How do you decide what's "genuine"? It comes back to hierarchies, and to valuing things because you want to *sell* them.'] ['What's wrong with *consumerism* anyway?']

CHAIR: We really must have questions in a more orderly way. The man in the mac over there . . .

MAN IN THE MAC: What would Adorno have thought about state subsidy of the arts, and is this really a way to increase democratic access to culture?

BEAUTIFUL SOUL: State subsidy would be part of the administered society, surely, the top-down directives of what has been called state culturalism, of which the middle classes are the economic beneficiaries. I'm all for *laissez-faire* in the arts. People should find their own levels. Subsidy is not the answer. Of course through education we try to train the sensibilities, but . . .

['Old-fashioned Thatcherite market stuff!'] ['Subsidy kills experiment!']

MAN IN THE MAC: [*with embarrassed vehemence*] I was thinking of theatre, actually. I'm a trustee of my local theatre, small theatre, very popular. We play to capacity audiences, our children's theatre too, all classes, varied programme. Theatre in Education and so on. But even if we play to capacity we can't break even, and we can't find big sponsors, only local garden centre, computer software shop, things like that. We bring people into town, help the local economy, but that's not the point. Government should help us, help us because we're successful, not because we're unsuccessful. It's a community theatre. There are small, *successful* theatres in England today on the brink of closure. The *Guardian* featured two a few days ago.[14] In the last eighteen years government has given all the wrong signals to the public. Theatre has been downgraded. Since 1991 a squeeze on theatre has meant ticket sales have dropped by well over a million annually. (And think what that does to the economy.) By *not* subsidizing, government becomes as directorial as any subsidy policy would be. Withdrawal of funding does not simply produce a neutral situation. Government cannot shuffle its obligations. Government is depriving people of choice, not giving it to them. That's not democratic choice. And our instrumental education system doesn't give people choice, either, because it doesn't value the imagination.

(*There is an uneasy silence.*)

BENJAMIN READER: We can't expect the arts to create democracy. Only political structures will do that.

['That's irrelevant!'] ['So why should thousands of taxpayers who don't go to the theatre subsidize those who do?'] ['What about the Royal Opera House fiasco?']

CHAIR: Girl in the knitted scarf?

GIRL IN THE KNITTED SCARF: [*Tentatively*] But, sort of, you can democratize beauty. You are being rather defeatist, really. People are like caddis-flies, you know. They strain water and take in what food they need. And they build up their cocoons from the most disparate things in the environment and make them their own, part of their bodies. Yesterday's popular kitsch can be today's high art in combination with something ordinary, like, for instance, the way people make little displays on their mantlepieces, and all that is made uniquely somebody's experience.[15] What am I saying? I'm saying that people make active choices that are about keeping them alive. I'm saying it isn't just a question of choosing what's on display. But that does mean having lots of opportunities for different kinds of experience. Lots of people don't have that chance. So the man in the mac is right about theatre. Government should be seen to back the arts, but they should work with local people, not from a centralized council. And as well as theatre and pictures and poetry *all over the place* you need something else. You need opportunities for people to do it themselves and take for granted that this is important. Things will only happen if people want them. My sister is working in Italy and she did a workshop sponsored by the local, well, what we would call town council, with Almateatro Di Torino. About twenty people worked with this professional women's theatre company over a part-time course towards a final presentation in public on multiculturalism. It was inspiring. They wrote a report afterwards. The whole thing was made their own... They –

BEAUTIFUL SOUL: BENJAMIN READER: You wouldn't find that happening here...

CHAIR: Well, on that *very* positive note I will close this discussion, which has shown us how lasting Adorno's concerns have been and how relevant they are to us today.

[*The hammering stops.*]

NOTES

1   Adorno's unfinished manuscript was published in 1970 after his death as *Asthetische Theorie*. The translation of *Aesthetic Theory* under review (1997, trans. Robert Hullot-Kentor) takes issue with many of the decisions of the 1984 edition (*Aesthetic Theory*, trans. C. Lenhardt). For issues of translation see Robert Hullot-Kentor's discussion of sentence structure,

vocabulary, the restoration of Adorno's paragraphing, and the order of the manuscript (pp. xiv–xvii). Hullot-Kentor claims that the 1984 translation was organized to become 'a model of what it protests against: the primacy of the constitutive subject' (p. xv).

2   Hegel's *Phenomenology of Spirit* introduces the Beautiful Soul, the unremitting but solipsist pursuit of the superior moral life, under the rubric of morality (paragraphs 667–71, pp. 405–9).

Goethe also takes up this theme in *Wilhelm Meister's Apprenticeship* (1795–6). Here the pursuit of the moral life as the beautiful life is taken up by a woman who progressively dissociates herself from communities, secular and religious, and relies on her inner integrity to achieve a 'beautiful' spiritual transcendence. Throughout, the kinship of aesthetic and moral experience is problematized: the following is a conversation between the 'saint' and her uncle, a connoisseur:

> With this view he had formed a beautiful series of works; and whilst he explained it, I could not help conceiving that I saw before me a similitude of moral culture. When I expressed my thought to him, he answered: 'You are altogether right; and we see from this, that those do not act well, who, in a solitary exclusive manner, follow moral cultivation by itself. On the contrary, it will be found that he whose spirit strives for a development of that kind, has likewise every reason, at the same time, to improve his finer sentient powers; that so he may not run the risk of sinking from his moral height, by giving way to the enticements of a lawless fancy, and degrading his moral nature by allowing it to take delight in tasteless baubles, if not in something worse.' (*Wilhelm Meister's Apprenticeship and Travels*, Book VI, vol. 1, p. 341)

3   Gillian Rose, *The Melancholy Science*, pp. 109–14 ('The sociology of culture'); pp. 140–1 ('The theoretical vacuum in Adorno's sociological analysis'). 'He has thus sacrificed the unique advantage of a Marxian approach: the derivation of political relations and of the state from an analysis of the productive and social relations of a specific kind of society' (p. 141). See also: Martin Jay, *Adorno*, pp. 155–60; Paul Crowther, *Critical Aesthetics and Post-Modernism*, pp. 188–224.

4   'Art after Auschwitz: Theodor Adorno', pp. 341–65.

5   See, for a full discussion of Iris Murdoch's collection, James Wood, 'Faulting the lemon'.

6   For the elaboration of 'aura' see Walter Benjamin, 'The work of art in the age of mechanical reproduction', *Illuminations: Essays and Reflections*, pp. 217–51. See also, for Benjamin's response to shock and modernity, 'Theses on the philosophy of history', XV1, p. 262. The dialectical image in an image-laden society is at one and the same time a mystified ideological construct and one which has explosive, emancipatory political potential in the force field of a particular historical moment. Susan Buck-Morss discusses the example of

Benjamin's analysis of flight, as conceived in Da Vinci's Utopian ur-images of planes, ideologized through images of the aeroplane as technological progress in Nazi Germany, but used for bombing and mass slaughter in the Second World War. *The Dialectics of Seeing*, pp. 244–5. Adorno was particularly sceptical of the dialectical image. See pp. 120–1.

7   Rose discusses Adorno's interpretation of reification as a linguistic or conceptual problem in which concept and property of object are assumed to be in identity with one another: words are turned into things, things are then turned into words: 'Reified concepts describe social phenomena, the appearance of society, as if it has the properties to which the concepts refer' (*The Melancholy Science*, p. 47).

8   Elaine Scarry, 'Imagining flowers'. The conditions under which sensuous experience occurs in reading and the relation of perception to physiology are the immediate concerns of 'On vivacity' and 'Imagining flowers'. They have wide implications, exploring the way aesthetic experience can be distinguished from other forms of imagining, and locating it both in commonsense perception and bodily structure as well as accepting its motivation in a range of objects and materials external to the self which need not necessarily be deliberately created as special 'aesthetic' objects.

9   Rose, *The Melancholy Science*, p. 148.

10   Rita Felski, *Beyond a Feminist Aesthetic*.

11   Roger Scruton, *The Aesthetic Understanding*, p. 237.

12   Scruton, 'Emotion and culture', ibid., pp. 138–52.

13   Nicholas Cook, *Music Imagination and Culture*. The concerns of this book are more subtle than the speaker's remark suggests. It explores the relation between technical knowledge and musical understanding, which do not necessarily depend on one another.

14   'Analysis: theatre costs', *Guardian*, 17 December 1997, p. 15.

15   This thinking could be developed further through Henri Lefebvre, *Critique of Everyday Life* (1947) and Michel de Certeau, *The Practice of Everyday Life* (1984).

Part IV

Feminism and Aesthetic Practice

7

Debating Feminisms

Of female misogyny

A *New Yorker* cartoon of February/March 1996 shows the chairman of four businessmen sitting round a table routinely asking the rhetorical question, 'Anyone here not a feminist?' Any successful movement finds that its successes are taken for granted and naturalized. Hence the idea that we exist in a post-feminist era. But such naturalizing processes assumed of post-feminism actually conceal the existence of the very problems feminism ought to be solving. Arguments that culture has been feminized (witness the outpouring of feeling at the death of Princess Diana), that women have access to power (witness Mrs Thatcher), not only ignore counterexamples – the violence of attacks on Hillary Clinton by the American media, for instance – but act as a cover for the necessity of rethinking feminist issues. To take a striking example of change, work for women, at the centre of the second-wave feminist agenda, is a different issue for the 'third' phase of feminism now that part-time work by women dominates the workforce and single mothers are being coerced into labour.

It is this masking of the necessity for argument that has enabled the emergence of attacks on feminism by women, attacks formulated less as critiques than as a series of rhetorical manoeuvres deliberately presented as performance art aimed at the media. They are 'aesthetic' in the weak sense of the word: the Kantian notion that the aesthetic assembles particulars without the concept. They are about style, executing moves, verbal performances, skilful at the level of assertion, not the least of which is the presupposition that 'feminism' is a unitary, homogeneous movement. It is these manoeuvres, simulacra of analysis, that require discussion. Arguably the powerful theorists of second-wave feminism have written in a 'strong' aesthetic mode, in the sense that for many writers – Luce Irigaray, Julia Kristeva, for instance – theory has involved writing what may quite properly be termed a poetics of gender and a form of discourse, which has distinguished their work, however different, from other philosophical discourses. But female anti-feminism has attracted wide attention. One of feminism's failures has been its inability to create a convincing popular forum, outside the universities and the middle classes, that might resist such attacks. On the contrary. Female anti-feminism makes an appeal, consciously or not, to female misogyny, to women's black, underground reservoir of hatred for themselves and for one another.

The terrified, panic-stricken alarmism of a recent review by Melanie Phillips is an example. Men, she claims, 'have been driven out altogether, neutralized, marginalized, emasculated' ('Losers in the war', pp. 4–5). She quotes Betty Friedan's self-castigations in her *Beyond Gender* (1997) to suggest that the 'women first' individualism of a rampant feminism has meant that 'Men are losing jobs and income to women'. The militant rights movement destroys community and society, and allows the teenage mother to reign supreme, because it fails to confirm family values. Phillips writes as if the presence of a working male with financial responsibility for the family would solve all problems. Yet this wild surmise ignores the fact that not feminism but late capitalism has created the part-time labour market in which women can be exploited at the expense of men: not feminism but the failure of a popular feminism that might enable self-worth to rest on other achievements than pregnancy has created the teenage mother. Arguments at this rhetorical level prevent careful analyses of the predicament, for instance, of young males, the predicament of masculinity, and ignore the historical fact that it is precisely feminism, deconstructing gender binaries, that has enabled us to consider the predicament of masculinity by making it visible. But because it attracts so much attention the rhetorical turn of female misogyny needs to be addressed. To this extent it dictates the terms in which we speak of feminist thought today. My intention in this chapter is to see how a taxonomy of those feminisms working with a 'strong' poetics of gender can lead us into the signifying spaces of new concepts; but the 'weak' aesthetic turn of female anti-feminism first has to be differentiated from other discourses of feminism.

The most aggressive critique of contemporary feminism, or of what is assumed to be feminism, has come from the United States. Though I shall discuss contemporary British versions of it, that critique is represented here by two American women of different generations, women who like each other's work and who regard each other as 'brave' for writing about 'unpopular' ideas. The first is Camille Paglia, libertarian diva and

Whitwomanesque drag queen of American academia, and pugilistic self-publicist well beyond it, whose latest book of essays, *Vamps and Tramps* (1994) does a lot to clarify her position.[1] The second is Katie Roiphe, ivy league princess, of the get-tough-with-feminism generation from Harvard and Princeton. Her widely read book *The Morning After: Sex, Fear, and Feminism* was published in 1993. There is, of course Germaine Greer in England, who has recently greeted the revival of forgotten women's poetry with shudders of disgust (*Slip-Shod Sibyls*, 1995). But she has always been a one-woman show. If the ideas of Paglia and Roiphe seem deeply immersed in matters relevant solely to American culture, this is only apparent. Paglia at least deals with issues important to western culture and beyond: in any case, American ideas are exported and resignified in Europe with extreme rapidity.

Paglia knows where she is. She is a libertarian from the sixties who has developed a unique Nietzschean populist anarchism around gender. She is always consistent and thoroughly sophisticated in her understanding of the publicity strategies required to advance herself. For it is herself she displays, with an almost impersonal egotism: she is medium and message, happening, mixed media event, a guerrilla activist who relies on surprise, outrage, abuse, the lewd, the aggressive, a larger-than-life priapic feminism. This is to defend herself and us against the etiolated 'office' culture of modern academia, drowned in the marketing techniques of business and multinational capital, with which she says she has not colluded. She utilizes the sixties techniques of pop art shock and display without embarrassment, with, on the contrary, robust, orgiastic glee. And true to her understanding of the principles of eternal opposition and dualism, an adaptation (and oversimplification) of Nietzsche's Apollonian and Dionysian poles of rational constraint and ecstatic passion and release, she relishes conflict. '[Andrea] Dworkin spouts glib Auschwitz metaphors at the drop of a bra' (*Vamps and Tramps*, p. 111), she says of the anti-pornography campaigner, and Paglia offers us the 'beauty, vitality, and brutality' of porn as antidote to the cerebral technological world. This love of a fight got her into the crude, knock-about feud with Susan Sontag – no sentimental female bonding for her. Paglia's commitment to the principle of dualism and opposition also leads her into something more difficult to sustain, a writing from the pressure of felt contradiction. For vamping – the technique of improvization, parody and Dionysian exaggeration which she has perfected – must be 'rude', must carry a style to extremes and must end up on the other side of it, outside, self-consciously aware of the limits of its own style, if the vamp-up is to be at all convincing. Paglia knows this. This is why the Sontag fight is carried out, Mahomet Ali style, like a slugging match from the boxing ring, at the same time as her rage and bitter disappointment at the shortcomings of a former idol are almost painfully exposed in her writing.

The necessity of living with eternal opposition, though, commits Paglia to a kind of double-speak. At times she seems to reduce her beliefs to the penis and paganism versus post-structuralism, Dionysian raunchiness against desiccated rationalism, and she invites this interpretation. Yet provisos and reservations lurk even in the blithest of her statements. She is a scholar, she claims, and this is true. She won't let herself get away with her own oversimplifications for long. So there is a curious tension between the vatic and the sensible in her writing. Abortion is a 'sword of self-defence put into their [women's] hands by Ares, the war god'. But she admits, unlike some campaigners, that it is 'a form of extermination' (p. 41). As for battered wives, 'Garish mugshot photos of women's bruised faces' evade the bracing necessity for women to have an 'equal responsibility in dispute and confrontation' (p. 43), which can be achieved without legislation if women are prepared to assert themselves. But she does not forget that we must 'continue to address the grave problem in economically underdeveloped countries of women treated as chattel or even killed by husbands or families for being a financial burden' (p. 42). The tension between overstatement and sense, hyperbole and reason, is often confusing, though sometimes fruitful.

A more confusing aspect of this double-speak is the adoption of the word 'feminist' both as a term of abuse and as a term of value. There is libertarian feminism (hers), and there is prim, repressive, self-righteous, coercive, cerebral feminism, corrupted by (as always) French thought, but Paglia uses the same word for both. Hence the collision course of these feminisms in the following passage on rape.

> Aggression must be returned to the centre of feminist thinking. The rape discourse derailed itself early on by its nonsensical formulation. 'Rape is a crime of violence but not of sex,' a mantra that, along with 'No always means no', blanketed the American media until I arrived on the scene. Feminists had an astoundingly naive view of the mutual exclusiveness of sex and aggression...That rape is simply what used to be called 'unbridled lust', like gluttony a sin of insufficient self-restraint, seems to be beyond feminist ken. (Camille Paglia, *Vamps and Tramps*, p. 41)

It would not be surprising if a reader were to carry away an impression of Paglia's complete hostility to any kind of feminism. It is the same with the battered woman and the Bobbit case, the famous case of the severed penis: 'But of course the feminist establishment, stuck in its battered woman blinders, learned nothing [about female violence] as usual from this lurid refutation of its normal views' (p. 42). 'As a feminist, I detest the rhetorical diminution of woman into passive punching bag, which is the basic premise of the "battered woman syndrome"' (p. 43). Then on to harassment: 'Whining and shrewishness are today's favoured campus style' (p. 46). 'Wavering, dithering, or passive hysterical fear will only intensify or prolong pursuit' [with intent to violence] (p. 47). 'White middle-class feminists', the 'feminist establishment', the 'feminist jabber' about victimization through fashion or the male gaze, the 'snippy neurotics' (p. 50) who police pornography – this reiterated abuse permits a reading of Paglia as misogynist all too readily, though she insists she worships the mythic, creative power of women.

The technique of flamboyant attack followed by modification actually means that the small print is obliterated by the sweeping gesture. More insidious, the celebration of women's oneiric and chthonic powers, the rhapsody of mythic woman, the violent hostility to the cerebral (can't women ever be allowed to think?) endorses familiar and even reassuring gender divisions, despite Paglia's own preference for a fruitful bisexuality. 'Women will never know who they are until they let men be men.' To find this sentence embedded in an attack on the anti-pornography campaign, on 'the delusionalism, sanctimony, prudery, and male-bashing of the MacKinnon–Dworkin brigade' (p. 111), is deeply reassuring to the conservative who harbours misogynistic feeling. Her sixties libertarianism actually converges at points with the neo-conservative libertarianism of the eighties and nineties, that free-for-all which nevertheless fiercely defends traditional hierarchical and gender boundaries. Her writing can easily be resignified to align with it.

This certainly accounts for her popularity in the British media, not known for its liberalism on gender issues. It chimes with a deeply sceptical response to feminism, or what is popularly thought to be feminism. The extent of populist anti-feminist feeling became apparent in the early nineties. A single issue of the *Evening Standard*, for instance, carried the following articles (10 September 1992): a discussion of a TV personality whose involvement in S & M had damaged his career, in which it was argued that the men who resort to S & M should not be punished but rather the women who administer it, supported as they are by their 'cleverer' educated sisters in the universities; a review by Fay Weldon of Neil Lyndon's *No More Sex War: The Failure of Feminism*, in which she argued that Neil Lyndon is 'an OK guy', that, regrettably, it's become 'culturally permissable for women to insult men', but quotes him insulting women on 'the pustulant lines of piss in the crock of cant which is modern feminism'; and an article on childbirth in which the presence of men at birthing is questioned and old-fashioned practices favoured – 'Now the role of mystery is denied. A New York psychiatrist, who is studying sexual behaviour after birth, has found that many men are less attracted to their wives after participating in birth'. Paglia might well say that if her priapic feminism and celebration of mythic woman is assimilated to neo-conservatism this is not her problem. It may not be, but it is a problem of her discourse.

To turn to Katie Roiphe: at first sight the single issue of date rape on American campuses (or rather, the campuses of Harvard and Princeton) might seem difficult to translate beyond the United States, but she sees the problem as part of a larger cultural situation, a mindless consensualism which is intolerant of argued dissent. In comparison with Paglia's large, Dionysiac scorn, Roiphe relies on steady belittlement. Where Paglia deals with a range of issues – battering, child abuse, rape, pornography – Roiphe builds her study round student concerns. The argument of her somewhat repetitive book can be summed up quite briefly. Feminism has become a narrow, coercive, conservative force, preaching a dogmatic, intolerant, often bigoted and fanatically legalistic fundamentalism which insists upon conformism to received dogma and presupposes, not only the bad faith of men in gender relations, but also the inevitability of female passivity, disempowerment, infantilization, 'silence' and victimhood. Thus 'rape is a natural trump card for feminism' (*The Morning After*, p. 56).

Her argument is familiar to those who have experienced conservative critiques of anti-racism – that campus feminism actually creates the evils it attacks. The blue-light policy of helpline phones, intended to create late-night safety for women, creates a culture of fear and a rhetoric of caution which turns women back into the overprotected, pure women of the fifties. Take Back the Night parades whip up hysteria, encouraging women to join 'the empowering universe of the disempowered' (p. 34). The 'rape epidemic' has been confected by alarmists whose casuistical definition of rape – which even extends to retrospective rape (p. 80) – proposes a definition so wide that almost any sexual discomfort falls into it. It encourages women to invent rapes. An essentialist account of rape as the ultimate feminine suffering has blocked analysis. (Roiphe does not remind us that men and boys are raped; Paglia does.) Sexual harassment rules actually regulate for gender opposition by presupposing it, and infantilize relationships into the bargain, destroying free communication between teachers and taught. Anti-pornography campaigners Andrea Dworkin and Catharine A. MacKinnon are fanatics, eliding sexuality and violence and refusing to distinguish between representation and reality.

Some of these arguments are sensible enough, and, without accepting the basic premise that feminism creates the problems it addresses, most people would agree that the inflation of sexual issues is counterproductive. But if this were all, Roiphe's book would hardly have been the best-selling success it has proved to be. Stripped of her flair for anecdote and burlesque, and their appeal to common sense, which is always persuasive and reassuring, her arguments do not seem particularly remarkable. But the attraction of the book is not its arguments, whatever it may claim, but a style. Rather more smoothly than Paglia, it executes a series of rhetorical manoeuvres. Roiphe includes a series of lampoons of typical (fictitious or at least unnamed) feminist students, which disclose the source of the book's allure for the general reader.

> As an undergraduate, Sarah wore baggy clothes in shades of brown and burnt orange. Looking at her, you couldn't see any curves or angles, just fabric. Her blond hair was short, and she wore an earring in the shape of a woman symbol...Sarah once told me about her fantasy of creating the ideal university. It would be free from all hierarchy...Every now and then she would wake up at six in the morning and go to Dollar-a-Pound in Boston and buy bags of faded clothes...Amanda is a graduate student in English...she dresses impeccably...She has no particular passion for literature, but she does have a passion for trends in literary criticism...feminists do relatively well in the job market...Amanda's remarks in class often included the word *other*, as in 'They appropriated the discourse of the other'. (Katie Roiphe, *The Morning After*, pp. 115, 126)

'The radical cover-girl chic feminist' (p. 126) and the new man and men in feminism come in for the same treatment. Roiphe is portrayed scrupulously disagreeing with her stereotypes in class and being put down by their hypocritical intolerance. But these gratuitous smears posing as parody, as much the prey of fashion as their subjects, tell us nothing about feminism. They tell us about the fantasy of a feminist conspiracy, perpetrated by the universities, funded by the universities (p. 57) and rewarded by the universities (p. 125). It is they who allow people to rise to power on 'the multiculturalist wave' (p. 107); they who collude with feminist extremists and their post-structuralist jargon; they who foster both intellectual permissiveness and cynicism.

This writing allows for a delicious indignation with the universities for teaching such feminist nonsense and simultaneously permits the voyeuristic pleasure of snooping on the young. It fuels female misogyny, reactionary hatred of the universities and generational prurience in one go. The frantic anorexic girls pounding the exercycles in the gym (p. 19), the parties where girls strip to their bras, 'black lace, pink lace, white lace' (p. 16), Ms Roiphe's musings in Adams House at the end of her Harvard undergraduate career and fights in Tommy's Lunch, all come alive in her excellent journalistic prose:

> Someone I knew in College had an admirable flair for putting offenders in their place. Once, when she was playing pinball in Tommy's Lunch, the coffee shop across from Adams House, a teenage boy came up to her and grabbed her breast. She calmly went to the counter and ordered a glass of milk and then walked over and poured it over his head. (Katie Roiphe, *The Morning After*, p. 101)

The gym, Tommy's Lunch, Adams House, you are allowed the vicarious pleasure of the assumption that you know all these places. The geography of Harvton or Princevard doesn't need to be explained: it is not meant to signify topography, but like equivalent Oxbridge place-name-dropping, it is the seductive signifier of a glimpse at the youth culture of a privileged group, the pleasure principle playing pinball and having fights at the tweak of a breast.

AIDS and economic recession form the background to this book, the shock of moving from free love to safe sex, the move from finding yourself to supporting yourself, as Roiphe's knack for the neat antithesis expresses it (p. 14). Part of the impetus of this book is disappointment: as she herself confesses in her introduction, damaged individualism is the context of an impatience with the regulatory 'excesses' of feminist puritanism. Whereas Paglia's anger has more radical origins in an emancipatory politics of freedom. But Paglia and Roiphe, different though they are, have the same relationship of mirror-double to what they think they oppose. What they see as a violent, regulatory fundamentalism around gender calls out in them an equally violent deregulatory impulse. They set up arguments in essentially the same terms, the dialectical opposites of each other. If Dworkin and MacKinnon call up hatred of men, Paglia and Roiphe call up hatred of women. Dworkin and MacKinnon want laws in the name of protection; Paglia and Roiphe don't want laws in the name of freedom. Each group is set up on one side of the 'rights' argument, rights for, rights against, so that both sides are fed by the same individualism. Nothing changes, because gender boundaries are never addressed. If rape really is the result, as Paglia suggests, of maddened male frustration with the superior power of women, rooted in mythic mystery and thetic aura, then it might be worth changing gender relations. We do not have to accept the maddened male deterministically. As for putting out the blue lights over campus and depending on the well-aimed glass of milk, adolescent fights are one thing, assault is another – and even then there are other ways of dealing with breast-tweaking teenagers.

What is striking about this polarized argument is that feminist issues have contracted to a single, obsessive theme – the control or deregulation of sexuality. The great Wollstonecraftian preoccupations of the past, not to speak of those of the more recent past, which made feminism into a philosophical project – concerned with education, work, politics and the social order, institutions, the alterability of gender relations, the categories of thought and discourse – have disappeared in these discussions. There have been searching discussions of the pornography debate – Frances Ferguson's for one – as an issue of civil society.[2] But for these two women the mode in which heterosexual sexuality is expressed or repressed, criminalized or decriminalized, classified, controlled or decontrolled is the central concern. Paglia and Roiphe raise serious issues, but all feminist concerns need not be narrowed to the drop of a bra, whether pink, white or black lace.

A rather more anodyne British version of this critique of feminism has appeared under the guise of a 'new' feminism, presenting itself as a more friendly, pragmatic, consumerist feminism, softer than the ideological, dogma-ridden gender politics of the past. Melissa Benn's somewhat naïve rediscovery of motherhood in *Madonna and Child: Towards a New Politics of Motherhood* (1998) and Natasha Walter's *The New Feminism* (1998) are typical. I shall concentrate on Walter, who is less well-meaning than Benn. Eschewing America, but actually absorbing much of its economic individualism, she offers us a 'revitalised British feminist debate' (p. 7). This 'debate', she says, will not be concerned with issues of either personal or cultural life, thus doing away with the central topoi of second-wave feminism. What's left? The new feminism will be, first, 'materialist' (p. 6) and, second, 'a celebratory and optimistic movement', full of 'laughter and celebration' (p. 7). By 'materialist' she does not mean that the material conditions of women's lives in different class contexts must come under scrutiny; rather women will be, as they are, 'flexing their muscles and demanding equality' (p. 6). It was Mrs Thatcher, the 'great unsung heroine of British feminism', who 'normalised female success', embracing power (p. 175). What Walter means by materialist feminism is meritocracy. Similarly, celebratory feminism is not the jouissance of delight in the widened boundaries of sexuality, but designer feminism, make-up and clothes. Men are OK too, constructing a new culture, not around shopping, but 'around the loss of power' which recognizes the 'frail' masculine body (p. 161), and indulging in ironic role-play, 'macho', or 'laddish', in order to distance themselves from these very stereotypes. Bland where her American counterparts are aggressive,

Walter nevertheless ends up where they are, rejecting the politics of feminist thought.

A serious project of feminism is to make gender issues important to people's daily lives, make them significant enough to argue about. This will not happen with indoctrination; altering people's perceptions is slow work. Nevertheless, for that very reason, the philosophical project of feminism, also an aesthetic project, is intensely important.

A taxonomy of feminisms

What is this project? It is a number of projects, of course, a number of different feminisms. Here is a taxonomy, advanced for the sake of clarifying future ambitions, for categories invite dispute. Though what follows charts some historical sequences, this is a taxonomy and not a history, recognizing that the clusters of thought described here, the three paradigms of feminism, overlap and co-exist. What they share, and this is why I describe them as a 'poetics', is the need to think and write experimentally to the limits of what Barthes called the 'doxa', the cultural and ideological boundaries of modernity, to remake the language of discourse. I am not describing a specifically feminine aesthetic, either, but a philosophical project mounted by women. There has been much discussion of the possibility of a feminine aesthetics. But though women's writing comes from a particular, gendered, place in the culture at any specific historical moment, and almost invariably – this is a truism – challenges a male dominant, it is hard to accept that an *intrinsically* feminine discourse is possible.[3] But second-wave feminists have certainly developed a poetics of gender, seeing gender through the prism of the aesthetic, using the resources of aesthetic language to explore gender. And Julia Kristeva's classic essay, 'Women's time', must come to mind, despite her anti-feminism, or dissociation from the feminist movement.

Over twenty years ago Kristeva initiated a classification of feminisms. Yet, because the change she figured in her analysis of what has been called a post-modern 'future perfect' has begun to take shape, intellectual patterns have reconfigured simply because of her intervention, and a new set of categories, new signifying spaces, have emerged. In 'Women's time', she argued that successive surges of feminist thought in the twentieth century had possessed a constitutively different ideological and psychic meaning. The post-Second-World-War western phenomenon of parity feminism, the move for equal rights and equality in the workplace, which was the logical consequence of former suffrage campaigns – and which crossed national and cultural boundaries at the same time as questioning them – overlapped with another project: attempts, both mythic and semiotic, to define the peculiar nature of feminine sexuality and sexual difference. She assigned different 'times' to each project. Parity feminism works with linear, goal-directed, 'masculine' time, the logical end of which is, today, control of experience by electronic media and virtual reality. The second time is mythic, cyclical. She called it 'monumental time' (implicitly 'feminine' time). Women's accommodation to the necessities of the 'Oedipal sacrifice' and the imperatives of castration and entry into the symbolic order govern both 'times' and make both uneasy. The Oedipal contract inflicts a damaged narcissism on women which is dramatized in the female terrorism (literally, Baader-Meinhof) that is the result of the violence of linear time. 'Monumental' experience, on the other hand, retreats into a feminine experience constantly folded back into itself. She saw the answer to this uneasiness as a fundamental renegotiation of sexuality and gender relations within the symbolic order through an act of the imagination – the aesthetic was to come to the rescue as the only mode of analysis sufficiently complex to open new gender possibilities and, perhaps, go 'beyond' gender division. This is an inexhaustible essay, but, arguably, feminism needs categories which will include not only the work of the last twenty years but ones which will include the essay itself. In a brilliant critique of Kristeva's essay, Carol Watts has argued that in placing the mother's body *outside* temporality – organizing primal separation as the moment when time enters the world for the child, yet giving the mother an autonomy that places her beyond time – Kristeva has ceded the possibility of the mother's relationship to the social. It is not simply that Kristeva works to a phallocentric model of Oedipal loss (although, surely, since the Oedipal moment propels the drive to separation, the primal separation from the mother's body is predicated on phallic power, and even Kristeva's potential emancipatory moment is limited by this):

> Her formulation of the maternal thus brings about an ethical reinforcement of the mother's symbolic burden, while denying the complexity of the mother's experience of differing, contradictory times governed by the social necessity of labour – the multiple interactions of the times of production and reproduction. In short, the figure of the mother becomes the over-determined site of the post-political in Kristeva's thought, the point at which social contradiction is condensed and internalized into the 'very nucleus' of personal and sexual identity. (Carol Watts, 'Time and the working mother', p. 13)

Arguably, therefore, Kristeva's categories, rather than being seen as authoritative, should be considered as part of a post-modern psychoanalytical and semiotic feminism belonging to a larger formation. Accordingly in what follows I sketch out a number of formations.

Categories which do not simply reproduce the determinants of race (black or Asian feminism, for instance) or nation (French or American feminism) or even disciplinary boundaries are essential. A good taxonomy puts together writings one would not normally expect to juxtapose. It has an element of surprise. Here are three categories, cutting across parity feminism and monumental experience and also across racial and national demarcations: Expressive, Phallic and Ludic feminism. This is not a survey but a morphological sketch. I look at the work of individuals to indicate patterns, not to suggest a hierarchy of writing.

First, Expressive feminism. The cry of rage or pain or ecstasy or demonic laughter comes from this group. It is women's experience, which is celebrated, passionately confirmed, sung, rhapsodized. 'Essentialism' is often the charge it lives with. But, aside from the fact that it is not possible to speak 'woman' at all without a certain minimal essentialism, as Rosi Braidotti has remarked, there is experience intrinsic to the feminine for Expressive writers, simply because women's experience is so firmly a given, even when we simultaneously acknowledge its constructedness ('The politics of ontological difference', p. 90). Women's experience is a cultural given, and it is in this sense that the feminine is given, not made. These are radical feminists because most believe, against all the odds, that what is given in women's experience unifies women, sometimes transcending, even if with difficulty, the barriers of race and class. An emancipatory universalism is the impulse of the cry of rage, pain, ecstasy, laughter. Expressive writers look to the future, to the transnational bonding of woman with woman. They look to the past to disclose a hidden tradition of women's texts. They look to the present to discover the felt abuses of women's lives. To them belong the activists, marchers, propagandists, anonymous workers; to them we owe helplines, rape crisis centres, hospices for battered women.

Hélène Cixous, Elaine Showalter and bel hooks would not expect to find themselves together, but, however different they seem, they share the same fundamental radical premises of Expressive feminism: that a specifically feminine experience is definable and that it is possible to derive an idea of commonality from it.[4] Cixous's intense celebration of the energies of women's creativity, the necessity that they write in the white ink of milk, the red ink of menstruation, writing their bodies, inscribing the feminine body insolently, defiantly, in their lives and texts, makes her the pre-eminent Expressive feminist. Her rage against binaries, which absolves her theoretically from a near-biologism and opens out the possibility of bisexuality, nevertheless does not prevent her from privileging, for strategic purposes, the feminine economy of expenditure without return, flow against fixity. The one-way movement of rhapsodic laughter is the instrument of the economy of feminine outflowing.

Elaine Showalter is the scholar of Expressive feminism in America. Unlike Cixous, she does not derive her poetics from the transgressive economies of Bataille. An American wit and toughness carries its principles into her theory and criticism. Always writing with an energy which embodies her understanding of women's power, Showalter almost single-handedly reconceptualized women's writing in the nineteenth century (making the nineteenth century the laboratory for feminist experiment) and introduced the important concept and practice of 'gynocriticism' into feminist criticism. She is an Expressive feminist by virtue of her ceaseless exploration of women's experience as defined through their texts or texts about them. She has always sought to historicize women's productions as cultural text and to retrieve a rigorously theorized understanding of the way women respond to a feminine experience organized, imaged and controlled by their culture. For her there is commonality because women's experience is organized in particular ways at particular times: in some circumstances, women can themselves construct sustaining traditions and networks in response to the constraints imposed on them, despite the conceptualization of the feminine as a 'malady'. Her refusal of this identification of the feminine and illness has been a dominant theme in her work. Her work on hysteria (*Hystories*) resists the identification of the feminine with the hysteric, and refuses the collapse of hysteria into the feminine.

bel hooks – the writer who did most to introduce race into white feminist discourse in the early 1980s, exploding into its complacency with her *Ain't I a Woman: Black Women and Feminism* – also belongs to the Expressive group, in spite of her antagonism to the narcissistic opportunism and flagrant individualism of so much white feminism. Parity feminism asks only for privileged white women's parity, she argues, sentimentalizing middle class experience as 'oppression' and turning the self-pity of the white housewife into a principle of sexual politics while exploiting and excluding other women – black women – to achieve its ends. It is her passion for 'solidarity', her belief that women can and must 'come together', and that they can do so without suspending rational critique, that makes her an Expressive feminist. Her analysis of class and race is strictly and bracingly Marxist, and saturated in anger, creative anger: though one might expect her position to lead to pessimism about unalterable ideological division between different groups of women, the opposite is the case. She subsequently clarified her position in *Feminist Theory*. She deprecates women's 'legacy of woman-hating' and argues that 'women need to come together in situations where there will be ideological disagreement and work to change that interaction so communication occurs'. Women need to 'develop strategies to overcome' negative disagreements. 'Women need to have the experience of working through hostility to arrive at understanding and solidarity if only to free ourselves from the sexist socialization that tells us to avoid confrontation because we will be victimized or destroyed' (p. 63). Division across sexual choices perturbs her: 'Feminist activists need to remember that the political choices we make are not determined by whom we choose to have genital sexual contact with' (p. 152). She reiterates that the object of feminism is a collective identity which is damaged by alignments round sexuality: 'Feminism will never appeal to a mass-based group of women in our society who are heterosexual if they think that they will be looked down upon or seen as doing something wrong' (p. 153). The solidarity born of interaction without false unity is her ideal.

Expressive feminism has probably done more to change the practical lives of ordinary women and, at the same time, more to alienate ordinary women, than any other kind of feminist thought. For this action-directed form of thought campaigns, sometimes vociferously and violently, against the abuses of a sexist society. Pornography is currently its great cause. If its hatred of violence seems doctrinaire and bigoted, and if women such as Andrea Dworkin and Catharine MacKinnon seem extremist, they have at least prompted a strenuous debate on the nature of pornography and representation which dramatizes the philosophical problems around the definition of the group and the meaning of action in civil society. Expressive feminism prompts intellectual work.

No one can doubt the cultural irrigation an impassioned Expressive poetics has accomplished. Its visibility has been greater than any feminism of the second wave. Its dance with essentialism has already been mentioned, and this is the criticism most frequently made of it. However, there are other problems: it is often charged with the jouissance of a superior feminine affect that demonizes masculinity, and this is not only true of the lesbian Expressive feminist. What the nature of this affect might be remains largely uninvestigated and often seems beyond representation, thus associating the feminine with the irrational emotions historically attributed to woman. The great project of this formation is surely the further investigation of affective life, the nature of its representation and the forms it might take in civil society. Indeed, so concerned is it with the energies, the pressure of feeling, that Expressive feminism tends to elide lived and represented experience.

Phallic feminism has been, until recently, the dominant form of feminist theory. Until the early 1990s it seemed set fair to produce the central,

generative debates in feminist thought. It always co-existed with Expressive and Ludic feminism, but it seemed to open new fields of knowledge
in a way that made it the theoretical wing of the women's movement. This
form of feminism is Phallic because its poetics derive from the two master
discourses of the twentieth century, the new knowledges evolving from
the work of Marx and Freud, and subsequently of Lacan. Phallic feminism works with the traditions of these forms of thought, questioning,
reconfiguring and remaking them for a new gender theory. Feminist
thinkers who are mutually hostile to each other intellectually can still
belong to the category of Phallic critique. It is not that the two traditions
are reconciled in Phallic feminism (though they sometimes are), but that
they form the theoretical and ideological ground which structures the
philosophical projects of women who *accept* the debates around Marx
and Freud as the starting point of their own thought. Swinging between
the different determinisms of both Marxism and Freudianism and the
different understandings of cultural construction available through the
theory of ideology and psychoanalysis, and bringing the insights of
semiotics to these discourses as heuristic tools, these thinkers often elaborate an analysis which has called out such deeply imagined thought
that this work has the force of poetry. This thought is so new that it
shimmers with the strangeness and beauty of a poem, partly because it is
aware that it is dealing with the stuff of the profound cultural myths of
the twentieth century – which is not to say that myths do not call out
belief. If the founding determinant of Marxist feminism is the anguish of
class, the anguish of the Oedipal sacrifice is at the centre of psychoanalytical feminism. These take on an explanatory, causal force, however
much they are re-read, re-visioned, re-described, understood as experience mediated through language and representation. The economic structure of women's oppression, the 'without' which organizes sexual
difference, women's psychic lives and their entry into the symbolic
order – these are the inexhaustible lyric themes of Phallic thought. And
I call them lyric because the very nature of identity is at stake in this
theory, how the 'I' is formed at the deepest psychic and social levels of
being.

Julia Kristeva, of whom I have already spoken, Juliet Mitchell and
Jacqueline Rose have been the formative critics of the psychoanalytical
tradition. Juliet Mitchell extended her classic early work in *Psychoanalysis and Feminism* (1974), sharing with Jacqueline Rose the introduction
to a collection of Lacan essays. These became the central text in a new
phase of Phallic feminism, shifting, through Lacan, the emphasis of
Freudian analysis from biologism to language and representation, from
a literalized reading of feminine sexuality in terms of penis envy to

the *structural* role of lack in the gender binary. 'Woman does not exist': the placing of woman in the space of lack, a fantasized other, the site of masculine self-elaboration, signifying the phallus through being its lack – these new conceptualizations promised an understanding of the genesis of gender formation and an explanation of the eternally unsymmetrical power relations constituted by sexual difference. It was undoubtedly the rigorous theorizing of a systematic symbolic order, which deterministic-ally organized gender relations, that attracted feminist thinkers to the Lacanian model, and still does. Mastery's secret is not only revealed but given a logic. To anyone puzzled by the acceptance of a seemingly negative understanding of feminine sexuality, the Phallic critic replies, as Mitchell did, that Freudian/Lacanian thought does not offer a recom-mendation for a patriarchal society but an analysis of one.

And this is an intensely creative genre of feminism still. *Between Feminism and Psychoanalysis*, a collection of essays edited by Teresa Brennan in 1989, brought a new debate about the possibilities of remain-ing inside or outside Lacanian feminism into circulation.[5] Mary Jacobus's first essay in the intricate and subtle *First Things* (1995), 'Freud's mne-monic: screen memories and feminist nostalgia', declares her intention to shift attention from the symbolic order to the function of the Imaginary in culture and psychoanalysis. In a delicate argument with Freud and two major figures, Adrienne Rich and Jane Gallop, she suggests that the Oedipal moment retrospectively creates the pre-Oedipal and acts as a screen memory for an originary feminine 'fall' into sexuality. Yet the myth of an unmediated primal relation to the mother's body, explored so poignantly by Rich, is, she thinks, untenable. Instead she turns to Jane Gallop's re-theorizing of phallic loss as nostalgia to consider the powerful cultural imperative which associates nostalgia and women. Regret for loss repeats itself backwards from self to the irreparable loss of the phallic mother, to which the subject can never return for compensation: nostalgia is not so much a longing for completion but the alienation of the subject in an amnesia which attempts to forget phallic absence.

Phallic critique incorporates materialist thinking. This is in eclipse, though it shows signs of reviving, because the breakup of communism has led to a premature assumption that the materialist project is irrelev-ant, though the analysis of Marxist feminism and its philosophical project is actually of more importance than ever. Gayatri Chakravorty Spivak, exponent of an intricately theorized materialist deconstructive feminism, brings to bear the textual insights afforded by semiotics in a way which distinguishes her from other writers (such as Michèle Barrett in England or Christine Delphy in France).[6] She has sharply criticized her psychoanalytical Phallic contemporary, Julia Kristeva (though she isn't averse to psychoanalysis), for an idealist and self-serving reading of the 'Third World' women of China, and for a retreat to the maternal body and motherhood as a principle of feminine existence. I single Spivak out because in her work a materialist analysis of the economics of gender and race comes together with a critique of the 'epistemic violence' of imperialism in a post-structuralist world. *In Other Worlds* (1987) gathers some of the most impressive of her work. She is an agonistic critic, proceeding by the deconstructive mode of putting into question. She strenuously attempts to rethink basic concepts (such as the labour theory of value), which she thinks have been written out of contemporary discourse, by recalling both economic and textual theories of value. Her demonstration that the dematerializing and abstraction of labour and use value in the post-modern economic discourse of global capitalism is dependent upon the exploitation of 'Third World' women is complex and intricate, but she makes the brute reality of exploitation obvious (p. 167). Refusing either to sentimentalize use value or to commit herself to the textualization of labour or money, she treads a path through these extremes: 'Within this narrative replay of my argument in the previous pages it may be pointed out that, whereas Lehman Brothers, thanks to computers, "earned $2 million, for... 15 minutes of work", the entire economic text would not be what it is if it could not write itself as a palimpsest upon another text where a woman in Sri Lanka has to work 2,287 minutes to buy a T-shirt. The "post-modern" and "pre-modern era" are inscribed together' (p. 171). Her virtuosity demonstrates the continuing possibilities of Phallic Marxism. The journal *Feminist Economics* and the work of Regenia Gagnier (*Idylls of the marketplace*, 1987), who is interested in developing a post-modern feminist economics, are indications of the vitality of these traditions.

Are there problems associated with Phallic feminism's acceptance of the grand narratives of Marxism and psychoanalysis? The necessitarian, deterministic aspect of these theories dictates an analysis of certain inevitable structures of power – the symbolic order, the interpellated subject who is organized through the economic pressures of material conditions – and works with a myth of power. It is a short step from analysis to acceptance, from describing what is to accepting what must be – the *structural* necessity of forms of power – organizing discussion around, and presupposing, the very models that are critiqued. Thus Kristeva can insist upon the harsh necessity of feminine entry into the symbolic order with Greek fatalism, and Spivak can allow her discourse to be so ordered by a Marxist paradigm of colonial oppression that she asks a rhetorical question, 'Can the subaltern speak?, expecting the answer, "No". Generally speaking what Phallic feminism has done is to "post-modernize" these modern knowledges, opening out their determinisms and the fixity of power relations and oppression implied in their epistemologies by giving both psychoanalysis and materialism a semiotic turn. A limited agency opens up when fractures in the determining order, whether psychic or social/material, precipitate epistemic crisis, a crisis of language in which the sign and what it represents are in disjunction, allowing the subject a space in which to apprehend contradictions exposed by the mismatch of sign and experience. But agency *is* limited and may only consist in the release from ideological blindness. Oddly, in both psycho-analytical and Marxist paradigms of Phallic feminism, the political has a tendency to fall away, to get lost or immobilized, inhibited by the totaliz-ing of political power itself. And gender issues themselves can disappear, can be absorbed by the myth of power.

Ludic feminism occupies the signifying space created by the disjunction of the sign and its object, seizing the initiative by reversing the priorities of Phallic feminism. Transgressive resignification that deconstructs hege-monic power, rather than the other way round, is its model of relation-ship. Actually, it distributes the relationship between the subject and the world in very different ways from that of Phallic feminism, and it con-ceives power very differently. Language and the body, marked by a history of compulsory gender construction, are its two terms, not self and world.

In the last few years, Ludic feminism has rapidly come to dominate feminist concerns. It is playful, of course, as the word suggests, but rather than putting in question, it puts things in play, the dance of an open semiosis that holds to the paradox of play, the acknowledgement of the rule-bound which makes deviation, 'free play', possible. Ludic feminism thus accepts at one and the same time both the coercive nature of hegemonic law, particularly the coercive nature of heterosexuality, and the possibility of transgression and therefore of change. The two consti-tute one another. It would repudiate the Phallic assumption that struc-tures, economic or Oedipal, can provide *causal* explanations for sexual difference and the asymmetry of power relations; rather, these are an effect of discourse. Power operates as a discursive field, but discursive fields can be disrupted. The Foucauldian thought of Judith Butler now dominates the arena of Ludic feminism, one of the most productive areas of lesbian theory. I shall discuss her work, which explores the perform-ative iterability of heterosexual identity along with the possibility of its alterability, in more detail in the next section of this essay. Here it is important to remember how many very different theorists are using models of sexuality which are structurally alike in their Ludic movement. What they share is an understanding that both discourse and the body are unstable, equally capable of transformation. That is why Donna Haraway's refusal of the dualisms, body/world, body/mind, belongs to Ludic paradigms. Dualisms are deconstructed in her account (*Simians, Cyborgs and Women*, 1991) of the post-modern cyborg culture that permits the invasion of technology into the body, not merely as prosthesis but as an element of consciousness – witness the personal stereo – rendering distinctions of gender subordinate to technology.

That is why Luce Irigaray, who attempts to institute a female symbolic order as an alternative or substitute for the Oedipal contract – which, Freud and Lacan insist, organizes the symbolic order, the order of language, into which both male and female are initiated – is a Ludic figure.[7] Seemingly the idealist antithesis of Haraway, Irigaray nevertheless shares the daring that envisages structural alterations in gender relationships. Both have an affinity with the theorist of 'Third World' identity Trinh T. Minh-Ha, who works towards a redefinition of the classic paradigm of colonial epistemology, self and other, by working with the idea of a more open, multiple subjectivity (*Woman, Native, Other*, 1989). Through this, her work asks a substantive question: what is it to identify oneself and be identified as belonging to a particular group or groups? Thus it avails itself of political questions more directly than some other Ludic texts. Irigaray conducts a dialogue with the law of the father, whether this is Marx or Freud, acknowledging its intransigence at the same time as she makes sophisticated sport with a new symbolic order where feminine jouissance has its own language. Her thought is audacious in a way rather different from that of Judith Butler, who has made a liberating conceptual leap in feminist thought by theorizing, not feminine jouissance, but lesbian jouissance, or rather the lesbian phallus. I shall return to some of the theorists of Ludic feminism in the next section, where I want to find a way of bringing the psychic experience of gender, language and the brute materiality of a dominated life-world together in the concept of space.

The labour of taxonomy: three instances of rape in three novels by Indian women writers

The taxonomy of feminisms mapped out in the first part of this essay is intended to serve as a series of interrogative classifications. Now I follow up on these interrogative classifications with some more specific questions. I ask these questions by returning to the 'trump card' for feminism that was treated with such scepticism by the writers with which I began: rape. Only this time it is in another cultural context altogether: three instances of rape in three novels by Indian women. These are Anita Desai's *Fire on the Mountain* (1977), Mahasweta Devi's 'Draupadi' (1978) and Shashi Deshpande's *The Binding Vine* (1993). Rape has different meanings in different cultures, and in the context of these novels the meanings of rape, male on female rape, figured as a limit case of oppression, raises questions crucial for Ludic writing. What does it mean to resignify the body? Who resignifies? Can resignification force hegemonic power to yield? In all three cases rape is a territorial issue, a matter of invasion, a matter of space.

Ultimately I want to arrive at a concept of space, of space rather than time, which rereads the postulates of some of the feminisms examined here. Since Ludic feminism has been so powerful recently, I shall reach the novels through a more detailed consideration of the work of Judith Butler and relate it to that of Trinh T. Minh-Ha. For Judith Butler's critique raises crucial questions about hegemonic power through the issue of sexual identity. Some of the possibilities of her work (along with its problems) can be dramatized if her thesis is transposed and extended to the terrain of post-colonial debate. If heterosexual hegemony is achieved, as Butler argues, by performative iteration, which makes the lesbian body unnameable by allowing no place for it in discourse, then the same might be said of colonial hegemony. This could be said to work likewise by the iteration of racial difference, and by excluding the alterity of the 'native' other and abjecting it. 'Which bodies come to matter – and why?' she asks, in *Bodies that Matter* (1993, p. xii). The same question could be asked of 'Third World' subjects.

What is the point of this transposition? In some ways it is retrograde. The enormous gain won in theorizing lesbian identity and making it visible beyond Adrienne Rich's 'lesbian continuum' seems to be given up if Butler's ideas can be elided so. It is not my intention, though, to efface queer theory, which, in the hands of Butler and Eve Sedgwick among others, has evolved so productively. On the contrary. But it is possible to give another meaning to Ludic logic by moving it to another context of inequality and power relations – the reality of post-colonial political and cultural experience, the materiality of economic and social constraints – which puts it under pressure and tests it out.

My purpose is to bring Ludic/discursive politics into relation with a dialectic of space, for space is felt internally, as well as experienced as *suffering* (that is, as that imposed from without), and is essentially *relational* and specific – the interpersonal as interspatiality produces a politics – in a way I believe Ludic discursive theory underestimates. The post-colonial context dramatizes this. I first look more closely at Butler's theory, and move on to consider Trinh T. Minh-Ha's post-colonial account of subjectivity and power, modified by a politics of space drawn from the work of Gaston Bachelard and Henri Lefebvre.

In *Gender Trouble* (1990) Butler challenged Kristeva's binary division between the semiotic and the symbolic. Remarking that the symbolic, the rule of language and law, was predicated on the non-rational semiotic, that repressed material which breaks the barrier of the unconscious, she noticed that for Kristeva its only function seemed to be to keep the symbolic in place by being repressed after momentary flickers of subversive, anti-rational life, a kind of waste product that was perpetually returned to the unconscious to maintain the subject's sanity. She complained that the semiotic, abjected in this way, could have no real discursive existence. In *Bodies that Matter*[8] she took this argument further. The lesbian body is a parallel case to that of the semiotic. Heterosexual performativity and iteration is predicated on the repression of the lesbian body. If this body is 'outside' discourse it cannot be represented. Thus to discover the lesbian phallus as signifier is a matter of revising and resignifying the existing signification of the phallus. This can be done because, like any hegemonic state, the phallus is maintained as privileged signifier only because 'it is always in the process of being signified and resignified' (p. 89) and in this compulsive heterosexual need to repeat is the possibility of designifying the signifier, making it open to 'variation and plasticity'. Further, Butler challenges Lacanian structures. She points out that a double instability is inflicted on Lacan's founding signifier, the phallus: first, effectively, if body parts – arms, legs, fingers, – can substitute for the phallus in a signifying system, they enact its vanishing; secondly, if the lesbian phallus displaces by signifying the phallus in excess of its 'structurally mandated position' in anatomy (p. 90), then its privileged status is threatened. The signification of the phallus is 'split' as a result, masculinist and not masculinist in its figuring of power (p. 89), thus enabling a resignifying which allows the lesbian to 'have' the phallus. Butler endorses her case for free play by arguing, first, that the morphology of the body is constructed through representation and desire: the 'bodily ego' (p. 91) is not identical with, or in mimetic relation to the anatomical body, and, since it is not bound by anatomical constraints, can therefore resignify and reshape morphology. Second, simply because heterosexual identification is 'historically contingent', this suggests that sexual bodies are constituted and reconstituted in 'variable ways' (p. 91), so that sexual difference itself is constantly reorganized through the historical continuum of culture.

The liberating aspect of this thought is its capacity to get round the refusal of discursive existence to abjected bodies, and its understanding that the excluded can enter into discursive play because the inherent instability even of that which holds signification in place, the phallus, permits the Ludic possibility of resignification. Three problems arise. Two are obvious, arising from the argument's assumption that change can occur by fiat, even by individual agency. First, bodies are matter as well as mattering, matter as well as morphology. Though they may be imagined as form, not strictly correlative with anatomical structures, it is an extraordinarily idealist reading of bodies that abstracts them from their nature as substance. It is not to adopt a literal reading of the body to say that it is subject to material experience. The pressures of labour, the history of its medication, feeding, pain. This is to accept the pathos of bodies, that they are acted upon, formed by the outside world as well as psychic needs: indeed, psychic needs are a response to the pressure of the material. Second, bodies are acted upon in history and culture. Butler appears to recognize this, but in fact she abstracts bodies from history as well as matter. Her preference for the term 'historically contingent' as a synonym for 'historically determined' suggests that the signification of bodies is a matter of historical accident or chance, and thus capable of an equally arbitrary resignification, rather than an irreducible specificity created by circumstance and mediated by social forms which require the full weight of cultural and political action if they are to be shifted, altered. Thus she swings between the coercive fixity of power in heterosexual iteration and the jouissance of lesbian nominalism without recognizing the agony of labour, the negotiation with material, substantive conditions. That is, what Jonathan Dollimore has recently called the 'cultural real'.[9]

Lastly, it is not simply that the body's sweat and tears are specific to history, important though this is: in order to 'mean', the lesbian body has to use the host discourse of heterosexuality and transform it. Because this is the only discourse available, the lesbian body has to cohabit within these discursive limits. Largely dependent on the host discourse for its life, it has to mime out an anti-discourse within the discursive limits set by heterosexual iteration, leaving that discourse intact. Resignification does not even 'steal' language to the extent of creating a new signifier out of a previous signifying system, as Barthes suggested of myth. Nor, in this structure, is there a possibility that heterosexual and lesbian signification might be *mutually* transformed. It is not logically possible for this to be.

Transposed to the asymmetry of race relations, the emancipatory possibilities are still there, but so are the problems. To transform the abjected colonial body by resignifying the language of power, forcing its hegemonic instability to yield meaning against itself, has been achieved in the case of the adjective 'black', once a term of abuse. But the enormous institutional and political labour and intellectual work concurrent with this minimal change is enough to suggest the difficulties of discursive theory. The Butler paradigm is set up as if limited to an agreement between two consenting adults, on a narrow model of individual sexuality. What would it mean to resignify the white phallus, the founding signifier of Eurocentric power, as the black phallus? How far would the black phallus reproduce the image of white power on the Butler system? If the resignification of the black body is to be controlled by the discursive limits of the language of colonial power, both are caught in the repetition compulsion of hegemonic imperialism. A double transformation is impossible. There is no gap for dialectic and for the generation of new concepts if one discourse is mapped on to the other.

Recently, Butler has responded strenuously to such critique. In an article republished from *Social Text* (1997) in *New Left Review* (1998) she has defended the necessary occupation of the field of a host discourse, or 'other', suggesting that, as in the act of parody, a kind of ambivalent complicity and imaginative projection, a living with, is necessary in order to understand the position from which one dissents. Parody for her is an example of a form that rejects the false unity of exclusion, an exclusion that refuses an opening out of difference. Queer politics is not an identitarian project but grows out of a revisionary Marxism. It is a neo-conservatism of the left that designates lesbian discourse as 'merely cultural' and refuses to accept the excitement and materiality of a political project that has to do with what Engels saw as the production of daily life. She refuses to make a distinction between the cultural and economic and argues that queer theory requires 'a fundamental shift in the conceptualizing of social relations' ('Merely cultural', p. 44). Indeed, the regulation of sexuality is tied to analagous forms of exclusion where race and class are concerned.[10] This is an impressive argument, though one wonders what kind of transformational possibilities are left for heterosexuals and heterosexual women in this analysis. Are they excluded *as* heterosexuals from advancing an emancipatory politics?

Butler's steady move into political critique (in 1997 she engaged in a dialogue with Ernesto Laclau on 'Equality' in *Diacritics*) is of great significance for Ludic feminism. Yet despite or perhaps because of this engagement, Butler seems to be working less with the paradigm of the discursive field than with a notion of difference opening up between self and other, inadvertently falling into a strangely contradictory Marxist individualism. Another Ludic feminist, Trinh T. Minh-Ha, offers another model of change. Her study, *Woman, Native, Other* (1989) is angry about the exclusion of so-called 'Third World' women from white feminist discourse and challenges its categories of self and other – western hegemony, 'Third World' alterity. The ideology of 'difference', of a

sanctioned 'authentic' colonial otherness, conceals a fierce racism under a
permissive liberalism of respect for difference. Multiculturalism is a form
of apartheid because in 'trying to find the other by defining otherness or
by explaining otherness through laws and generalities' (p. 75) it designates or imposes an identity of irreducible difference on the other, which
is the creation of a privileged master discourse and its dualisms, a one-
way definition which leaves no space for the other to define itself.
(Compare lesbian sexuality here.) The doctrine of 'authenticity' creates
a subjectivity which is an 'i', the master's subject. The solution is to
conceive the subject as 'I/i'. This is not a composite in which the 'I' of
power and the 'i' of powerlessness are reconciled but a radical reconfiguration of subjectivity. There is a false binary I/i which simply reconsti-
tutes the big I and the little i of colonial power, and Minh-Ha occasionally
designates this oppressive relationship in such a way. But in a newly
understood, fluid reading of subjectivity, I/i has liberating potential,
pointing to the way subjectivity is actually lived. The 'I' within the 'I/i'
stands for difference as 'critical difference from myself' (p. 89), not an
indivisible identity of pure origin or true self, but the power to conceptualize differences between and within the subject. Thus lower case 'i' is
the not-I constructed by the subject itself. It is not organized through the
dualisms of self and other.

All subjects are I/i, multiple configurations of I/i layered through time.
She refuses to recognize an essentialist East / West subjectivity. Far from
making the subject a separate and separatist consciousness, the principle
of critical difference 'both between and within entities' (p. 94) creates
multiple, overlapping subjectivities: 'A critical difference from myself
means that I am not i am within and without i. I/i can be I or i, you and
me both involved. We (with capital W) sometimes include(s), at other
times exclude(s), me. You and I are close, we intertwine ... you may also
be me, while remaining what you are and what i am not' (p. 90). 'I/i' and
'you' are always already pluralized, because 'I/i' and 'you' can constitute
different overlapping groups as well as individuals, and thus the individualist paradigm of self/other disappears. Political action 'within and
between' different groups becomes a possibility. I/i is the ground of a new
commonality. The possibility of overlapping relations between one I/i and
another I/i, 'you and me both involved', means that a process of resignification is continuous, as new, mutually transformed configurations of I/i
emerge – eventually. For Trinh T. Minh-Ha the paradox is that a recon-
ceived I/i would mean profound political change and cultural work at the
same time that it is the prerequisite of change. I/i may well be the correct
way to understand the epistemology of self, but to achieve the alteration
of political structures which would be entailed by the recognition of this

reality is an arduous pursuit. Nevertheless, I/i opens up a dialectical space for negotiation.

'Difference does not annul identity. It is beyond and alongside identity' (p. 104). The plural identity does not mean that parts of subjectivity can be subtracted at will. Trinh T. Minh-Ha will not accept Kristeva's dissolving of the identity of 'woman' to a series of 'beyond-the-sex' attributes, because such a dissolution follows a 'logic of acquisition' in western constructions of gender and ethnicity alike. Her understanding of difference – not as an irreducible quality but as a drifting apart within 'woman' [which] articulates upon the infinity of 'woman' as entities of inseparable 'I's' and 'Not-i's' (p. 104) – enables her to retain a notion of identity which includes both gender and ethnicity. There is no point outside identity to be, culturally constructed or not: one's womanhood and ethnicity are indivisible and unique and this is where one starts from politically. This is why she strategically holds on to the notion of 'Third World' women, despite its western condescension. Such a notion of identity does not contradict the possibility of plural, overlapping womanhoods. Nor does it contradict Minh-Ha's understanding of interactive subjects of difference rather than irreducibly different subjects, 'western Eurocentric', 'colonial'. The whole point of the I/i structure is that it establishes crossings, the occupation of mutual space, drifting apart, convergence, an almost infinite variation of relationship within and between subjects.

This relational interactivity is not the hybridity explored by Homi K. Bhabha in *The Location of Culture* (1994), though it might resemble it. Bhabha's hybridity depends on a deconstructive moment, when binaries are exposed as impure, permeable, and when, therefore, the hierarchical colonial structure of self and other breaks down. For Minh-Ha the experience of what she refuses to call the colonial subject is always already free of hierarchy and oppositional identities. Hence, despite the freedom of a post-modern identity, the I/i is located confidently in a kind of cultural imaginary, in the 'felt' experience of ethnicity and womanhood. The I/i has to have somewhere to start from. This is why she reconciles a free-floating I/i with the immediacy of felt identity.

Such a felt experience of womanhood and ethnicity is worth investigating further because it is this culturally 'felt' experience among and between groups that has to be negotiated if change is to occur. It has been misunderstood by Sara Suleri, who upbraids Minh-Ha with a naïve return to the literalness of 'lived experience'. But Suleri's is itself a superficial reading. Minh-Ha is considering 'felt' experience rather than 'lived experience', and 'felt' experience is not necessarily 'lived' experience at the literal level. It is more a function of the way the most intimate sense of the self is represented as subjectivity and context, as subjectivity-in-community.

Minh-Ha's paradoxical, even contradictory, position points to something materially important, the territorial nature of identity when it is imagined, its locatedness in space. Thus any understanding of the subject of difference rather than the irreducibly different subject, any attempt to consider the interrelatedness of the I/i, has to address the interpenetration of a double condition. Subjects of difference encounter both one another's psychic representations of space and the material conditions of socially produced space, which are marked, sometimes with violence, on the body and mind. That is why it is no contradiction to bring together the seemingly idealist psychic phenomenology of Bachelard's *The Poetics of Space* (1958; translated 1964) and the Marxist politics of space that theorize the instrumental space of capital in Henri Lefebvre's *The Production of Space* (1974; translated 1991). In what follows I offer an outline for thinking of change interspatially, rather than in terms of the discursive site which is obliged to mirror or double the host discourse from which it dissents.

This is where Bachelard's conception of 'vital space' is useful, for it is the space the I/i occupies. To build on his hints: vital space is imagined, never known; it cannot be known in its primal nature; but it is the representation of the primal, sheltering space once lived in, which lives in the subject and continues to define its being in interaction with subsequent experience. S/he carries vital space around as part physical sense, part image, part memory, throughout her or his life. It is not the psychoanalytical space of origins, of the womb or of the *chora*, because it is part of the earliest social and cultural life of the self. It is thought of as a dwelling, a place to be in, and it is a sensory composite – things touched, seen, heard – derived from the first dwellings or protective enclosures of early life, the first experience of setting limits to the self and of limits being set. It is a praxis of space, associated with the concrete, primary function of inhabiting, 'the non-I that protects the I' (*Poetics of Space*, p. 5). Bachelard's phenomenological poetics will not allow this to be a regressive, pre-Oedipal space, deliberately challenging this interpretation by risking it. Nor is it the habitus ordained by status and class envisaged by Pierre Bourdieu in *Distinction*. It must be the place of nostalgia, the lost, but it is carried around in the body and the mind. Bachelard thinks of vital space as the first experience of the house and though his account of the structure of the house is European, the essential element of vital space as dwelling is transposable to other cultures. Individuated, concrete, sensuous, it is where thought and daydreaming begin, and where, by extension, community is first imagined as well as experienced. The primal dwelling is made from the inside out by the self, from the outside in by human labour. This space is simultaneously sexual and social.

However, this space is always already negotiated. It is intra- and inter-personal space – 'interspatiality'[11] as it has been termed – and, as Lefebvre insists in *The Production of Space*, it is always already mediated political space, dominated space. Far more complex than that of Bache-lard his model is the production of three non-symmetrical relationships, spatial practice, representations of space and representational spaces, each intersected by the abstract, instrumental space of capital. Every social space is demarcated and produced, each implying a network of superimposed relationships and practices organized by work, economics, state bureaucracy, capital and, he might have added, the ethnic mapping that followed the expansion of capital. The emergence of globalized abstract space, which resembles Benjamin's 'empty' homogeneous time,[12] as the space of capital is Lefebvre's deterministic theme. The relation between mental and material space is not 'transparent'. Even though the mirage effect of capital makes it seem so, the effect of trans-parency is ideological. Thus, identifying 'the foundations upon which the space of each particular society is built, the underpinnings of that space's gradual development' (p. 188) is actually obfuscated by the mirage-like clarity offered by that society's own representations of space. By Lefebv-re's reading it would seem a naïve project to envisage the transformation of interspatial relations as a political project, since Bachelard's vital space would be a misrecognized ideological zone. This clinging to a primal 'anthropological' space is, after all, what helps to perpetuate the territor-ial violence of Ireland, Jerusalem, Bosnia.

Yet it is precisely this realism that Bachelard's paradigm requires. The intense difficulty of negotiating mental and material space has to be recognized as a prerequisite of opening genuinely new spaces. And per-haps because vital space is so resistant to negotiation, this is the place to begin. And perhaps, also, without indulging in bland optimism, it may be that the gap between discourse and materiality is actually the opening that makes possible not only the opening of new mental space but the changing of the literal shape of materially lived space. Though space appears objective, Lefebvre writes, 'it exists in a social sense only for activity'. Because the 'way in which it presents itself and the way in which it is represented are different' (p. 191), space is a multiform principle, a given field of action and a basis for possible action, actual and potential, quantitative and qualitative.

To return to vital space as an integral element of the I/i with Lefebvre's realism in mind, the ideological aspect of vital, ontological, space may be actually what offers the possibility of change, enabling the interstices between represented space and dominated space to become evident.

Vital space is what makes the I/i concrete to itself and to others, what makes it a social entity. This roundedness has a double movement of interaction and alienation. The overlapping pluralities of I/i, are approached through the accommodation of vital spaces one to another. The convergence, the mutuality of space, comes from a capacity to imagine a space, from an interspatiality which can either be easily ima-gined and granted if it is culturally shared, or, if it is not, puts the imagination in difficulties. 'Home' is the terrain of shelter, but it is always territorial as well. With those conceived as other – the immigrant, the 'native', for example – the negotiation and modification of vital space, the *changing* of vital space to imagine the not-I which is not known, both psychic and social, must be a strenuous cultural and political work. It often fails, as Bosnia and Africa attest. It is an effort of mind and body, self and society – it is labour. And, as we have seen, it is predicated on the material shaping of *literal* space and its constraints. Yet if this is an imagined space it can be re-imagined, creating a transitional area, cultural and personal, between entities.

D. J. Winnicott reminds us of the openness of transitional space and the way in which it opens up the revision of cultural traditions.[13] He thought of this revisionary, psychoanalytical space as one within and between groups in the same culture, but the same necessity for mutual revision governs subjects of difference, the I/i. There are times when cultures have to re-imagine the transitional space of the house to create a gap for the new. Post-colonial experience is an imperative example. Interspatiality means the double modification of space, within and between cultures. In a passing, virtually parenthetical comment in 'Women's time', Kristeva mentions the possible conceptualization of Oedipal separation as spatial separation between child and mother rather than the temporal moment of violence which we see as the act of castration. Is the double modification of space a possibility from the earliest moments of life?

To turn to the novels. We could see the moments of assault in each text as a portrayal of the complete breakdown of heterosexual iteration. We witness its total failure and essential violence as the signifying systems around phallic power collapse and the symbolic is taken for the real. One could say that in rape the performative function of heterosexuality noted by Butler has collapsed into literal performance. The melancholia she perceives in heterosexual relations has issued in violence. Certainly there is a concurrent crisis of power and signification. Yet one can stay with her thought only so far. The terrible literalism of rape, its absolutism, suggests a fury which is transcultural and over against history, and thus Butler's supra-historical structures might seem to have a certain appropriateness. But to escape from the European context, and to consider the anguish of rape in novels from and about India, is to discover that each rape signifies something different because its significance depends on the 'felt experience' of its culture, the felt experience of the protagonist caught in very particular complexes of power. The bodies of the assaulted cannot be abstracted from history, and different violations of vital space occur as different vital spaces become irreconcilable. A failure to negotiate the space of the highly specific and individuated I/i, a failure to imagine vital space, is the source of violence. In each case the power relations are different: in colonial relations between indigenous peasant farmer and Indian anglophile (Desai); in guerrilla warfare and anti-terrorist action between different classes (Devi) and in kinship structures (Deshpande).

Anita Desai's *Fire on the Mountain*: Ila Das, an educated Indian who is a welfare officer employed by the government on a pittance, depends for her self-respect on her long-past but over-idealized connections with the prestige of colonial rule and her subaltern standing. She needs this self-respect because she is a figure of fun in the peasant village in which she now lives, in the mountains above the Punjab plains. 'All her life mobs had taunted and derided her' (p. 110). In terms of the binary of I and i, master and slave, she is the i of two cultures, Indian and British, for both now exclude and reject her as other. Living through the anachronistic code of the English shabby genteel spinster (she recited 'The boy stood on the burning deck' at school), she is actually on the point of starvation, and lives in a hut with a lean-to in which cows are 'comfortably mooing and chewing' (p. 142) virtually next to her. This is nevertheless 'home' to her (p. 141) and she can live with the contradictions of living in a dwelling poorer than most of the peasant farmers around her because she believes in her reforming mission derived from her British-inspired training and education, which has seen to the formation of her I/i. She has tried to prevent a child marriage, which is now against the law. A girl of seven is being given in marriage 'to an old man in the next village because he owns a quarter of an acre of land and two goats. He's a widower and has six children but, for a bit of land and two goats, they're willing to sacrifice their little girl.' She has 'argued with her mother', and 'I even tackled the father, Preet Singh, in the potato fields the other day. But he's a sullen lout, I could see I wasn't making any headway with him' (p. 130). The 'I' here is definitely that of post-colonial power – 'i' asserts itself as 'I', however well-intentioned her horror at the seven-year-old child as chattel.

Preet Singh, the father, strangles and rapes her. The old woman's rape – she is described as a 'child-sized' creature (p. 137) – doubles the violation of the seven-year-old girl. She is on her way home down the dark hill when 'a dark shape detached itself from the jagged pile of the rock, that last rock between her and the hamlet, and sprang soundlessly at her' (p. 142). Preet Singh is a 'shape' to the short-sighted, bespectacled Ila Das, just as the rocks she descends, imagined through the aesthetic of western nostalgia for the oriental exotic, are transmuted by her limited vision from Indian hills to the 'shapes' of another culture, 'a Chinese landscape – an austere pen-and-ink scroll, of rocks and pines and mountain peaks, all muted by mist, by darkness' (p. 141). Ila Das, horrified by the child marriage, is nevertheless ideologically short-sighted. She insists peremptorily on the hygienic abstractions of her adopted European code of ethics: she simply occludes the factor of dowry, without enquiring whether, to the subsistence farmer with a virtually dowryless girl child, the quarter of an acre might ensure her future; to the parents this would not be the 'sacrifice' of but an insurance for the child. She doesn't understand the pull of endogamy. Perverted though this use of girl children as object of exchange may be by western standards, her zeal for reform fails to recognize that the economics of land occupation and cultural practice have not created a structural context for reform. Ila Das speaks the language enabled by what Spivak calls the 'artificial inscription' of the culture of 'colonial monopoly capital' as against the 'harvest calendar' of peasant experience. This is a tragedy which comes from a failure to imagine how space feels in peasant life, an inability to imagine the importance of land and a praxis of land, an imperviousness deriving from a colonial society which has abstracted itself from the land, despising native custom while exploiting native labour. Preet Singh's hatred is the accumulated fury, fury and despair, of years of past Anglo-Indian occupation which is stamped indelibly on the landscape even though Indians replace British in new power relations. It is a mutual breakdown. On both sides it is the i failing to see that the i might be an I/i.

Singh's hatred is a hatred of women, engendered by the sapping demands of the dowry system and a loathing of the female subaltern's rhetoric. The whole incident is an ironic intertextual reference to an earlier, western, representation of the Indian as rapist: E. M. Forster's *Passage to India*. As Jenny Sharpe has noticed in her *Allegories of Empire: The Figure of Woman in the Colonial Text* (1993), an insistent, over-determined discourse of the Indian as rapist emerged in the years after the Indian Mutiny of 1858 and persisted into the twentieth century. This was a direct inversion of the colonial realities of military rule, where white rapes were perpetrated and military power deployed in the name of a rhetoric of 'protection', which figured the white woman's virginity at risk. Forster explores this hysterical discourse in his novel. After 1947 (Indian independence), Desai notes, 'Maiden ladies were not thought to be safe here any more.' They were packed on to the last boats to England, 'virginity intact' (*Fire on the Mountain*, p. 9). Preet Singh terrifyingly confirms the rhetoric of rape on the residual legatee of western values, Ila Das. But what is not 'safe', Desai shows, is not the white woman's body but the values associated with it. Yet, of course, fatally, he too cannot read Ila Das's space, or rather its contradictions. She bears both the sign of western power and Indian abjection. He takes revenge on both. She is a memsahib with some of the characteristics of the independent English woman (she walks by herself, she lectures the natives), but without the privilege or protection of that status. Forced by poverty to walk home alone at night, to live in a hovel, she is despised and hated as the abject projection of their poverty by the peasants of her village. She carries the marks of power, but she is powerless. She is i rather than I, assaulted by another i.

In Devi's 'Draupadi', I assaults i, or *conceives* itself as belonging to this structure, living out the power relations of self and other as irreducible difference. This short story, translated with an informative and brilliant introduction by Gayatri Chakravorty Spivak, is set in West Bengal in 1971. Draupadi, or Dopti, is a Santal tribal, a landless peasant and farm-worker (not an untouchable but a member of an abjected group, illiterate and way outside the class position of the intellectuals with whom she collaborates) who is taking part in guerrilla insurgence. The guerrillas are fighting the oppression of a landlord–government collusion which extracts virtually unpaid labour from tribals. Dopti, whose husband has been shot, is wanted for the killing of a landlord who refused water to the village in a time of drought. She is tracked down by Senanayak, military theorist and liberal intellectual subaltern, who is actually theoretically sympathetic to the tribal cause. A higher class Bengali, he prides himself on inwardness with Santal guerrilla codes. She suffers multiple rape. Spivak reads this relation in terms of an unreconstructed I tracking its binary other, the i, and as an allegory of the 'First World' reader who tracks down the 'Third World' subject, not by direct but by indirect violence, in a predatory breaking of its codes, by occupying the space of the other. Arguably, she understates Senanayak's misrecognition of his subaltern 'i' and occludes the strength that makes Dopti an I/i as subject.

Senanayak appropriates vital space, or thinks he does. He uses the sophisticated technologies of 'superior' western knowledge to do so, importing the epistemological techniques of code-breaking along with the brute materiality of arms and methods of torture to enter and transform vital space into dominated space. Yet, despite the horror of the story, he fails to deprive Dopti of vital space. In an absurd parody of the soldier as researcher, Senanayak has specialist linguists imported to interpret Dopti's song, true to his watchword, 'in order to destroy the enemy, become one' (p. 189). This is liberal empathy by violence, in which a practice of oppression is disavowed in theory. Spivak believes that the story brings about the possibility of throwing the liberal reader into uncertainty, the classic deconstructive moment, but hints that a reading of the reader as rapist could also be included in this allegory. Rape as a weapon of war must be the ultimate appropriation of vital space at the same time as it is the ultimate refusal of the interspatial. This must mean that the reader fails as Senanayak fails. Is there an alternative to readerly violence?

Draupadi was translated in the context of an ongoing discussion of the Subaltern Studies Group and its analysis of change. Spivak admires the shift of emphasis in their Marxist analysis to 'confrontations rather than transition', to histories of exploitation, and to epistemic theory (p. 197). But, as in her earlier essay, 'Can the subaltern speak?', she is doubtful that an 'authentic' subaltern consciousness can be retrieved by western discourse. Yet she writes as if western discourse cannot discover the authentic because of its position as western discourse, rather than repudiating the concept of the authentic as such: for her, it seems, the authentic is discoverable only by itself, only by those who are it. Yet perhaps the project of this dream binary should be entirely relinquished. It is a dream of power, if we are to believe Minh-Ha, that is founded on a false premise, the master (Senanayak) and the irreducible difference of the colonial subject (Dopti/Draupadi). Because there *isn't* such an 'authentic' subject, the tentative meeting of I/i and I/i could replace this paradigm as a model of reading. What difference would this make to a reading of 'Draupadi'? To begin with, Senanayak and Draupadi/Dopti are part of a continuum of Bengali experience, albeit that Draupadi uses a tribal language mocked by sophisticated Bengali speakers, and albeit that they are hunter and hunted. The relation is not between imperialist outsider and subaltern indigenous subject: it is between subaltern and oppressed peasant. For Senanayak is indigenous subaltern class, doing the work of oppression from within by adopting sophisticated western military strategies, but arguably insecure as man of power, a subordinate himself. These are not structurally the same positions. Far from being 'authentic' other, Dopti/Draupadi has two names. Draupadi is the name given to her by the mistress who brought her up and used her as a servant. Dopti is the name she knows herself by. Dopti's language of ululation and gnomic song is fused with the language of the intellectuals who fight alongside of her (Spivak, aware of the perils of sentimentalizing Dopti, writes as if her experience of intellect is merely to learn by rote what intellectuals tell her, but she has surely internalized this language). Dopti is already I/i. Living in the same camp with them, she has lived, as they have, interspatially, revising vital space. In her final confrontation with Senanayak, she realizes herself as I/i.

'Draupadi comes closer...Draupadi's black body comes even closer' (p. 196). In the last moments of the story (before she is finally murdered, we assume) Draupadi comes toward Senanayak, displaying her horribly mutilated body and pushing her 'mangled breasts' against him. She forces an encounter with him, in the literal sense, as Spivak points out, rather than its euphemistic sense (in the language of war) as torture, refusing the 'cover-up' of language just as she refuses to put on her cloth. Senanayak is 'terribly afraid', but what occurs is not a simple, if temporary, reversal of power. Draupadi desecrates his physical space, spitting blood at his 'virginal' white shirt, an act which effaces him as I, the master. She writes her blood on him. 'Are you a man?' She cannot be ashamed of her nakedness because there are no men in the camp, she says. The trauma for Senanayak is that his vital space has been assaulted and negated because he has excluded everything except his instrumentality from his identity. It is this which allows Dopti to come, literally and symbolically, close to him. If his standing as a man, linked as it is with pure instrumentality, can be even temporarily destroyed, he falls out of the space of representation as both 'I' and 'i'. He has repressed all except the I, male, master, and can *only* go on being this: 'What more can you do?' Logically the 'more' Senanayak can 'do' is to kill her, but this is only an extension, of his earlier actions, and the more he asserts male power the less he is a man. Draupadi assaults the category 'man' and exposes it as empty, a mere I, whereas she takes her own self-definition into her own hands, becoming an I/i, refusing to accept a definition of herself as irreducibly other. 'A fictional change in a sign system is a violent event', Spivak writes (p. 197). The birth of the non binary I/i is violent and temporary. Spivak refuses idealism: a prior gap for changing signification will be opened up by crisis and crisis precipitates gaps, 'a space for change', in the sign system. Language and event work symbiotically but with difficulty and discontinuously. Draupadi's mutilated body is the price of attaining a new sign, I/i.

With Shashi Deshpande's novel, *The Binding Vine*, urban culture – and its discontinuities – is the context of an assault on Kalpana by her uncle. Crisis comes about when sophisticated, educated middle-class values confront traditional interpretations of rape – as shame for the woman. Urmila attempts to resignify rape as shame to rape as violation, ultimately by taking political action on behalf of Kalpana: the upheaval of the sign system parallels an upheaval of events. Urmila's confidence arises from her sense of power: her earliest spaces are the privileged spaces of an old

Raj palace, much and eccentrically partitioned for an extended family, but nevertheless the space of intellectual privilege. The fatherless Kalpana comes from a poor family who want to suppress the rape. Here Kalpana's mother speaks:

> 'The man', she says after a small silence. 'What use is it blaming him? Women like you will never understand what it is like for us. We have to keep to our places, we can never step out. There are always people waiting to throw stones at us, our own people first of all. I warned Kalpana, but she would never listen to me. "I'm not afraid of anyone", she used to say. That's why this happened to her... women must know fear.'... Suddenly ...I find myself rampant with anger. (Deshpande, *The Binding Vine*, p. 148)

Kalpana's abused mother, constantly excluded, like an animal, from one contracted space after another, accepts what she thinks of as a cultural real, the need for women to go in fear of the shame of rape. Sara Suleri invokes such a fear in her dispute with Trinh T. Minh-Ha. She puts what she supposes to be the 'parochialism' ('Women skin-deep', p. 769) of Minh-Ha's 'lived experience' – what we might call Asianism – against the realism of the Hudood ordinances of 1980 in Pakistan, which can put a fifteen-year-old raped by her uncle in prison for fornication. In other words, lived experience as the experience of the law is a destructive, not cohesive force, hardly confirming women's identity. But as I have already said, Suleri misinterprets Minh-Ha as an Asian essentialist, whereas she is arguing a more subtle position. Minh-Ha's analysis of the plural terms, I/i can be inflected both positively and negatively. It makes possible a reading of this novel as the breaking down, the dispersals, of I/i under cultural pressure, a violent reversion to the old, binary I/i.

Deshpande would have been aware of the feminist controversy over the Hudood ordinances, which emerged in the early 1990s, while she was writing her novel. As an Indian, Kalpana is not subject to the cruelty of such a law, but she is subject to a culture which conceives rape as shame. Urmila takes up the position of the strong 'I' of enlightened discourse against the weak 'i' of Kalpana's mother – she comes after all, from the devastated grandeur of a palace with, as in Ray's film *The Music Room*, its mark of status and western illumination, the crystal chandelier. She is not averse to bullying. She sees herself also pitted against the strong 'I' of the (at first) unknown male rapist, allied with the dying Kalpana, who, before the rape, asserted her power as a strong 'I'–'I'm not afraid of any one'. It looks as if 'I' (female) is aligned against 'I' (male), and the same female 'I' is aligned against another female 'i', the traditional feminine subjectivity of Kalpana's mother, locked in irreversible opposition. When the rape finally becomes public, however, the voracious publicity insists on Kalpana's 'guilt'. Both the girl and Urmila are cast as 'i' in the debate, which polarizes subjectivity, realigning all women as 'i', the subjugated sex. This is compounded by Urmila's own domestic situation, whose husband casts her as 'i', arbitrarily leaving her and returning to her at will. Her husband was her first love, worshipped from childhood, co-occupier of her earliest vital space. Urmila's I/i is deeply conflicted. She cannot occupy the overlapping subjectivities which constitute the plural I/i. Though she tries to achieve it, her selfhood falls into the oppositional, essentialist I/i of colonial discourse, the master/slave. When the rape becomes the subject of publicity, Kalpana's aunt burns herself to death, and it is clear that her uncle, who, with the childless aunt's terrified collusion, had wanted his niece as a (by this time illegal) second wife, is the rapist. A tortured figure, tortured by an anachronistic male will to power once sanctioned by the law but now defunct by virtue of the law, he never appears in the narrative except through the mother's description. The strong 'I' of the rapist is reduced to the weak 'i' of a desperate male sexuality tied to a defunct hegemony, an obsolete primal space. Urmila's hubris, her failure to consider why some women's abjection is so habitual that they accept oppression as their vital space, their designation as 'i', is brought low.

But the sombre point of the novel is not this. Some women can remake their vital space, as Urmila does at the close of the story by ending her marriage, and reconstitute the I/i of the self. Some women cannot. They are literally 'oppressed' – in the sense that to 'oppress' means to press against, press or bear down physically – 'We have to keep to our places, we can never step out'. Kalpana's brave refusal of the 'i' position demanded a political context it did not have. Some women are forced to remain as 'i' – the aunt, the mother. Vital space cannot easily be remade. The anguish of the rape is at the terrible junction of two signifying systems thrown into crisis: it is both cause and effect, the physical dereliction created by that crisis and the literal event occasioning it. The 'old' code of male power and female shame and the 'new' code of female autonomy and the refusal of violation are irreconcilable. Both codes, however, can polarize I/i as master and slave: the fruitful generation of difference within and between, embodied by the non-binary I/i, is not only difficult to achieve but is constantly in danger of collapsing back into the simplified opposition of the powerful and its other. Tragically, events organize and are organized *by* this unstable constitution. There is a gap for change and for changing space in the cultural real, but the struggle to alter cultural space is prodigious.

The texts I have discussed suggest that, in the context of post-colonial writing, resignification of cultural and sexual meaning is an arduous and agonistic process, a violent event in the sign system (as Spivak terms it), paralleled by political upheaval which is as much cause as effect of discursive change. To transpose the issue of resignification from the heterosexual body to the context of post-colonial discourse is to dramatize the difficulties of resignifying the racialized body as discursive site. Intractable material and social obstacles, the obstacles of political structures and economic arrangements, intervene. At the same time, discursive change is constrained by the paradigms it seeks to modify, and reproduces them. Of course, crises in the sign system *do* occur, as Spivak demonstrates, and the opportunities for resignification can be seized. But such crises are knotted together with the upheaval of political and economic conditions. I have suggested that a politics of space might replace the politics of resignification. Would this be just as likely to run into the arbitrariness of performative change? One would hope not, because of the double nature of space as both material and psychic experience. Experience in space negotiates both the brute given of irreducible territorial power and psychic imagining of space as felt experience. It links the intransigent material world and the cultural imaginary and provides more hopeful ground for thinking through the possibilities of cultural and political change and reaching *new* models of relationship rather than reproducing, albeit oppositionally, the old patterns. The double subject of difference, I/i, creates another way of avoiding hierarchies. How does all this look if we move it back to the context of queer theory? In what ways does the subject of difference, I/i, allow a more open reading of gender, and in what ways can issues of lesbian identity be realized through a spatial politics? And how might a philosophical project for feminism be renewed?

Different and conflicting primal spaces make, perhaps, for an intransigent politics which does not seem to open transformative possibilities. But it is worth remembering here the tradition from which both Bachelard and Lefebvre derive, however differently they take it up, the phenomenological tradition of Martin Heidegger. It is possible to extrapolate a spatial politics from Heidegger's thought, even if it is one he himself would not have recognized. And here I sketch one out as a coda, perhaps an idealist one, to this discussion of interspatiality.

Heidegger's spatial politics rests on the repudiation of Cartesian space, in which a single, free, abstract subject stands separate and alone, confronting an objectified abstract universe in a relationship of power (*Being and Time*, pp. 122–34). Pronouns such as 'I' and 'he' need to be replaced by locative adverbs, 'here', 'yonder', to convey the refusal of an 'I' seen 'as from a certain privileged point' (p. 155). Since, for Heidegger, Being is always a manifold, Being-in-the-World, it is always already environmental, horizoned, produced as belonging inseparably to a region: it can never stand over and against space, for it is with it and in it. Correspondingly, the environmental world must inevitably be one that is inherently social, lived in by others, and cannot be conceived except with people, or 'Others', as he terms them. This is the position argued out in chapter 4, 'Being-in-the-World as Being-with and Being-one's self, the 'They' (pp. 149–68). A world that contains other people is *constitutive* of Being-in-the-World and vice versa. Thus this social aspect of Being or *Dasein* is not simply added on numerally – Being and other people – but a structural element of experience, a 'with-world' (p. 155). *Dasein* recognizes itself as Being-in-the-World only because this is predicated on others, who cannot be subtracted from the experience. The 'Others' 'are not somehow added on in thought' (p. 154): reciprocally, 'Others' cannot recognize themselves without predicating Being-in-the-World on the existence of another. Consequently, so this argument can be extended, the *bodily* being of others is paramount, for Being-in-the-World is never an abstract experience. In this reading bodies *do* matter materially.

There are two moments to this experience, a positive, Utopian, and a negative, 'realest' (p. 166) moment. They are signalled by two different terms for sociality, 'Others' and 'They'. Both are relevant to gender, to politics and to a feminist project.

To take the moment of the 'Others' first. Being is in a condition to 'free' a space for 'Others' rather than to see itself oppositionally and abstractly: 'freeing something and letting it be involved' (p. 146) is essential to *Dasein*. *Dasein* is not fully Being-in-the-World unless it has lost its immediacy to itself and become one among others, or come to accept that it is a somebody else to a somebody else. This is a condition in which the world is 'not everyone else but me' but 'those among whom one is too' (p. 154). One might read this recognition as an accommodation of vital space to the phenomenologically *relational* status of *Dasein* (certainly and perhaps inevitably Heidegger veers between seeing this as a structure and an ethics). But the structure of this recognition is more extreme. Being is fully grounded only when a negation or displacement to the space of 'Others' has occurred: 'Everyone is the other, and no one is himself' (p. 165), a statement that has both an egalitarian and a pathological moment, as we shall see.

A transformative egalitarian politics is the obvious possibility to be envisaged in the freeing up of space for 'Others' and the mutuality of permeable interspatial relations. This is a condition Heidegger expresses as a 'Being-with that is something encounterable for others' (p. 157), deliberately stressing the way Being achieves meaning because it can be responsively perceived by entities external to it. The mutual project of 'understanding the stranger' (p. 163) actually dissolves the strange into the different – lesbian to heterosexual, heterosexual to lesbian, immigrant to indigenous dweller and vice versa – and is brought about by a process of radical re-envisaging or re-seeing that must mean that both entities change. It is associated with special kinds of sight, or seeing, a spatial relation lost in translation, where words suffixed 'sicht' are rendered by terms such as 'forebearance'.[14] This linked visual and spatial accommodation is important, for a freeing up of space for others has a double political and territorial and *imaginative* movement that has consequences for civil society. 'Empathy', the duplication of being in the Other as an act of domination is, Heidegger insists, a misreading of the relational conditions of Being-with-one-another (p. 162), though there will always be a struggle between 'that which leaps in and dominates' and that which 'leaps forth and liberates' (p. 159). 'Empathy' is essentially a power-ridden construction of relations and a sentimental understanding of 'community'. It is an individualist reading of what must belong to a collective experience.

In this movement of reciprocal and radical reconceptualizing of relations in an egalitarian order there can surely be no structural difference between gender politics and politics more widely defined. Both need to be worked out in the political *and* cultural sphere, where, in aesthetic work in particular, the palpable being of bodies can never be forgotten. But there are reasons why a feminist movement would be particularly responsive to the demands of 'Being-with-one-another'. Rosi Braidotti's conception of woman as nomad, traversing spaces and crossing boundaries (in 'The politics of ontological difference'), may be an over-optimistic reading of women's ideological freedom of movement, but her model does suggest why women, homosexual and heterosexual women, black and white women, might be particularly receptive to a radical politics of 'Being-with-one-another'. It is not so much that they share the designation 'Woman', but because, the space they occupy, even in the western world, and even across class and ethnicity, is still a space *self-consciously* occupied, a space *thrown into question*. The recent history of feminism itself has seen to that. The new concern with masculinity will not alter the radical opening up of feminine subjectivity that has occurred. Indeed, as I said earlier, the legitimizing of an enquiry into masculinity is a direct consequence of feminist politics, however unintentional, which has freed a space for masculinity, just as it has freed a space for lesbian poetics and politics. The 'right kind of objectivity', Heidegger says, frees the Other by enabling its condition to become transparent to itself (p. 159).

But there is a grimmer inflection of all this, and for Heidegger it is the dominant condition of modernity. His theorization of Being-in-the-World is a reworking of Hegel's Master-Slave dialectic, in which the Master's exploitation of the Slave actually becomes a dependency upon him. The complement of understanding, alertness, re-envisaging, is indifference, a not-seeing. A hardening of 'distantiality' (p. 163) occurs. The 'Others' become the 'They'. Once *Dasein* can be conceptualized as one among others, 'dissolved completely in the Being of the 'Others' (p. 164), the negation of its specificity can, as a corollary, be handed on to the 'Others' themselves. Both Being and 'Others' become abstracted as a solid, undifferentiated unit, the 'They'. The dictatorship of the 'They' as a homogenized mass occurs. 'Everyone is the other, and no one is himself' (p. 165). Being is 'given' in terms of the 'They' (p. 167) and consequently 'misses itself' and 'covers itself up' (p. 168).

The pernicious aspects of this thinking are notorious. The creation of the 'averageness' (p. 164) of the masses through democracy, as much as the way capital instrumentalizes and abstracts subjects as the 'masses', is Heidegger's target. The iron surveillance of movement (public transport), intellectual life (newspapers) and pleasures (mass media) crushes individual creativity so that any discovery of 'authentic Being' (p. 167) becomes a violent struggle to free itself and its creativity from the 'They'. Since Being is not freed by others, it takes the task upon itself. If one reads this reactionary politics against the grain, however, and phenomenologically as Heidegger requires, one could formulate his model of modernity rather differently as a *structural* condition in which relations are *posited* as the opposition between a homogenized unit and the individual subject. Thus individualism set against the local or global conglomerate is the necessary ideological form of imaginative and political life. Indeed, this has been extrapolated from the Heideggarian tradition by thinkers as different as Sartre and Lacan. Sartre's sense that freedom is posited against external definitions of the self – the Jew, for instance – and Lacan's theorization of the misrecognized autonomous subject whose subjecthood is constituted from the place of the other, are variant readings of Heidegger's 'They'.

What Heidegger does demonstrate is modernity's capacity to harden and homogenize definitions of groups as 'They'. Abstracted for different political purposes by states, media or market, 'frozen' categories (a Marxist would term this reification) emerge as part of the syntax of modernity, obfuscating political complexities in the name of a taxonomy of identities. The project of understanding the stranger emerges as a response to the alien through obdurate classifications rather than as a response to difference – the Third World, Islam, the lesbian (to the heterosexual), the heterosexual (to the lesbian) – the 'They', alien, closed, hostile.

How do the imperatives of such classifications recall us to a project for feminism or at least to a gendered way of knowing things? The other side of a Utopian egalitarianism and interspatial relations is critique, and the necessity of tearing apart definitions, 'accomplished as a clearing away of concealments and obscurities, as a breaking up...of disguises' (p. 167). Gender may not be *the* foundational experience, but it is worth provisionally *behaving* as if it is; however we may dispute the ground of difference, it is one of the few shared differentiating markers that we have – and one of the few readily presupposed in discourse. Gender's business *is* with difference. For that reason a frank strategic universalism is pragamatic. It is the assumption of gender enquiry that it will not only examine itself but reach out and enquire into taxonomies that take the gendered subject for granted – the black male, the single mother. Such a way of knowing is well equipped to deal with Heidegger's 'They'. A gendered way of knowing reconfigures conceptual fields. That gendered discourse works both at the cultural and the political level, engaging with the theoretical and practical simultaneously, is another reason for retaining gender as a foundational category. Feminism has always been a double practical and philosophical project. Finally, a gendered way of knowing remembers palpable bodily experience. Here I am not regarding the materiality of the body as the ultimate ground of experience; but a gendered way of knowing notices the body's passions and sufferings – love between women, the time-bound work that refuses the mother time to dream, the imposition of emotional dryness on masculinity – and gives it space in the world.

I have written as if there is no distinction between a gendered way of knowing and feminism. There is a distinction, but gender underwrites feminism. Rather than wondering if there is a place for either, it is worth considering what our world would be like if feminist thought were subtracted from it. The third phase of the feminist project might not possess the coherence of earlier phases, but it will find a new content. Women, dramatically thrown into question, now ineradicably self-conscious about their place in culture, are beckoned by the task of modernity, the discovery of a new subjectivity and the political conditions of it.

NOTES

I am grateful to Diane Chisholm for her response to a draft of this paper, which made me rethink many aspects of it, and to seminar discussion at the Department of English, University of Alberta, Edmonton.

1   Most of my quotations come from the most substantial essay in *Vamps and Tramps*: 'No law in the arena'. This book indicates the range of Paglia's work in film, media and cultural criticism in a way her first book, *Sexual Personae: Art and Decadence from Nefertiti to Emily Dickinson*, does not.

2   Frances Ferguson, 'Pornography: the theory': 'I see MacKinnon as addressing a central question for modern self-governing societies, namely, how can such societies modify their own tendencies to replicate the power structures that already exist?' (p. 673) This searching discussion, ranging over political philosophy, considers the limitation of both libertarian and liberal discourse.

3   As can be seen from anthologies such as *Feminism and Tradition in Aesthetics*, ed. Peggy Zeglin and Carolyn Korsmeyer, which gathers a number of writings on feminism and aesthetics, there is a range of ways of describing a feminine aesthetic, but such arguments tend to be drawn to the trans-historical, or drift towards endowing the feminine with an exclusive capacity for affective, non-rational life.

4   Hélène Cixous has remained remarkably consistent in her views, elaborating the same position in innumerable and highly creative ways. Her best-known essays, 'The laugh of the Medusa' and 'Sorties', are still a fair representation of her work. See *The Feminist Reader: Essays in Gender and the Politics of Literary Criticism* (ed. Catherine Belsey and Jane Moore). Elaine Showalter, *A Literature of Their Own: British Women Novelists from Brontë to Lessing*, established a more powerful critical tradition than the notorious *The Mad Woman in the Attic*, by Sandra Gilbert and Susan Gubar, even though, for a time, their account of the anxiety of influence in female writing in the nineteenth century was widely used as paradigmatic feminist critique.

5   See Juliet Mitchell, *Psychoanalysis and Feminism*, particularly parts 3 and 4, 'Towards another symbolic', pp. 87–185.

6   Some of Gayatri Chakravorty Spivak's major work is collected in *In Other Worlds: Essays in Cultural Politics*. Her essay 'Scattered speculations on the question of value' and the work on subaltern issues in section 3 of this collection are particularly impressive. Her argument is extended in the essay, 'Can the subaltern speak? Marxism and the interpretation of culture'. Michèle Barrett's *Women's Oppression Today: Problems in Marxist Feminist Analysis* shows a hostility to psychoanalysis which was more characteristic of Marxist feminism of the 1980s than of feminism today.

7   Luce Irigaray has always insisted that it is possible to transform psychic and social structures. In her most recently translated work, *I Love to You: Sketch for a Possible Felicity within History*, she argues for a fundamental transformation of the institution of marriage, which means changing love relations. Ludic energy throws situations into play in the most serious possible way. Teresa de Lauretis, notable for her work on film, has extended Ludic criticism in her recent *The Practice of Love: Lesbian Sexuality and Perverse Desire* (see particularly 'Re-casting the primal scene', pp. 81–148).

8   As Butler has substantially altered her earlier position I concentrate on this text.

9   In a lecture, 'Sexual disgust' (Harvard University English Graduate Confer-
     ence, *Dirt*, March 16 1996). Jonathan Dollimore discussed Butler's first
     book, *Gender Trouble*, with considerable sympathy in *Sexual Dissidence:
     Augustine to Wilde, Freud to Foucault*, pp. 319–20. He expressed reserva-
     tions similar to mine about *Bodies that Matter*.
10   'Merely cultural' is part of an ongoing argument with Nancy Fraser, whose
     reply, 'Heterosexism, misrecognition and capitalism', argues that the decon-
     struction of the cultural/economic binary is not useful at the level of social
     theory because it does away with dialectic.
11   I owe the term 'interspatiality' to Dr. Shannon Jackson, a colleague in the
     Department of English, Harvard University.
12   Walter Benjamin developed the notion of 'empty, homogeneous time' in the
     'Theses on the Philosophy of History', sections XIII and XVII (completed
     1940, first published 1950). See *Illuminations: Essays and Reflections*, pp.
     253–64.
13   Transitional space was 'invented' by D. J. Winnicott, who considered it a
     crucial element in the formation of psychic and social experience. For a more
     detailed discussion of transitional space, see chapter 1.
14   Heidegger, *Being and Time*, pp. 157, 159, translator's notes 3 and 4.

8

Women's Space: Echo, Caesura, Echo

Some meditations on Echo

Juliet Mitchell makes a passing reference to Echo when she considers Freud's exploration of narcissism. Narcissus seems to have a female double. An echo is to an originary sound as a reflected image is to a body. This nymph, she hints, forgotten by Freud, might lead us to the devious pathways of feminine sexuality and desire, always mysterious to him. But she also forgets Echo and pursues the problem of Narcissus and reflection. And since forgetting is as miraculous as remembering, this is important. In Ovid's *Metamorphoses* Echo is allowed just to wander off into the woods after the crisis of the death of Narcissus. He forgets her too.

There has been a forgetting over the last decade in feminist thought. Perhaps one project cannot be pursued unless another is forgotten. Remarkably, because there seems no good reason why this should be so, the philosophical project of feminism has been quenched in preference to the pursuit of the politics of sexual identities and the regulation of sexuality through the legal control of pornography. If the first debate is about the extent to which a society can open up its response to gender choices and reform categories of sexuality, the second is about the extent to which a society can close down on the sexual market. These debates may even be opposite forms of one another. Both debates raise philosophical and ethical questions and enquire deeply into the meaning of civil society. But maybe by remembering that other project, some of these debates could be clarified. That project is no less than to think a new kind of knowledge, or new ways of thinking about knowledge.

Ovid, it seems, invented the presence of Echo as looker-on at Narcissus when he falls in love with his own image in water. Actually, Echo was less metamorphosed than depleted. She was a chatterbox, a frivolous compulsive talker who knew the secrets of the Gods' sexuality: she kept Juno talking to enable the nymphs disporting with Jupiter to make a getaway. Knowing too much, she was dangerous. It was Juno who punished her by taking away her voice, just as she blinded Tiresias in revenge for taking Jupiter's part in their dispute about the degree of sexual pleasure men and women experience (Tiresias came down on the side of women's jouissance). Jupiter gave Tiresias the compensating gift of knowledge, and it was Tiresias who prophesied in a riddle that Narcissus would live long if he did not come to know himself, meaning, that is, if he did not meet his own image reflected in the fateful pool. Echo was not allowed a similar compensating gift. She was sentenced to the vicarious reproduction of sound – she could only repeat. She must be secondary. Her language, if it was one, was made out of endings and depended on the structure of other people's speech. What is the syntax of a sigh such as this? It has none of its own. The properties of an echo as residue, the weak mimesis dependent on a prior sound, are not promising. But if myth is a culture's way of asking questions, what questions does the myth of Echo pose? What *new* questions could it pose?

> A *'feminist cogito'*, as it has been expressed, is the philosophical project erased or lost sight of recently. It is surprising how quickly Teresa Brennan's important collection of essays by women prominent in Anglo-American discussions of psychoanalysis and cultural politics, Between Feminism and Psychoanalysis, *published in 1989, a densely theoretical book, has disappeared from discussion. Its enquiries seemed to set the agenda for a decade and required arguing out, testing, research, response. The epistemic ambitions of this collection were immense – to work towards a new understanding of knowledge, not as an* alternative feminine knowing, *a kind of optional choice, but as a transforming female symbolic order which would reorganize experience in our culture. That is why Rosi Braidotti ('The politics of ontological difference') argued that one cannot afford not to be essentialist, because only by accepting herself ontologically as a 'female sexed subject who is mortal and endowed with language . . . born and constructed as a woman' (p. 101), could a woman in a collective movement claim a part in the reinvention of the subject and arrive at new structures of thought. It is not possible, she argued, to rinse gender out of this project, because one's affectivity and sexuality play a dominant role in 'what makes a subject want to think' (p. 95) and*

thus in how she thinks. The social and political work to be done in altering the asymmetry of women's experience must be grounded on that experience as an ethical prerequisite.

Similarly, the reassessments of Luce Irigaray and Hélène Cixous emphasize ways their thought aims to change what knowledge is. Margaret Whitford ('Rereading Irigaray') argues that Irigaray's challenge to Lacanian thought arises from a critique which refuses to abandon women to a pathologized space outside the symbolic order; the symbolic order which, of course, brings both the law and the social into being and creates the shared experience which keeps us sane. In Lacanian thought the mother/daughter relation remains unsymbolized, lacking mediation in the symbolic for the operations of sublimation. No representations of this relation are culturally available, and thus women are left with nothing but the position of other to the male, and nothing but the position of the maternal in a civilization organized round the destruction of the maternal and the possession of the phallus. Repeatedly Whitford returns to Irigaray's understanding that, under the structures of the Lacanian symbolic, the feminine is threatened with the psychosis which comes from its inseparability from the mother's body and subject position. The merging of the female subject with the mother is such that self and other cannot be unfused. No exchange can occur, and no form of symbolic representation or primary metaphorization can come about because there is no language in which the feminine can represent its desire to itself. This is partly because the feminine is devalued by being assimilated to masculine models of representation (the possession of the phallus) presented deceptively as neutral models. Phallic loss is representable: what the woman has lost is not, and is not valued anyway. But because the woman occupies the identical space of the mother in oneness with her, it is impossible to detach herself from that which could be symbolized. The consequence of this is that the repression necessary for symbolization and the symbolization necessary for repression cannot occur. Thus the energies of desire cannot be rerouted through representation and released for contemplation, thought and intersubjective relations. The consequence of this is twofold: the feminine is a weak or negative image of the masculine subject and vulnerable to its cruelty; women are cruel to one another, competing as they do for the unique place of the mother.

Whitford is aware how precarious it is to think a female symbolic and a female imaginary as if by fiat, and she insists that Irigaray repudiates such a course. The psychoanalytical diagnosis has to be followed by cultural work, which is nevertheless clarified by diagnosis.

For, she says, if we assume that the symbolic actually organizes the imaginary, and that the two orders come into being simultaneously, then we can see that the male symbolic is a prey to the epistemologies of control, mastery and domination. Releasing the mother's body for representation is a way of restoring the link between knowledge and its origin in the passions and 'raising the question: What is knowledge for?' (p. 120).

As Whitford seeks a political-epistemological reading of Irigaray, so Morag Shiach ('Their "symbolic" exists') seeks to demonstrate that Hélène Cixous is concerned with 'a kind of knowledge which does not seek to destroy' (p. 166). Bringing out her affinities with Jacques Derrida, but casting her work in a daemonic, or perhaps we should say maenadic, register far from his, she argues that Cixous's strategies of disruption and disorder are a way of breaking traditional categories of thought and structures of oppression, a form of writing in excess of the binaries which organize knowledge. The theatre as the space for the mobility of non- hierarchical knowledge in which subjects are caught up in an incessant process of exchange, the becoming-time of space, and the becoming-space of time, is above all the place where, captured by the primitive hermeneutics of what will happen next, no one can have 'prior, or superior, knowledge' (p. 162). Rather than asking 'What is knowledge for?', the theatre is the very enactment of a new order of knowing.

A nymph without a body, empty, invisible, all hollowness, hollowed out into the cavernous spaces which create the replication of sound. Can it be imagined, an orifice, an internal cavity, a void space, without the excavated body from which these are hollowed out? Pure emptiness? Ovid seems to imagine Echo like this. She is the dreamwork inversion of Daphne, Io, Arachne, whose bodies are essential to the labour of metamorphosis. The hot breath of the panting Apollo on the neck of Daphne, his frantic beating on her breasts while they are already encrusting over with bark at the instigation of her father; Io, who sees herself as a cow reflected in a pool (a faintly ludicrous antithesis of Narcissus); Arachne the spider, weaving representations of violated bodies, all these women begin as fleshly creatures and end as figures heavy with the organic life into which they are absorbed. The violence done to Echo passes without comment. Though Ovid remarks that the anguish of Narcissus weeping for the love of his image is compounded by the repetitions of Echo, who loved the self-absorbed Narcissus. Yet he is seemingly impervious to her cries. Does he hear them at all? The man in love with himself or his visible double pines away in death: a wand-like flower grows exactly where he died; death initiates the displacement of symbol. And again, and again.

So Echo, true to her name, is an afterthought in the myth and in the history of Narcissus's story. If her experience is the disembodied duplicate of the 'real' scene of repetition and love in which Narcissus is paramount, it is not surprising that she seems to be legitimately forgotten. Freud is as enthralled with the image of that young man as the man with his own image. Gaston Bachelard, too, rewriting Freud in water and dreams which both hold and dissolve images. Not to speak of Lacan. But what is Echo actually doing? Seemingly unheard by him she repeats or partially repeats a man's cries, or the termination of his words and phrases. She overlooks him overlooking his own image, a looker-on as consumed by gazing as Narcissus himself. Except that her gaze is not returned, even in imagination, as that of Narcissus is. She looks, as it were, at the back of his head as he gazes into his pool. An echo is to a sound offered up to the air as a reflection is to a body offered to the water? Is she the rival of the golden image in the pool or does she love the man loving his image, loving both the image and the man? Or she could be in another place. The pool is a hollowed space filled with water from which cries resound. This hollowed space is the medium by which the image comes into being.

Thus in 'Echo and Narcissus' Naomi Segal argues that the pool of Narcissus serves man as his mirror, the mother mirroring her child to provide both the security and severance which is a basis for its existence. But she goes further: the woman is not simply a mirror before which a child can 'practise the fiction of a self' (p. 171). For Irigaray (Irigaray again) the feminine mirror becomes the means by which 'men wish to hold women as other, to guarantee their own position as knowing subjects' (p. 171). But because to desire the mother is not to have the phallus, feminine sexuality must become the 'unthought' of the Oedipus complex. Feminine sexuality both lies behind and is excluded from the Oedipus complex. Fear of feminization, of women's desire reflected from the mirroring pool, of a castrated mother (the hollow) who is a threat to the phallic monopoly of knowledge, means that an epistemophilia emerges wherein the son can know only at the expense of destroying the mother's body. In order that there can be no end-point to knowledge, the mother's body must be endlessly epistemologically penetrable. There can be no place for the mother to know.

Perhaps this deterministic reading is possible at a primal moment, but it forgets that interface between the body and the social which many of the writers in this volume want to consider. The playing out of knowledge on the woman's body is precisely what moves Braidotti to reject psychoanalysis as a mode of knowledge for feminism. She wants to return to the metaphysical body made by the totality of representations of the feminine in history in order to take on an ethical responsibility for her gender as historical essence (p. 99). Such a responsibility gives her the power of remaking representations of the feminine by actively engaging with the social and cultural sphere, to think 'rigorously through the discursive conditions of enunciation' (p. 99). Asking the question, 'how does a collective movement re-invent the definition of the subjective self?' immediately entails the possibility of new structures of thought and a new notion of community as a legitimating agent, possibilities ignored, she argues, by psychoanalysis (p. 95). Only in this way can two prerequisites of feminism be achieved: first, a self that can exist at the juncture of the socio-political and the subject, so that the subject is agent enough to project a driving desire which relays the self to the many 'others' that constitute her/his "external" reality', thus mediating and changing relationships (p. 97); second, a sociality which fastens on the otherness of the other woman, an otherness which recognizes 'our common sameness, our "being-a-woman"' (p. 98). Only in this way can the mastery of the analyst be avoided, a mastery which also subordinates the subject to the deterministic narrative of psychoanalysis and thus to 'Time, the great master' (p. 98).

Braidotti considers a Nietzschean unity to combat the dualism which would put subject and social in antithesis and speaks of the 'philosophy of as if' (p. 103) as a political project which acts as if 'a common ground of enunciation existed among women' (p. 103). Joan Copjec and Toril Moi, however, offer different and more rigorous solutions to a feminine cogito.

At least we can be aware that whatever its function in pairing and doubling sound, an Echo's status in the act of repetition is quite different from the golden, complicit man in the pool, smiling and weeping in unison with the man above him. Sometimes the reflections of trees and objects in the water grow from what they represent so exactly that they resemble roots, so things above are strongly rooted in images steeped in the underworld of water. A reflection is always simultaneous with its object. It is always caught in Time. It may be that the dark gloss of water sharpens the lineaments of reflected objects with a gleaming outline; or that its depths hold incandescent concentrations of light and radiance unseen in the world above; or that one may actually see in the water secret parts of the reflected object – a gleam, a contour, a pattern – which cannot be seen in the object above because the watery light reflects at an angle the eye above cannot perceive; or that the tangle of drifting green weed entangles with reflected branches in the subaqueous world and the limpid image of the body itself. Nevertheless, though the reflection may be in excess of its object, it can never be different, never can be other than simultaneous, never can but exist in perfect symmetry with what beholds it, steeped in the gaze of the other. It never can be other than *literal*. Passive, specular, coercive. Ovid and his renaissance translator, Goldman, stay with the anguish of the literal image which is not *real*. It depends on the Master, Time. But an echo does not have this simultaneous and immediate manifestation. There is a gap between its manifestation and originary sound. And an echo never is a literal reproduction of sound but a vestige or variant made by shadowy harmonics.

It would be a shock, and perhaps the world would never recover, if the visual image appeared in the pool in slight dissymmetry with its object, after a blank, or a time lag; or if the water yielded an extra branch, a snapped twig where there was an unbroken twig above, an extra bird flying in the air in the water. Dorothy Richardson thought of that possibility in the second volume of *Pilgrimage* (*The Tunnel*) when she imagined a series of identical rooms, but in one a single narcissus stem in the vase of flowers was snapped, whereas there were no snapped stems in the other rooms – the only difference. No doubt because consonance in the world is so desirable – one might go mad without it – and no doubt because such identity is so unbearable, so limiting, so coercive – one might go mad *with* it (and Narcissus suffers from the two kinds of madness) – some kind of separation, some kind of break, has to be envisaged.

For a long time the Oedipal break or sacrifice has been the violent determinant around which discussions of gender and sexual difference have configured, a narrative which obeys Time, the Master, as the threat of severance and mutilation observes a sequential plot – and then if this, that, and then . . . and then . . . Linear time, death and time, come into the world with the phallus and its law. And a substitutive world – power is exchanged for gratification, language for lack, the first bargains of the symbolic order. This is a too familiar story. There are other breaks to consider. In a finely argued and intricate piece, 'Cutting up', Joan Copjec considers two breaks: the break which means that the construction of the historically defined and limited subject can be thought and can think without being 'obliged to reduce her to the images social discourses construct of her' (p. 242); and the conceptual break which organizes a new understanding of psychic relatedness to the 'real' by redefining the fundamental notions of cause and law. Both breaks turn on the intransigence of the real.

Copjec refuses the openness of the subject in process or the adoption of multiple subject positions in fantasy as the easy answers to the possibility of either social or psychic change, and is right to do so. And she rejects two other fallacious readings of the real. The real is neither what is opposed to psychical and imaginary experience, nor is it the 'ideal' social representations which are deemed to construct the subject's being and which it recognizes as the full equivalent *of its nature.*

For Copjec it is not the pleasure principle but the death drive which organizes and is organized by the real. Repetition, the compulsion to repeat, is life, and the aim of life is death. They are the inevitable corollaries of symbolic life (or perhaps symbolic life is their inevitable corollary) because signification comes into being retroactively, and thus presupposes the loss of the past and with it the loss of immortality. Two consequences follow from this. First, there can never be an equivalent *representation of the subject, because the subject constructed by language finds itself detached from a part of itself: language splits the subject by failing to make visible a 'lost' or 'missing' part of the self which it represses and can never include within its definitions. Far from recognizing itself in language, the subject cannot discover itself there and thus does not find itself conforming to social limits. Second, this lack opens up a gap for critique and a gap for desire. Signification makes it possible to think the negation of signified realities. This is the saving nature of language. Failure of representation actually* 'produces rather than disrupts identity' *(p. 242). Fantasy is the response to the impossibility of discovering this repressed, invisible element. But desire, won out of negation, produced by and producing doubt, is the central experience of the subject. It has no content: it doesn't* want *something, but something* more. Desire keeps us alive while killing us. *The female subject is not organized by the masculine image of the Other's desire so much as unable to image the Other's desire. This lack causes her desire, and thus – though this is to extrapolate from Copjec, who is no optimist – has different epistemic possibilities than those of simply occupying the place of masculine fantasy or the space of negation. She is offered both the possibility of critique and the possibility of knowledge, as desire ceaselessly precipitates and abolishes representation. This – together with a reworking of old theories of cause as constant conjunction, elaborated by a covering law in terms of* norms *and deviation from norms – provides the conditions for a kind of knowledge which is organized by the real, even as the real provides the conditions of testing out the real itself.*

So the same knowledge and desire are offered to male and female subjects on the same terms? What of the structural conditions of sexual difference? Cultural positioning? Biology? Surely not. The very terms we want to refuse, with their binary antithesis, come back as explanatory concepts, as gender slips out of sight in a seemingly ungendered knowledge? Does this matter?

Narcissus gazing. Desire. Desire keeps us alive. Desire kills twice over. Wanting empties the present. And the future too. Death drive and pleasure principle chase one another. Are they simply the same, then, Echo and Narcissus – only Narcissus gets the better deal? No body, no voice, looking at the back of someone looking. Emptiness filled with the fictions of rage as the body she hasn't got and the phallus she hasn't got are revenged. Duplicating Narcissus, repetition or mimesis of that loved reflection, other to that other, in loving she only imitates another kind of love, a simulacrum of someone else's love. The phallus displaces what it signifies with signifying *power*. We know all this. An echo can never say 'I', following the predicates of another, never being answered, only replying. Such negations *are* and have been entertained. The Ovidian fallacy of seeking equivalences and doubles. Hollow caves.

The temptation to write out gendered knowledge is strong. Indeed, any 'strong' theory of knowledge obliterates sexual difference and it is clearly a relief to achieve this because so many of the embarrassments of either gender inferiority or 'special' feminine knowledge are circumvented. Toril Moi contests the meaning of the binaries, masculine/feminine, reason/emotion, in which femininity becomes the support of the signifier of male rationality in separate systems of cognition/feeling. But in arguing for a radical, new construction of knowledge, based on Freud's reversal of the traditional roles of speaker and listener in analysis, the possibility of different positions from which knowledge is experienced disappears. We lose that possibility of a transforming female symbolic order. Does it matter? Moi argues that the model of transference and counter-transference, dialogic but not dualistic, is the foundation of a new knowledge. Moi approaches this new knowledge by way of a critique of Evelyn Fox Keller, and what she takes to be an admirable epistemology which has been unduly distorted by the influence of Nancy Chodorow's understanding of 'permanent' and fundamentally different male and female personality structures. This genders knowledge unequivocally. But why should we not claim this new mode of thought as 'universal'? 'Simply as the way to do science? Why imply that this new mode somehow is less suitable for males? Nor would I want to call traditional science "male" – why not "patriarchal"? Just as all women are not feminist, not all males are patriarchal' (p. 190).

Hence she calls her essay 'Patriarchal thought and the drive for knowledge'. She respects the onslaught on binary categories mounted by both Hélène Cixous and Michele le Doeuff, because sexual opposition manifests itself in the very structure of the sign, and the effort to deconstruct phallogocentric logic constitutes a more radical solution to the problem of knowledge, the undermining of all forms of cultural essentialism, than the 'weak' solution of Keller and Chodorow, which reintroduces the oppositions which were responsible for the problem of the patriarchal epistemology of science as mastery in the first place.

In pursuing her new 'universal' knowledge Moi implicitly recognizes that new knowledge is theorized from the place of the feminine simply because it is woman who has suffered through history from the binaries reason/unreason, cognition/emotion, mind/body, where the unprivileged binary has been sounding board to the privileged term. How to construct a knowledge not predicated on what Le Doeuff describes as the philosophy which must take unreason as its repressed other? Though no thought can avoid boundaries and exclusion (it could not happen without them), it ought to be possible to establish new boundaries and limits – or perhaps, I would suggest, new concepts of the limit. These are to be found in the discourse of the counter-transference and through the Freudian theory of epistemophilia.

Freud did at least incorporate the discourse of the hysteric into positivist language, and, despite the colonizing impulse of patriarchal rationality, radically changed knowledge, or scientificity, as a consequence. The construction of a transferential network triangulates interchange: it is not simply between two egos, because 'two participants encounter each other in the place of the Other, in language'. This reorders the subject/object relation, 'dividing' subjects differently, imbricating them in one another, which, Moi argues, is a different form of relation than Keller's 'commingling' of subject and object, which leaves the terms untouched. Epistemophilia, the second model of knowledge, questions another binary, the body/mind dichotomy. Epistemophilia begins with the infant's urgent researches into sexuality, generally when a wound or shock to narcissitic contentment occurs (the paradigm being the Oedipal wound). Thus intellectual work begins in and with the body; though it is ultimately sublimated or 'diverted', the desire for knowledge is characterized by Freud as a 'drive' because, like other drives, oral and anal drives, for instance, it is generated by and organized by the horizons of the body, and has an 'anaclitic' or metonymic relation to it. That is, it is independent of the body and the parts of the body to which it relates, but it has been shaped by them. Moreover, because intellectual labour is both pro-

duced by and thwarted by the body – the infant's knowledge is always incomplete, doomed to failure because its own physical being is not sufficiently developed to produce understanding – the idea of mastery becomes a fantasy of omnipotence. Intellectual labour is also shot through with the energies of libido, arising from them, and thus it is impossible to posit to be intellectual as the opposite of 'being emotional or passionate' (p. 203).

Actually, Moi seems to be offering two opposing forms of knowledge. One is the Space *of the transference, in which two egos are reconfigured and* have *to be three. The other is the* Time *of epistemophilia. The drives involved in the anaclitic chain of displacement that initiates and continues intellectual work operate along a temporal axis in which, very easily, they could shed their early connection with libido and become abstracted from it. Abstraction in all senses, indeed, could be said to be the aim of this mental labour. Correspondingly, the aim of mastery, though thwarted, is the constitutive objective of the epistemophilic drive. This new universal (temporalized) knowledge could easily become the old universal knowledge, and perhaps it was all the time.*

What is knowledge for? The truth?

Narcissus gazing. The image in the bronze water, penetrating each other's eyes, holding each other there, exchanging the longing mutual gaze. Looking is reversible. Two-sided. The image can be substituted for the originary self, self can be displaced by image. Dyadic simultaneity of literal body and reflected body, dyadic displacement through time of one for the other. Which is what Narcissus is longing for. Out of this is born the logic of the chain of displacement and substitution, as something stands in for the reflected, watery body, not absent but not there, never lost and never found, made by the water, not of it. But the originary sound can never be substituted for the echo, sound, the same sound, in transit, coming into being in the gap, the caesura of the echo, depending on space. Not reversible, radiating from the moment of sound, spreading in waves like a pebble thrown into a pool, in ever-expanding circles, disrupting the image in the water, concentric circles cutting up the bronze-gold image and its coercive duplication. But not the phantom proxy of the reflection. Nor the reflection of sound.

Empty vessel, hollowness, hollow caves reverberating to the reverberate hills. Unseen and chthonic, the echo's element is space, and the earth, the matter which returns sound in altered form. Not water and time. The wound of Narcissus takes away what he already has, the phallus; the wound of Echo is the womb, empty until it receives something. What kind of knowledge would this imply?

The girl child in mourning opens herself up to space, dances, chants, inscribes patterns with her body as a form of delineating and redrawing boundaries, limits. She gyrates, in circular movement, singing. A quasi symbol, a doll, is the only form of substitution she achieves, and it appears to be a symbol for herself, not mistaken for the other. So Luce Irigaray genders mourning. And in insisting on gendered mourning she implicitly here genders knowledge. In 'The gesture in psychoanalysis' she settles upon the Fort–Da *game – the game Freud watched his grandson play to compensate for the departure of his mother – in order to gender both mourning and knowledge. It was the game which enabled Freud to understand more about repetition compulsion and the death drive, the other side of the pleasure principle. The cotton reel the boy repeatedly throws away and retrieves with such remarkable intensity – repetition is life and the aim of life is death, remember – enables him to free himself from dependency on the mother and to express his mourning by making and* controlling *symbolic substitutions. Both the cotton reel and the action of rejection and retrieval, separation and restoration, form a network of symbolic substitution as the cotton reel becomes the mother he separates from and who separates from him, and the action of throwing becomes not simply a mimesis of her departure but an empowerment over it. And presumably he can split in different places in the symbolic network and reverse the displacements: the cotton reel can represent him as he represents the mother throwing him away – research by reversal. Irigaray insists that these substitutions are not available to the girl child because, unlike the boy, she occupies the same subject-position as the mother and thus cannot detach herself sufficiently from the mother to represent her through symbol – or herself. A symbol requires that the object and that which represents it are independent entities. The girl cannot achieve this differentiation.*

Are we to assume that the girl is a different kind of subject? If symbol-making powers are not so strongly at her disposal, what kind of knowledge can she avail herself of or create? Where does she stand in relation to the repetition which is life – and death? What about her access to the signification (systems of substitution) which enables her to think 'the full-scale destruction of our entire signified reality', as Joan Copjec puts it (p. 238)? What about the desire born out of lack, the failure of representation which, Copjec says, produces rather than disrupts identity? Irigaray – it is not in her brief – does not pursue these questions. But it is worth guessing at the answers.

Because, as Rachel Bowlby shows in 'Still crazy after all these years', Freud is shaky on what actually founds sexual difference, and often appears to be undecided whether or not gender is something one falls out of or into; it is not clear whether masculinity is the place we all begin from, some of us falling into a feminine which has to be repudiated, or whether the feminine is something which holds masculinity in place, a place from which it can fall. It would be a question of reversing figure and ground, and knowledge would be intrinsically gendered. But this reading is a matter of dispute, and it might be as well simply to claim Braidotti's knowing essentialism in assigning herself to the category 'Woman'? 'Woman', a cultural representation which does not coincide with the experience of particular women but nevertheless moulds their experience in important ways, would become a term one could use strategically, at least when thinking about knowledge. So knowledge would not be intrinsically gendered, but would come to be gendered by virtue of the subject-positions enjoined on Woman. Nevertheless, she would have to come at the purposeful symbol formation of Fort-Da knowledge differently – obliquely, perhaps? How far would she be able to think the full-scale destruction of signified reality, the act, according to Copjec, which emerges from symbol formation and emancipates the subject from the domination of one system, freeing him to think another? If this were done, perhaps, it would not be through the logic of substitution (on which the symbolic order and the sign subsist) but through the retracing of boundaries and categories, the questioning of limits and conceptual groupings? In other words, she would take up differently what Kleinians call the depressive position, the position from which the subject constructs new wholes out of the intellectual and psychic elements it has split? Would the more confident trajectory of epistemophiliac knowing – the form of thought we might align with Fort-Da knowledge, and which can collapse into what Moi calls patriarchal knowledge – be less amenable to Woman? It might be that, since Woman is seen as structurally lacking (to accept the Lacanian terms provisionally here), she is both more and less able to confront the failure of representation which produces identity, experiencing extremes of negation and possibility. The space for desire opened up by hermeneutic failure both confounds and precipitates mental work. Whatever moment of the experience she occupies, however, negation or representation, it is likely that Woman will belong to the condition of desire rather than to the compulsion to epistemophiliac sublimation?

Or would it simply be that one would ask different questions about what knowledge is for? But that in itself would change the nature of knowing. The collection of essays I have been reviewing prompts a move to another text, Wilfred Bion's Caesura (1977), *with which I shall conclude. A caesura is a cut, a pause between two words in a metrical foot. Bion thinks through an epistemology with it.*

Hollowing out, space. Echo reduced to an orifice, a mouth. To resound. Sound comes from the inside out, seeing from the outside in. Seeing fixes, static, holding the glassy image in its place, even the images of the falling tears, dissolving the vigilant eye, falling into the water and momentarily, but only momentarily, destroying the weeping face in it, the burnished bronze dented with tears. Returning sound like a decoy or dupe, redundant, transforming verbs into imperatives or vocatives, reduplicating the threnody of the voice, obeying another's syntax, an echo is secondary but mobile. Echo is secondary but extra. And echoes collect, resound, are aggregative, ululations sent outwards by the voice, returning with the contours of the world inscribed in their cadences.

An echo is a third. The longing gazer, his double in the water, the longing listener who replies to the air: then comes the fourth, the father who forbids and cuts and threatens mutilation. So the law and politics is not what Freud said it was: the father is not the third; he has to shout his threats against the echoing hills.

Sound, from the inside out, is shaped. The image is given. Does space ground the seen? It enables the echo's flight. An echo researches. Researching sound by traversing space, the same space, in the cavity of the ear, in the whorl of the shell, bending to the helix, returning on the undulations of the air, or water, learning the grammar of the boundaries which respond to it, turning. An echo searches for a predicate, made by rocks, stones, the broken columns of a ruin, iron, glass, cement, unique vibrations, sonic lyric, of unique matter. The sinister song of underwater, the shape of the submarine. Sound's intervention changes the space it enters: it is a different space. The tower block. An echo breaks upon the glass sides of the tower block. A new harmonics, a new space.

Is an echo a repetition? Repetition multiplies, successive, not simultaneous, remaking sound, not imitating it, turning it back on itself in a new form. Every repetition turns and varies sound working on the possibilities derived from something else. Every repetition is a rhyme.

No word uttered is ever acoustically the same. Unique sound doubled and redoubled, duplicated and reduplicated in echo. Different all the time, belated all the time, new. Could there ever be sounds without echoes? The echoes take responsibility for the sound. What would an echo-less world be like? More dead than a world without shadow, without reflection?

An echo is everywhere, heard from many places at once, ululating from the hills before, the valleys behind, utterance, a multiple, voluble universe.

Hegel thought art involving sound the most ideal because reflexive, contemplative, where things return upon themselves, after the necessary disjunction.

A piercing scream, a drill, sighs, whispers, susurration, doubled shadowy noise, a football crowd's roar, a surf of wind in the trees, the swish of corn, an explosion in Bosnia, the explosion out of the void which began the universe and which we hear to infinity, a water-filled glass ringing, the echo quickens these sounds, depending on them, they on it.

Echoes radiate from the human and things in nature: is it ever possible to separate out these secondary harmonics from originary sound?

However could it be possible to subtract an echo, the second sound from the first sound, beginning as it does after the minutest interval, a caesura, often before the cessation of the first? Would the first *be* without an echo?

Echoes go beyond the beyond of the first sound. And sometimes we encounter an echo before the sound which produced it. An echo arrives as messenger of sound.

The break, the disjunction, is what makes the echo, what makes the sound. The caesura.

Bion proceeds in a series of discrete statements, whose connection is enigmatic, miming the pause of the caesura, the breaks which are both barriers and disjunctions and which enable thought. The essay is about the kind of thinking required in and between the participants in an analysis, but beyond the horizon of the analysis is the world. He is not thinking consecutively or in terms of the metonymic connection between signs. He is rigorous in this. The logic of the caesura is not temporal, even though statements have to follow one another. It is spatial. Thinking comes about in the breaks between people and in the breaks in experience. 'There is much more continuity between intra-uterine life and earliest infancy than the impressive caesura of the act of birth allows us to believe' (p. 37): this is the founding quotation from Freud. Which means that it is necessary for Bion to re-imagine the womb: what knowing for the foetus in the womb and for the being in the break beyond it might be. The boundaries and horizons inscribed by its and the mother's body constitute at once a limit and the primal, unbounded experience of the universe. The leap over a space, or perhaps one should say the leap to a different space, is the essence of thought. If we know in the womb, then that knowing is going to shape knowing out of it, in the cavernous body, in the cavernous universe. But it is only by constituting spaces that we actually think, and it is thinking that constitutes spaces.

Nymph of orifices, openings – mouth, ear, birth passage, ear, mouth. Maker of gaps. Sound pauses, in the air, in the ear, suspended. Nymph of spaces.

The discipline of the caesura in the search for truth (which of course involves lies, fantasies and fictions) – Bion always maintained that psychoanalysis is a rational, scientific enquiry – is the discipline of the non sequitur, *the discipline of unthinking customary logic. This necessitates a suspension of customary syntheses and categories and an examination of conceptual boundaries. Is a feeling an idea, for instance? Does embryological intuition, intense and unformed as it is, avail itself of our usual categories of feeling and thought, and how far would this be relevant to post-natal experience (p. 42)? Or we might think in terms of 'times' and 'levels' of mind co-existing rather than of thought and feeling (p. 45). We know that foetal optic pits respond to pressure, and that sub-thalamic life is so insistent that experience of more than ordinary intensity in analysis might not only relate to this foetal 'past': to move between the break in pre- and post-natal experience might persuade us to conceptualize the past and future differently. Crossing one another, contained in one another, they would be configured as repetitions of one another. A fear of the future 'repeats' a fear impossible to remember, and the future 'repeats' an experience which has not 'occurred' because it has not been remembered: unshaped experiences or ideas are so because they are 'buried in the future which has not happened, or buried in the past which is forgotten' (p. 43), a caesura which alters the nature of temporality. (Wordsworth called this the fear gone by which seems like a fear to come.) This imbrication of time can come about because Bion insists that the discourse of the analysis has only the present as its data. We think we are discussing the past, but we are actually discussing the present. The analysis creates a new caesura between what is inside and outside the session.*

Ululations sent from the past to be repeated in the future, returning to the present with the contours of the future inscribed in their cadences.

The caesura insists upon a breaking apart of concepts without content and of the intuitions which 'fill' them. The gap between the analyst and analysand in a transferential situation, as 'one constantly changing personality talks to another' (p. 47) – a gap analogous to the gap between East and West (p. 45) (we remember Bion's experience as Anglo-Indian) – enjoins a deferral of the concept as one listens to the patient's scream. To match concept and intuition prematurely is to force form and content together by violence. On the other hand, this break has to be traversed in order for interpretation to emerge. At different times Bion thinks of 'penetrating' or 'traversing' the caesura, but, in this somewhat misleading terminology, he is thinking rather of a two-way passage between entities or across barriers, 'effective in either direction' (p. 45), rather than a 'breakthrough' (p. 47). The woman's body as the ground of knowledge makes an appearance here: 'it is like penetrating the woman's inside either from inside out, as at birth, or from outside in, as in sexual intercourse' (p. 45).

Echo from the womb. The voice traversing. Moulded from within. From the inside out. Made from the air out of the pressure of the body's sinews.

There are undoubtedly moments, particularly when he thinks of the caesura as obstacle or barrier rather than pause (p. 53), when Bion's language leads him to think in terms of transcendence and development, though he seems to insist on a metaphysic which, despite its affinities with evolutionary psychology and even ego psychology at times, is radically charged with the spatial meanings generated by the caesura as break or cut. Three ways of knowing emerge from his discourse. The first is splitting, a form of creative repression. To choose or to 'know' an interpretation is to be able to move through a non-pathological splitting-off process in which a considerable number of alternative interpretations are envisaged, and the 'whole' personality has to be analysed into parts in order to foreground one meaning rather than another (p. 46). In other words, rationality consists in the form of the analysis and its process rather than in the ultimate conclusion, which is always a matter of value, of choice of interpretation. There is no law of cause and effect, no law of objectivity, which leads to an impeccably correct judgement of psychic experience – that only applies to things.

Keep still, keep still, you say to the image, or I can't get you. Got you. Snap.

The second way of knowing is transitional or transitive knowing which accepts being-in-transit as the condition of knowledge. Transitive knowledge is provisional, in movement, accepts no permanent halting place where investigation ceases. Transitive knowledge moves from the known to the unknown, the unknown to the known. It is prepared to accept any number of caesura, the dramatic caesura of marriage, for instance, which could be ordered by a person's intra-uterine experience (p. 48), and the undramatic event which could be equally powerfully inflected by pre-natal life. How to use change and mobility, to get used to the transitive method of thinking, to arrive at an interpretation which is itself arriving at an 'immediately changing situation' (p. 50) is its intention. The risk of transitive thoughts and ideas is great and is often undertaken only by artists, musicians, scientists and discoverers (p. 53). Accepting that the analyst lives in the world of reality of which the analysis is a part, that interpretation itself represents a change in the situation we analyse, is paramount (p. 49).

In transit, an echo multiplies its flight across the sky and turns back to a different sound, but not quite, and another sky, but not quite.

Lastly, perhaps an aspect of transitional thought, but sufficiently distinct in implication to be discussed separately, hypothesis is the hermeneutic tool of this form of knowing. The hermeneutics of the womb – positing an unknown, echoes, as it were, from the womb – must be the model of inquiry. The infant's knowledge is partial, and not only in analysis but in other forms of relationship (the example is, again, marriage (p. 52)) we are encountering a total personality who, consciously or unconsciously, has 'chosen a particular view or a particular vertex from which to see the view' (p. 52). One might extend this to most encounters, which are between those who see from particular vertices – a mountain, for instance, which is a different mountain from different perspectives – and who are all, to a greater or lesser extent, involved in an inhibition of the 'capacity to see the views that one does not want to see' (p. 52). But it is not only a matter of positing another vertex from which to see and hear, the other's vertex: it is a matter of going beyond the available facts, positing an unknown. To limit ourselves only to what we understand is a failure to entertain the incomprehensible, a denial of the raw material on which 'present and possibly future knowledge and wisdom might depend' (p. 52). Language is not held in common. The differing vertices of knowing ensure this. Thus the perpetual task of translation, translation of the uninterpretable, in order to bring it into the realm of articulate speech and thought, is enjoined upon the subject. This is what transference seems to be about – translation into an unstable language which is always catching up with the mobility of the subject.

Echo, caesure, echo – the translation of sound.
At the vertices of sound waves.
Echo – sound heard from the other side of a sound, and from another side of that.

Bion's work can often, though not always, be extrapolated from the analytical situation to experience outside it, if only because he was so consistently concerned with what was generalizable as rational method. Here he performs the feat of bringing the order of the traditionally conceived 'irrational' and the material horizons of the body into the sphere of analytical discussion without conceding to phallic or patriarchal knowledge as defined by Moi. This essay is particularly amenable to a more general theory of knowledge. We catch a glimpse of the knowledge organized through space in Kristeva's essay, 'Women's time', when she speaks briefly and parenthetically of the space *between mother and child as an alternative to the Oedipal sacrifice, a gap, a space made by the boundaries of two bodies rather than the* cut, *the act of violence which founds the symbolic order. Bion did not gender his account of knowing. Though to all intents it is an epistemology of the womb; the womb is where we all come from. Nor did he suggest that it might unthink the symbolic order as we customarily know it. But by starting with echoes from the womb and the caesura of birth, rather than the caesura of castration, and by working with the* gap *rather than the sign, with the different vertices from which we talk and with the apparently unknowable which grounds the known, he surely made it possible to envisage the failure of representation which produces identity (to use Copjec's terms), the hermeneutic failure to grasp the 'incomprehensible' which opens desire. Thus he begins to elaborate a poetics of space. It would be inappropriate to merge his thought with that of Moi and Copjec, who are avowedly Lacanian where he was not. The incomprehensible does not mean the same thing in the two systems. But he does seem to be describing a non-phallic knowledge which does not have to do with having or not having but with the gap where possibilities can reverberate and 'where knowledge is not there to be used' (p. 56). This was Bion's new 'universal' knowledge. So it could be. But in terms of strategic essentialism it might be termed feminine.*

Nymph of orifices and orisons.

Bibliography

Adams, Parveen, 'Of female bondage', in Teresa Brennan (ed.), *Between Feminism and Psychoanalysis*, London and New York, Routledge, 1989, pp. 247–65.

Adorno, Theodor W., *Aesthetic Theory* (1970), trans. C. Lenhardt, New York and London, Routledge & Kegan Paul, 1984.

—— *Aesthetic Theory* (1970), ed. Gretel Adorno and Rolf Tiedman, newly translated, edited and with an introduction by Robert Hullot-Kentor, London, Athlone Press, 1997.

Appadurai, Arjun (ed.), *The Social Life of Things: Commodities in Cultural Perspective*, Cambridge, Cambridge University Press, 1986.

Armstrong, Isobel, 'English in higher education: "justifying" the subject', in Martin Dodsworth (ed.), *English Economis'd: English and British Higher Education in the Eighties*, London, John Murray and Atlantic Highlands NJ, Humanities Press, 1989, pp. 9–24.

—— 'Thatcher's Shakespeare?', *Textual Practice* 3:1 (Spring 1989), pp. 1–14.

—— 'So what's all this about the mother's body? The aesthetic, gender and the polis', in Judith Still and Michael Worton (eds), *Textuality and Sexuality*, Manchester and New York, Manchester University Press, 1993, pp. 218–36.

Bachelard, Gaston, *The Poetics of Space* (1958), trans. Maria Jolas (1964), Boston: Beacon Press, 1969.

Barrell, John, *Poetry, Language and Politics*, Manchester, Manchester University Press, 1988.

Barrett, Michèle, 'Material aesthetics', *New Left Review* (1981), pp. 86–93.

—— *Women's Oppression Today: Problems in Marxist Feminist Analysis*, London, Verso, 1984 (2nd edn 1988).

Barthes, Roland, *S/Z*, trans. Richard Miller, New York, Noonday Press, 1974.

—— *Image, Music, Text*, trans. Stephen Heath, Glasgow, Collins, 1977.

—— *Camera Lucida: Reflections on Photography* (1981), London, Vintage, 1993.

Bataille, Georges, *Visions of Excess: Selected Writings, 1927–39*, ed. and with an introduction by Allan Stoekl, trans. Allan Stoekl with Carl R. Lovitt and Donald M. Leslie, Minneapolis, University of Minnesota Press, 1985.

—— *Literature and Evil* (1957), trans. Alastair Hamilton, New York, Marion Boyars, 1985.

Battersby, Christine, *The Phenomenal Woman; Feminist Metaphysics and the Patterns of Identity*, Cambridge, Polity Press, 1998.

Baudrillard, Jean, *Simulations*, trans. Paul Foss, Paul Patton and Philip Beitchman, New York, Semiotext(e), 1983.

—— *Seduction*, trans. Brian Singer, Basingstoke and London, Macmillan, 1990.

Belsey, Catherine, and Moore, Jane (eds), *The Feminist Reader: Essays in Gender and the Politics of Literary Criticism*, London, Macmillan, 1989.

Benhabib, Seyla, 'Feminism and postmodernism', in Linda Nicholson (ed.), *Feminist Contentions: A Philosophical Exchange*, New York and London, Routledge, 1995, pp. 17–34.

Benjamin, Walter, *Illuminations: Essays and Reflections*, ed. and with an introduction by Hannah Arendt, trans. Harry Zohn, New York, Schocken Books, 1968.

Benn, Melissa, *Madonna and Child: Towards a New Politics of Motherhood*, London, Jonathan Cape, 1998.

Bhabha, Homi K., *The Location of Culture*, London and New York, Routledge, 1994.

—— 'Aura and Agora: On negotiating rapture and speaking between', in Richard Francis, *Negotiating Rapture: The Power of Art to Transform Lives*, Chicago IL, Museum of Contemporary Art, 1996, pp. 8–17.

Bion, Wilfred, *Learning from Experience*, London, William Heinemann, 1962.

—— *Elements of Psycho-analysis*, London, William Heinemann, 1963.

—— *Second Thoughts*, London, Karnac Books, 1967.

—— *Caesura*, London, Karnac Books, 1977.

—— *Cogitations*, ed. Francesca Bion, London and New York, Karnac Books, 1992.

Black, Max, 'Metaphor', in *Aristotelian Society Proceedings*, vol. LV (1954–5), pp. 273–94.

Blake, William, *Songs of Innocence and of Experience*, ed. Sir Geoffrey Keynes, Oxford and New York, Oxford University Press (in association with Trianon Press, Paris), 1970.

—— *Jerusalem, the Emanation of the Giant Albion*, in *The Complete Poems*, ed. W. H. Stevenson, London, Longman, 1989.

—— *The Marriage of Heaven and Hell*, in *The Complete Poems*, ed. W. H. Stevenson, London, Longman, 1989.

Blanchôt, Maurice, *The Siren's Song: Selected Essays*, ed. and with an introduction by Gabriel Josipovici, trans. Sacha Rabinovitch, Brighton, Harvester Press, 1982.

—— The Writing of the Disaster, trans. Ann Smock, Lincoln NB, University of Nebraska Press, 1995.

Bollas, Christopher, The Shadow of the Object: Psychoanalysis of the Unthought Known, London, Free Association Books, 1987.

Bourdieu, Pierre, The Love of Art: European Art Museums and their Public, trans. Caroline Beattie and Nick Merriman, Cambridge, Polity Press, 1991. First published as L'Amour de l'art: les musées d'art européens et leur public, Paris, les Editions de Minuit, 1969.

—— 'The market of symbolic goods' (1971), in Randal Johnson (ed.), The Field of Cultural Production, Cambridge, Polity Press (in association with Blackwell, Oxford), 1993, pp. 115–27.

—— Distinction: A Social Critique of the Judgement of Taste (1979), trans. Richard Nice, London, Routledge, 1986.

Bowie, Andrew, Aesthetics and Subjectivity: From Kant to Nietzsche, Manchester, Manchester University Press, 1990.

Bowlby, Rachel, 'Still crazy after all these years', in Teresa Brennan (ed.), Between Feminism and Psychoanalysis, London and New York, Routledge, 1989, pp. 40–59.

Braidotti, Rosi, 'The politics of ontological difference', in Teresa Brennan (ed.), Between Feminism and Psychoanalysis, London and New York, Routledge, 1989, pp. 89–105.

Brennan, Teresa (ed.), Between Feminism and Psychoanalysis, London and New York, Routledge, 1989.

Brett, R. C., and Jones, A. R. (eds), Wordsworth and Coleridge: Lyrical Ballads, London, Methuen, 1965.

Buck-Morss, Susan, The Dialectics of Seeing: Walter Benjamin and the Arcades Project, Cambridge MA and London, MIT Press, 1991.

Burke, Edmund, A Philosophical Enquiry into the Origin of Our Ideas of the Sublime and the Beautiful, ed. James T. Boulton, London, Routledge & Kegan Paul, 1958.

Butler, Judith, Gender Trouble: Feminism and the Subversion of Identity, London and New York, Routledge, 1990.

—— Bodies that Matter: On the Discursive Limits of 'Sex', New York and London, Routledge, 1993.

—— 'Equality', Diacritics 27 (1997), pp. 3–12.

—— 'Merely cultural', New Left Review 227 (January/February 1998), pp. 33–44.

Calhoun, Craig, Lipuma, Edward, and Postone, Moishe (eds) Bourdieu: Critical Perspectives, Cambridge, Polity Press, 1993.

Caygill, Howard, The Art of Judgement, Oxford, Blackwell, 1989.

—— A Kant Dictionary, Oxford, Blackwell, 1995.

—— 'Stelarc and the Chimera: Kant's critique of prosthetic judgment', Art Journal 56:1 (1997), pp. 46–51.

Chodorow, Nancy, Reproduction of Mothering: Psychoanalysis and the Sociology of Gender, Berkeley LA, University of California Press, 1978.

Cixous, Hélène, 'The laugh of the Medusa', in Elaine Marks and Isabelle de Courtivron (eds), *New French Feminisms: An Anthology*, Brighton, Harvester Press, 1981, pp. 245–67.

—— 'Sorties', in Catherine Belsey and Jane Moore (eds), *The Feminist Reader: Essays in Gender and the Politics of Literary Criticism*, London, Macmillan, 1989, pp. 101–16.

Connor, Steven, *Theory and Cultural Value*, Oxford, Blackwell, 1992.

Cook, Nicholas, *Music, Imagination and Culture*, Oxford, Clarendon Press, 1990.

Copjec, Joan, 'Cutting up', in Teresa Brennan (ed.), *Between Feminism and Psychoanalysis*, London and New York, Routledge, 1989, pp. 227–46.

Cousins, Mark, 'The culture of fear', *Tate: The Art Magazine* 15 (Summer 1998), pp. 51–3.

Crowther, Paul, *Art and Embodiment: From Aesthetics to Self-Consciousness*, Oxford, Clarendon Press, 1993.

—— *Critical Aesthetics and Post-Modernism*, Oxford, Clarendon Press, 1993.

Dadlez, E. M., 'Fiction, emotion, and rationality', *British Journal of Aesthetics* 36 (1966), pp. 290–304.

Darwin, Charles, *The Expression of the Emotions in Man and Animals* (1872), with a preface by Konrad Lorenz, Chicago and London, University of Chicago Press, 1965.

De Certeau, Michel, *The Practice of Everyday Life* (1984), trans. Stephen Randall, Berkeley LA and London, University of California Press, 1988.

De Lauretis, Teresa, *The Practice of Love: Lesbian Sexuality and Perverse Desire*, Bloomington and Indianapolis, Indiana University Press, 1994.

De Man, Paul, *Allegories of Reading: Figural Language in Nietzsche, Rilke, and Proust*, New Haven CT, Yale University Press, 1979.

—— 'Sign and symbol in Hegel's *Aesthetics*', *Critical Inquiry* 8 (1982), pp. 761–75.

—— 'CRITICAL RESPONSE: reply to Raymond Geuss', *Critical Inquiry* 10 (1983), pp. 383–90.

—— 'The rhetoric of temporality', in *Blindness and Insight*, London, Methuen, 1983 (2nd edn), pp. 187–228.

—— *The Rhetoric of Romanticism*, New York, Columbia University Press, 1984.

—— *Aesthetic Ideology*, ed. Andrzej Warminski, Minneapolis and London, University of Minnesota Press, 1996.

de Sousa, Ronald, *The Rationality of Emotion*, Cambridge MA and London, MIT Press, 1987.

Deigh, John, 'Cognitivism in the theory of emotion', *Ethics* 104 (1994), pp. 824–54.

Deleuze, Gilles, *Difference and Repetition* (1968), trans. Paul Patton, New York, Columbia University Press, 1994.

—— *Cinema 1: The Movement Image* (1983), trans. Hugh Tomlinson and Barbara Habberjam, London, Athlone Press, 1986.

—— *Cinema 2: The Time Image* (1985), trans. Hugh Tomlinson and Robert Galeta, London, Athlone Press, 1989.

Derrida, Jacques, 'Economimesis' *Diacritics* 11 (1981), pp. 3–25. This article first appeared in *Mimesis des articulations*, Paris, Aubier-Flammarion, 1975.

——*The Truth in Painting* (1978), trans. Geoff Bennington and Ian McLeod, Chicago and London, University of Chicago Press, 1978.

Desai, Anita, *Fire on the Mountain*, Harmondsworth, Penguin, 1981.

Deshpande, Shashi, *The Binding Vine*, London, Virago, 1993.

Devi, Mahasweta, 'Draupadi', in Gayatri Chakravorty Spivak (ed.), *In Other Worlds: Essays in Cultural Politics*, London and New York, Methuen, 1986, pp. 179–96.

Dewey, John, *Art as Experience*, New York, Minton, Balch and Company, 1934.

——*The Child and the Curriculum and the School and Society*, Chicago IL, University of Chicago Press, 1956.

Dollimore, Jonathan, *Sexual Dissidence: Augustine to Wilde, Freud to Foucault*, Oxford, Clarendon Press, 1991.

Dworkin, Andrea, *Pornography: Men Possessing Women*, London, Women's Press, 1981.

Eagleton, Terry, *The Ideology of the Aesthetic*, Oxford, Blackwell, 1990.

Empson, William, *Seven Types of Ambiguity* (1930), London, Chatto & Windus, 1947 (2nd edn).

Feagin, Susan, *Reading with Feeling*, Ithaca MI, Cornell University Press, 1996.

Felski, Rita, *Beyond Feminist Aesthetics: Feminist Literature and Social Change*, Cambridge MA, Harvard University Press, 1989.

Ferguson, Frances, 'Justine; or, the Law of the Road', in George Levine (ed.), *Aesthetics and Ideology*, New Brunswick NJ, Rutgers University Press, 1994, pp. 106–23.

——'Pornography: the theory', *Critical Inquiry* 21 (Spring 1995), pp. 640–95.

Fish, Stanley, 'Why literary criticism is like virtue', *London Review of Books*, 10 June 1993, pp. 11–16. Adapted from two of the Clarendon Lectures given in Oxford, May 1993.

Forrest-Thomson, Veronica, *Collected Poems and Translations*, ed. Anthony Barnett, London, Lewes and Berkeley, Allardyce, Barnett, 1990.

Francis, Richard (ed.), *Negotiating Rapture: The Power of Art to Transform Lives*, Chicago IL, Museum of Contemporary Art, 1996.

Fraser, Nancy, 'Heterosexism, misrecognition and capitalism', *New Left Review* 228 (March/April 1998), pp. 140–9.

Freud, Sigmund, *The Interpretation of Dreams* (1900), trans. James Strachey, Penguin Freud Library Vol. 4, Harmondsworth, Penguin Books, 1953.

——*Fragment of an Analysis of a Case of Hysteria* (1901), trans. Alix and James Strachey, Penguin Freud Library Vol. 8, Case Histories 1, Harmondsworth, Penguin Books, 1977.

——*Introductory Lectures on Psychoanalysis* (1916–17), trans. James Strachey (1963), Pelican Freud Library, Vol. 1, Harmondsworth, Penguin Books, 1973.

—— Beyond the Pleasure Principle, Leipzig, Vienna and Zurich, Internationaler Psychanalytischer Verlag, 1920; trans. C. J. M. Hubback, London and Vienna International Psychoanalytical Press, 1922.

—— *New Introductory Lectures on Psychoanalysis* (1933), trans. James Strachey, London, Hogarth, Press, 1974.

Friedan, Betty, *Beyond Gender: The New Politics of Work and Family*, ed. Brigid O'Farrell, Washington DC, Baltimore and London, Johns Hopkins Press, 1997.

Frow, John, *Cultural Studies and Cultural Value*, Oxford, Oxford University Press, 1995.

Gagnier, Regenia, *Idylls of the Marketplace: Oscar Wilde and the Victorian Public*, Aldershot, Scolar Press, 1987.

Geuss, Raymond, 'CRITICAL RESPONSE: a response to Paul de Man', *Critical Inquiry* 10 (1983), pp. 375–82.

Gilbert, Sandra and Gubar, Susan, *The Mad Woman in the Attic: The Woman Writer and the Nineteenth-Century Literary Imagination*, New Haven and London, Yale University Press, 1979.

Goethe, Johann Wolfgang von, *Wilhelm Meister's Apprenticeship and Travels*, trans. Thomas Carlyle, London, Chapman and Hall, 1871.

Green, André, *Le Discours vivant: La Conception psychoanalytique de l'Affet*, Paris, Presses Universitaires de France, 1973.

—— *The Fabric of Affect in the Psychoanalytical Discourse*, trans. Alan Sheridan, The New Library of Psychoanalysis 37, London and New York, Routledge, 1999.

Greenblatt, Stephen J., 'Invisible bullets: Renaissance authority and its subversion, *Henry IV* and *Henry V* ', in Alan Sinfield and Jonathon Dollimore (eds), *Political Shakespeare: New Essays in Cultural Materialism*, Manchester, Manchester University Press, 1985.

—— *Learning to Curse*, New York, Routledge, 1990.

—— *Shakespearean Negotiations: The Circulation of Social Energy in Renaissance*, Clarendon Press, Oxford, 1990.

Greer, Germaine, *Slip-Shod Sibyls: Recognition, Rejection and the Woman Poet*, London, Viking, 1995.

Greimas, A. J., and Fontanille, Jacques, *The Semiotics of Passion: From States of Affairs to States of Feeling*, trans. Paul Perron and Frank Collins, Minneapolis, University of Minnesota Press, 1993.

Griffiths, Paul E., *What Emotions Really Are: The Problem of Psychological Categories*, Chicago IL, University of Chicago Press, 1998.

Giullory, John, *Cultural Capital: The Problem of Literary Canon Formation*, Chicago IL and London, University of Chicago Press, 1993.

Hacking, Ian, 'By what link are the organs excited?', *Times Literary Supplement*, 17 July 1998, pp. 11–12.

Hans, James S., *The Question of Value: Thinking through Nietzsche, Heidegger, and Freud*, Carbondale IL, Southern Illinois University Press, 1989.

Haraway, Donna J., *Simians, Cyborgs and Women: The Reinvention of Nature*, London, Free Association Books, 1991.

Harré, Rom, *The Social Construction of Emotions*, Oxford, Blackwell, 1986.
—— *The Singular Self: An Introduction of Psychology of Personhood*, London, Sage, 1998.
Hegel, G. W. F., *The Phenomenology of Spirit* (1807), trans. A. V. Miller, Oxford, Clarendon Press, 1977.
—— *The Encyclopaedia Logic* (1830), trans. T. F. Geraets, W. A. Suchting and H. S. Harris, Indianapolis and Cambridge, Hackett Publishing Company, 1991.
—— *Introductory Lectures on Aesthetics*, trans. Bernard Bosanquet, London, Penguin, 1993 (originally published in Georg Wilhelm Fredrick Hegel Werks, Berlin, Dunker and Humblot, 1832–45).
Heidegger, Martin, *Being and Time* (1927), trans. John Macquarrie and Edward Robinson, Oxford, Blackwell, 1962.
Hjort, Mette, and Laver, Sue (eds), *Emotion and the Arts*, Oxford, Oxford University Press, 1997.
hooks, bel, *Ain't I a Woman: Black Women and Feminism*, London, Pluto Press, 1982.
—— *Feminist Theory: From Margin to Centre*, Boston MA, South End Press, 1994.
Housman, A. E., *The Name and Nature of Poetry*, Cambridge, Cambridge University Press, 1935.
Irigaray, Luce, 'The gesture in psychoanalysis', in Teresa Brennan (ed.), *Between Feminism and Psychoanalysis*, London and New York, Routledge, 1989, 127–38.
—— *I Love to You: Sketch for a Possible Felicity within History*, trans. Allison Martin, New York and London, Routledge, 1996.
Jacobus, Mary, *First Things: The Imaginary in Psychoanalysis and Culture*, London and New York, Routledge, 1995.
James, Henry, *The Princess Casamassima* (1886), ed. Bernard Richards, London, Everyman's Library, 1991.
Jameson, Fredric, *The Political Unconscious: Narrative as a Socially Symbolic Act*, London, Methuen, 1981.
Janowitz, Anne, *Lyric and Labour in the Romantic Tradition*, Cambridge, Cambridge University Press, 1998.
Jay, Martin, *Adorno*, Cambridge MS, Harvard University Press, 1984.
Jenkins, Richard, *Pierre Bourdieu*, London, Routledge, 1992.
Joyce, James, *Ulysses* (1922), ed. Hans Walter Gabler with Wolfhard Steppe and Claus Melchior, intro. Richard Ellmann, Harmondsworth, Penguin Books (in association with Bodley Head), 1986.
Kant, Immanuel, *The Critique of Judgment* (1790), trans. James Meredith, Oxford, Clarendon Press, 1952.
—— 'An answer to the question: what is Enlightenment?' (1790), in David Simpson (ed.), *German Aesthetic and Literary Criticism*, Cambridge, Cambridge University Press, 1984.
Kaplan, Cora, 'Language and gender', in *Sea Changes: Culture and Feminism*, London, Verso, 1986, pp. 69–93.

Keller, Evelyn Fox, *Reflections on Gender and Science*, New Haven CT, Yale University Press, 1985.
—— and Hirsch, Marianne (eds), *Conflicts in Feminism*, New York and London, Routledge, 1990.
Kristeva, Julia, *Desire in Language: A Semiotic Approach to Literature and Art* (1977), ed. Leon S. Roudiez, trans. Thomas Gora, Alice Jardine and Leon S. Roudiez, Oxford, Blackwell, 1980.
—— 'Stabat Mater' and 'Women's time', in Toril Moi (ed.), *The Kristeva Reader*, Oxford, Blackwell, 1986, pp. 160–86, 187–213.
—— *Black Sun: Depression and Melancholia* (1987), trans. Leon S. Roudiez, New York and Chichester, Columbia University Press, 1989.
Lacan, Jacques, 'The insistence of the letter in the unconscious' (1957), trans. Jan Miel, in David Lodge (ed.), *Modern Criticism and Theory: A Reader*, London and New York, Longman, 1988, pp. 80–106.
—— *Ecrits: A Selection* (1966), trans. Alan Sheridan, London, Tavistock, 1977.
Langer, Susanne K., *Feeling and Form*, New York, Scribner, 1953.
Le Doeuff, *The Philosophical Imaginary*, trans. Colin Gordon, London, Athlone, 1989.
—— *Hipparchia's Choice: An Essay Concerning Women*, trans. Triosta Selous, Oxford, Blackwell, 1991.
Leask, Nigel, *The Politics of Imagination in Coleridge's Critical Thought*, Basingstoke, Macmillan, 1988.
Lefebvre, Henri, *Critique of Everyday Life* (1947), trans. John Moore, London and New York, Verso, 1991.
—— *The Production of Space* (1974), trans. Donald Nicholson-Smith, Cambridge MA and Oxford, Blackwell, 1991.
Levinas, Emmanuel, 'The transcendence of words' (1949), in *The Levinas Reader*, trans. Seán Hand, Oxford, Blackwell, pp. 144–90.
Levine, George (ed.), *Aesthetics and Ideology*, New Brunswick NJ, Rutgers University Press, 1994.
Levinson Marjorie, *Wordsworth's Great Period Poems: Four Essays*, Cambridge, London and New York, Cambridge University Press, 1986.
Lloyd, David, 'Race under representation', *The Oxford Literary Review* 13 (1991), pp. 62–94.
Lyndon, Neil, *No More Sex War: The Failure of Feminism*, London, Sinclair-Stevenson, 1992.
Lyons, William, *Emotion*, Cambridge, London and New York, Cambridge University Press, 1980.
Lyotard, Jean-François, *The Postmodern Condition: A Report on Knowledge* (1979), trans. Geoff Bennington and Brian Massumi, Manchester, Manchester University Press, 1984.
MacKinnon, Catharine A., *Only Words: Towards a Feminist Theory of the State*, Cambridge MA and London, Harvard University Press, 1989.
Marcuse, Herbert, *The Aesthetic Dimension: Towards a Critique of Marxist Aesthetics*, Boston, Beacon Press, 1978.

Middleton, Peter, *The Inward Gaze: Masculinity and Subjectivity in Modern Culture*, London and New York, Routledge, 1992.

Migoshi, Masao, 'Radical art at Documenta X', *New Left Review* 228 (1998), pp. 151–60.

Minh-Ha, Trinh T., *Woman, Native, Other: Writing Post-Colonialism and Feminism*, Bloomington and Indianapolis, Indiana University Press, 1989.

Mitchell, Juliet, *Psychoanalysis and Feminism: Jacques Lacan and the Ecole Freudienne*, London, Allen Lane, 1974.

Moi, Toril, 'Patriarchal thought and the drive for knowledge', in Teresa Brennan (ed.), *Between Feminism and Psychoanalysis*, London and New York, Routledge, 1989, pp. 189–205.

Mossetto, Gianfranco, *Aesthetics and Economics*, Dordrecht, Boston and London, Kluwer Academic Publishers, 1993.

Murdoch, Iris, *Existentialists and Mystics: Writings on Philosophy and Literature*, ed. and with a preface by Peter Conradi, foreword by George Steiner, London, Chatto and Windus, 1997.

Norris, Christopher, 'Introduction: Empson as literary theorist – from ambiguity to complex words and beyond', in Christopher Norris and Nigel Mapp (eds), *William Empson: The Critical Achievement*, Cambridge, Cambridge University Press, 1993, pp. 1–20.

Nussbaum, Martha C., *Passions and Perceptions: Studies in Hellenistic Philosophy of Mind. Proceedings of the Fifth Symposium Hellenisticum*, ed. Jacques Brunschwig and Martha Nussbaum, Cambridge, Cambridge University Press, 1993.

Paglia, Camille, *Sexual personae: Art and Decadence from Nefertiti to Emily Dickinson*, New Haven and London, Yale University Press, 1989.

—— *Vamps and Tramps: New Essays*, New York, Random House, 1994.

Parret, Herman (ed.), *Peirce and Value Theory: On Peircian Ethics and Aesthetics*, Amsterdam and Philadelphia, J Benjamins, 1994.

Philips, Melanie, 'Losers in the war: in search of a new sexual settlement', *The Times Literary Supplement*, 20 March 1998, pp. 4–5.

Poovey, Mary, 'Aesthetics and political economy in the eighteenth century: the place of gender in the social constitution of knowledge', in George Levine (ed.), *Aesthetics and Ideology*, ed. New Brunswick NJ, Rutgers University Press, 1994, pp. 79–105.

Rich, Adrienne, *On Lies, Secrets and Silence: Selected Prose 1966–1978*, London, Virago, 1980.

—— *Blood, Bread and Poetry: Selected Prose 1979–1985*, London, Virago, 1986.

Richards, I. A., *Practical Criticism: A Study of Literary Judgment*, London, Kegan Paul, 1929.

Richardson, Dorothy, *Pilgrimage, Vol. 2: The Tunnel* (1919), London, Virago, 1979.

Ricoeur, Paul, *Fallible Man* (1965), trans. Charles A. Kelbley, New York, Fordham University Press and London, Eurospan, 1986.

—— *The Rule of Metaphor: Multi-Disciplinary Studies of the Creation of Meaning in Language* (1975), trans. Robert Czerny with Kathleen McLaughton and John Costella, SJ, Toronto, University of Toronto Press, 1977.

—— *Freud and Philosophy: An Essay on Interpretation* (1965), trans. Denis Savage, New Haven CT, Yale University Press, 1970.

Roiphe, Kate, *The Morning After: Sex, Fear and Feminism* (1993), republished with new introduction, Boston, New York, Toronto and London, Little Brown and Company, 1994.

Rorty, Amélie Oksenberg (ed.), *Explaining Emotions*, Berkeley, University of California Press, 1980.

Rose, Gillian, *The Melancholy Science: An Introduction to the Thought of Theodor W. Adorno*, Basingstoke and London, Macmillan, 1978.

—— *Hegel Contra Sociology*, London, Athlone, 1981.

—— *Dialectic of Nihilism: Post-Structuralism and the Law*, Oxford, Blackwell, 1982.

—— *The Broken Middle: Out of Our Ancient Society*, Oxford, Blackwell, 1992.

—— *Love's Work*, London, Chatto and Windus, 1995.

Scarry, Elaine, 'On vivacity: the difference between daydreaming and imagining-under-authorial-instruction', *Representations* 52 (1995), pp. 1–26.

—— 'Imagining flowers: perceptual mimesis (particularly delphinium)', *Representations* 57 (Winter 1997), pp. 90–115.

—— *On Beauty and Being Just*, Princeton NJ, Princeton University Press, 1999.

Schiach, Morag, 'Their "symbolic" exists, it holds power – we the sowers of disorder know it only too well', in Teresa Brennan (ed.), *Between Feminism and Psychoanalysis*, London and New York, Routledge, 1989, pp. 153–67.

Schiller, Friedrich, *On the Aesthetic Education of Man in a Series of Letters*, trans. Elizabeth M. Wilkinson and L. A. Willoughby, Oxford, Clarendon Press, 1967.

Scruton, Roger, *The Aesthetic Understanding: Essays in the Philosophy of Art and Culture*, London and New York, Methuen, 1983.

Searle, John R., 'The mystery of consciousness', *New York Review of Books*, 2 November 1995, pp. 60–6.

Sedgwick, Eve Kosofsky, and Frank, Adam (eds), *Shame and its Sisters: A Silvan Tomkins Reader*, Durham and London, Duke University Press, 1995.

Segal, Hanna, *The Work of Hanna Segal: A Kleinian Approach to Clinical Practice*, Northvale NJ and London, Jason Aronson Publishers, 1981.

Segal, Naomi, 'Echo and Narcissus', in Teresa Brennan (ed.), *Between Feminism and Psychoanalysis*, London and New York, Routledge, 1989, pp. 168–85.

Sharpe, Jenny, *Allegories of the Empire: The Figure of Woman in the Colonial Text*, Minneapolis and London, University of Minnesota Press, 1993.

Shibles, Warren, *Emotion in Aesthetics*, Dordrecht, Boston and London, Kluwer Academic Publishers, 1995.

Showalter, Elaine, *A Literature of Their Own: British Women Novelists from Brontë to Lessing*, Princeton NJ, Princeton University Press, 1977.

—— *Hystories, Hysterical Epidemics and Modern Culture*, London, Picador, 1997.

Sim, Stuart, *Beyond Aesthetics: Confrontations with Poststructuralism and Post-modernism*, Toronto and Buffalo, University of Toronto Press, 1992.

Sinclair, Iain, *Lights Out for the Territory*, London, Granta, 1997.

Sinfield, Alan, 'Royal Shakespeare: Theatre and the Making of Ideology', in Alan Sinfield and Jonathan Dollimore (eds), *Political Shakespeare*, pp. 158–81.

—— and Dollimore, Jonathan (eds), *Political Shakespeare: New Essays in Cultural Materialism*, Manchester, Manchester University Press, 1985.

Smith, Barbara Hernstein, *Contingencies of Value: Alternative Perspectives for Critical Theory*, Cambridge MA, Harvard University Press, 1988.

Solomon, Robert C., *What is an Emotion? Classic Readings in Philosophical Psychology*, Oxford, Oxford University Press, 1984.

Spivak, Gayatri Chakravorty, *In Other Worlds: Essays in Cultural Politics*, London and New York, Methuen, 1987.

—— 'Can the subaltern speak?', in C. Nelson and L. Grossberg, *Marxism and the Interpretation of Culture*, Basingstoke, Macmillan, 1988, pp. 271–313.

Still, Judith, and Worton, Michael (eds), *Textuality and Sexuality*, Manchester and New York, Manchester University Press, 1993.

Sulerie, Sara, 'Women skin-deep: feminism and the post-colonial condition', *Critical Inquiry* 18 (Summer 1982), pp. 757–69.

Tomkins, Silvan, *Affect, Imagery, Consciousness*, 4 vols, New York, Springer Publishing Company, 1962–92.

Volosinov, V. N., *Marxism and the Philosophy of Language*, trans. L. Metejka and I. R. Titanik, Cambridge MA, Harvard University Press, 1986.

Vygotsky, Lev Semenovich, *The Psychology of Art* (1925), ed. A. N. Leontiev and V. V. Ivanov, Cambridge MA and London, MIT Press, 1971.

—— *Thought and Language* (1934), trans. Alex Kozulin, Cambridge MA, MIT Press, 1986.

—— *Mind in Society: The Development of Higher Psychological Processes*, ed. Michael Cole, trans. Michael Cole, Sylvia Scribner, Ellen Souberman, Vera John-Steiner, Cambridge MA and London, Harvard University Press, 1978.

Walter, Natasha, *The New Feminism*, London, Little, Brown and Company, 1998.

Warminski, Andzrej (ed.) *Aesthetic Ideology*, Minneapolis and London, University of Minneapolis Press, 1996.

Watts, Carol, 'Time and the working mother: Kristeva's "Women's time" revisited', *Radical Philosophy* 91 (September/October 1998), pp. 6–17.

Welsch, Wolfgang (ed.), *Undoing Aesthetics*, trans. Andrew Inkpin, London, Sage, 1997.

Whitford, Margaret, 'Rereading Irigaray', in Teresa Brennan (ed.), *Between Feminism and Psychoanalysis*, London and New York, Routledge, 1989, pp. 106–26.

Williams, Raymond, *Culture and Society 1780–1950*, London, Chatto and Windus, 1958.

Wimsatt, W. K., and Beardsley, Monroe C., 'The affective fallacy', *The Verbal Icon: Studies in the Meaning of Poetry*, Lexington KY, University of Kentucky Press, 1954, pp. 21–39.

Winnicott, D. W., *Playing and Reality*, Harmondsworth, Penguin Books, 1971.

Wittgenstein, Ludwig, *Philosophical Investigations* (1953), trans. G. E. M. Anscombe, Oxford, Blackwell, 1989.

Wood, James, 'Faulting the lemon', *London Review of Books* 20 (1 January 1998), pp. 13–15.

Zeglin, Peggy, and Korsmeyer, Carolyn (eds), *Feminism and Tradition in Aesthetics*, Philadelphia, Pennsylvania State University Press, 1995.

Žižek, Slavoj, *Tarrying with the Negative: Kant, Hegel and the Critique of Ideology*, Durham NC, Duke University Press, 1993.

Index

Harré, Rom 133
Hartley, David 100
Hegel, G. W. F. 1–2; Adorno 179,
 184–5; artwork 132; Beautiful
 Soul 193 n2; consciousness 61,
 71; Deleuze on 62; *Encyclopaedia
 Logic* 13, 16–17, 50–1, 58, 65,
 116; equivocation 76; 'I' 51;
 immediacy 62, 66, 70–1;
 Introductory Lectures on Aesthetics
 73; de Man on 16, 45–6, 50–3, 54,
 55, 56; master/slave 94, 235;
 mediation 66, 67, 68, 70; poetics
 61, 65; post-modernism 17; post-
 structuralism 17; repetition 71;
 Rose, G. 13, 63–5, 76; sound
 253; symbol 50–1, 52; thought
 71–2
hegemony 31, 32, 216
Heidegger, Martin 20, 232–5
Heraclitus 71
hermeneutics of suspicion 13–14,
 16
heteroaffection 48, 49
Hjort, Mette 146
hooks, bel 208, 209–10
Hopkins, G. M. 89
Housman, A. E. 109–10
Hume, David 28, 159
hybridity 59, 70, 221
hysteria 54, 209, 248

'I': artwork 75; decentred 73; Hegel
 51; 'I/i' dichotomy 220–1, 224,
 225; as symbol 53; universal/
 particular 73–4
Id 117, 120, 124
identification 52, 53, 102
identity 215–16, 220–1, 222, 232,
 239, 257
ideology: aesthetic 16, 33, 46, 86;
 art 42
illusion 180–1
imaginary 29, 34–5, 40, 241
imagination 186
immediacy 62, 66, 70–1
impressment 100–1
individualism 32, 235

intentionality 6, 134, 173 n5, 186
interpersonal relations 134
interspatiality 223, 224, 238 n11
Irigaray, Luce 198; gender/aesthetics
 20; knowledge 241; Ludic
 feminism 215; marriage 237 n7;
 mirroring 243; mourning 250

Jacobus, Mary 212
James, Henry 1, 2, 3–4, 5, 22 n4
Jameson, Fredric 133
Johnson, Randal 160
Jones, Tim 174
jouissance 46, 55, 87
Joyce, James: *Ulysses* 151, 171
judgement 161, 168, 189

Kant, Immanuel: Adorno on 50, 179,
 183, 184; aesthetics 1–2, 30, 32,
 33, 49, 160, 162; body 50;
 culture 12; Derrida on 16,
 45–50, 54, 55, 56; difference 35;
 Eagleton on 28–9, 32–4;
 epistemology 32; free play 12, 23
 n7, 30, 33, 34; gender 27;
 imaginary 29; intentionality
 134, 173 n5; middle 68; mirror
 stage 35; pleasure principle 32,
 33, 48; reason 9, 27; Scruton 8
Kaplan, Cora 42
Keats, John 168–9
Keller, Evelyn Fox 247, 248
Kierkegaard, Søren 31–2, 64
Klein, Melanie 124–5, 251
knowing: Bion 255–7; feeling 134
knowledge 67; Cixous 241, 242;
 emotion 59, 115–16, 118;
 gendered 244, 247, 248, 249, 250;
 infant 249, 256; Irigaray 241;
 mediation 68–9, 79–80;
 non-phallic 257; patriarchal 251,
 257; thought 240–1;
 transitive 256; universal 248
Kristeva, Julia 20; affect 18, 54, 81
 n7; classification of feminisms 206–7;
 depressive position 111; feminist
 theory 198; fetish 40, 79; Oedipal
 separation 224; poetry 112, 113;